Managing Business Marketing & Sales

Per V. Jenster, H. Michael Hayes & David E. Smith

Managing Business Marketing & Sales

An International Perspective

Copenhagen Business School Press

Managing Business Marketing & Sales
An International Perspective

© Copenhagen Business School Press
Printed in Denmark by Holbæk Amts Bogtrykkeri
Cover design by Morten Højmark
1. edition 2005

ISBN 87-630-0147-0

Distribution:

Scandinavia
DJØF/DBK, Mimersvej 4
DK-4600 Køge, Denmark
Phone: +45 3269 7788, fax: +45 3269 7789

North America
Copenhagen Business School Press
Books International Inc.
P.O. Box 605
Herndon, VA 20172-0605, USA
Phone: +1 703 661 1500, fax: +1 703 661 1501

Rest of the World
Marston Book Services, P.O. Box 269
Abingdon, Oxfordshire, OX14 4YN, UK
Phone: +44 (0) 1235 465500, fax: +44 (0) 1235 4656555
E-mail Direct Customers: direct.order@marston.co.uk
E-mail Booksellers: trade.order@marston.co.uk

Table of Contents

Preface

Our Objectives for the Book

The aim of this book is to marry leading academic thinking about business marketing and sales force management, with the reality of global management practice. The book distinguishes itself from other marketing books, by insisting that the management of marketing and sales activities must be thought of as sides of the same coin. As such, our philosophy is that business marketing is concerned with the identification and orchestration of profitable opportunities in the marketplace, and that sales and distribution management focus on the conversion of these opportunities into orders and long term relationships for the firm. We trust that the concepts and practical applications of this book will aid the readers in developing a comprehensive approach to the management of business marketing and sales.

Few aspects of business are as complex and intellectually challenging as business marketing. How organizations buy, with multiple influences in the customer's organization interacting with others in the organization and with suppliers, is in and of itself a fascinating study of human behavior. The relationship between buying and selling organizations, with both cooperating and conflicting objectives, is not only complex but dynamic as firms adapt their strategies to changing circumstances. In formulating marketing strategy, marketers are faced with an almost infinite array of product-market choices.

Product or services customization is the norm. Markets can be segmented horizontally, vertically, or both. With few exceptions, goods and services for business markets travel easily across country borders, expanding market choices but requiring further consideration of customization.

This complexity leads to our second and broader objective, which is to develop the student's ability to formulate implementable business marketing strategies. We believe this has three dimensions. The first is the ability to understand the complexity of business marketing situations in a global context. The second is the ability to formulate good strategies, recognizing that there is no one "right" strategy but rather that the key to strategy determinations is the selection of the best strategy from a number of competing alternatives. The third is an appreciation of the issues that must be managed in order to implement the chosen strategy.

The Scope of the Book

The structure of the book reflects our belief that these objectives are best accomplished through rigorous analysis of a large number of business marketing situations, guided by certain fundamental concepts and leavened by an exposure to marketing literature that reports on recent empirical research and conceptualizations. Again, we are biased. Our experience in researching, writing, and teaching cases to graduate students, undergraduate students, and executives have led us to conclude that, short of the opportunity for hands-on experience of real-world analysis, one of the best ways to acquaint the student with the complexity and intellectual challenge of business marketing is through the analysis of cases. Clearly, no reasonable set of cases can fully encompass all possible marketing situations. Still further, we recognize that the historical nature of cases precludes the opportunity to consider immediately contemporaneous situations. For that reason, we have elected not to include cases, but to provide this freedom of choice to the instructors for chosing cases that best fit the specific course. Their study will assist the student's development of analytical skills that can then be applied to many other situations. Case studies will also assist the student's discovery of basic concepts that will generalize to other situations.

Our objective for the text material is to provide the student with basic frameworks or ways to think about business marketing situations. Some of these are fundamentals that have stood the test of time. Others have been developed from the extensive and ongoing research in the field or have been adapted from research in some of the basic social sciences. We have avoided extensive comparisons of business marketing to consumer goods marketing on the premise that business marketing merits its own and separate treatment. As is inevitable with any textbook, some aspects of the subject are treated only modestly, and we expect that the text will be supplemented by the instructor and, where appropriate, by the students' own experiences.

The Context of Business Marketing

Historically, there has been a tendency to equate business marketing with heavy smokestack industries. Early textbooks tended to focus on products for large, capital-intensive industries and gave minimum attention to services. Today, the scope of business marketing is much broader. Steel companies still buy heavy rolling mills, and electric utilities still buy turbine generators and large transformers, but new products and new industries have emerged as major elements of business marketing. Computers, once sold only to large organizations, are now sold to thousands of organizations, both large and small. The medical industry has emerged as a major purchaser, not just of health care equipment, but of all the other products and services necessary to the functioning of a large industry. Attention to services, once of concern principally as an adjunct to related products, is increasing both because of the importance of services in their own right and as they are being unbundled from their related products. The dynamic nature of corporate organizations suggest that this broadening of scope will continue as new products and services are developed, as new industries emerge, and as firms focus on their core competencies and use external suppliers for many products or services that once were produced in-house. No textbook can enumerate all the possible products or services that are part of business marketing or treat all their idiosyncrasies. For the student it is important, therefore, to recognize that using this book in the study of business marketing is just a starting point for learning about a fascinating field.

The global dimension of business marketing adds to its excitement and intellectual challenge. Goods and services for business markets have always traveled easily across country borders. Statistics about the large U.S. merchandise trade deficit ($804,596 million in 2004) mask the fact that in 2004 the United States exported $535,435 million in capital goods and industrial supplies, more than 66% of total merchandise exports. Similarly, with perhaps the exception of automobiles and consumer electronics, the exports of most other industrialized countries are heavily weighted toward business markets. While not all firms may elect to pursue markets outside of home country boundaries, few producers of business products and services can ignore their consideration. In the text material, we have attempted to demonstrate the importance of such consideration and to provide the necessary understanding for it.

For the student pursuing a career in business marketing, we hope our book will materially assist in ensuring a rewarding career. For those who pursue other careers, we believe that the analytical skills and concepts developed in the course of studying this book will apply to a broad range of marketing situations. In either case, we hope you find the study of the subject as fascinating as we do.

Features of the Book

Several features of the book merit special mention:

(1) Unique to business marketing books, our book includes, in one volume, text that presents major concepts.

(2) A global perspective is integrated throughout the text. Our basic premise is that marketing concepts are fundamentally international. We elected therefore, to integrate international aspects of marketing as extensions of fundamental concepts where appropriate rather than to have separate international sections.

(3) The book has a strong strategic and managerial orientation. The first five chapters establish the context of marketing planning and include corporate and business planning and a separate chapter on industry analysis. The remaining chapters address segmentation and product, pricing, and communication and distribution decisions.

Acknowledgements

Few textbooks are the work of just the authors, and our book is no exception. We first want to express our sincere appreciation to those who gave us the opportunity to develop a different approach to a business marketing textbook and whose advice and counsel during the development of the book were invaluable.

We are especially indebted to Ole Wiberg, managing director at CBS Press, who, together with Hanne Thorninger Ipsen and Denise Ross did marvels in editing and polishing the text and kept us on track and on schedule when it frequently appeared an impossible task.

We sincerely thank the reviewers, whose valuable input helped to shape the text.

We are indebted to the University of Colorado at Denver for the encouragement given to Michael Hayes to undertake this task and to the Copenhagen Business School and National University and its outstanding faculty for their generous support of the writing work of Per Jenster and David Smith. Without their support this book would not have been possible.

Lastly, but most importantly, we are indebted to our families who supported us throughout the writing of this book.

Per V. Jenster
H. Michael Hayes
David E. Smith

September 2005

Chapter 1

An Overview of Business Marketing

Over half the world's economic activity consists of exchanges between organizations. Most of these organizations are commercial enterprises, existing to provide products or services to other organizations or to an ultimate consumer. Others are government entities or not-for profit institutions such as schools or hospitals, also engaged in providing products or services to others. The term "Business Marketing" has evolved to indicate the marketing of any product or service to an organization that is involved in the production of products and services for others, regardless of ownership. More formally, we define business marketing as the marketing of products and services to commercial enterprises, governments and other not-for-profit institutions for use in the products and services that they, in turn, produce.

This book is about the formulation and implementation of strategies for business markets. For the student embarking on a study of this subject we believe it is important to provide an overview, a road map if you please, that will indicate the territory we plan to cover, as well as convey the basic premises, logic and structure of the book.

The Nature of Business Marketing

The issues which business marketers face are significantly different than those that face marketers of consumer products or services. The fundamentals, of course, are similar. That is, all marketers are concerned with the selection of target markets, with segmentation within these markets, and with decisions regarding product, promotion, pricing and distribution. It is the context within which these decisions are made that varies enormously and which justifies separate study.

The nature of organizational buying, characterized by multiple influences, professional buyers and long-term relationships, is very different from that of consumer buying. Because organizations buy in order to achieve organizational purposes, there is more emphasis on functionality. As a result, most products and services produced to meet the needs of organizations find markets in many countries. Selection of markets, the critical decision, has the horizontal dimension of consumer goods plus a vertical dimension. Horizontally we can, for in-

1

stance, select customers on the basis of industry, size of organization or nature of purchasing practice. Vertically, we can target component manufacturers, equipment manufacturers or end users. Products (for the sake of avoiding awkward phrasing we will frequently use the term products to include both goods and services) are often custom built and, in a surprising number of instances, new product ideas themselves come from customers. Promotion relies heavily on personal selling. Hence, management of the sales force as an orchestrator of organizational resources to satisfy customer needs is a major concern. Price determination is heavily influenced by the prevalence of both sealed bidding and negotiation with skilled professionals. Distribution decisions must take into account a high degree of specialization of distributors as well as the relationships that distributors have established with end customers and the very complex set of tasks performed by industrial distributors.

Business Marketing Strategy

At the heart of business marketing is the formulation of strategy; strategy that takes into account the nature of demand for the particular product or service, the industry in which the firm competes and events and trends in the broader external environment. Marketing strategy, however, is not conceived in an organizational vacuum. Its purpose is to assist the firm to achieve its objectives. It must take into account the capabilities and aspirations of the firm and it must work closely and in harmony with other functional strategies. In Chapter 2, therefore, where we discuss a number of marketing strategy concepts and analytical frameworks, we place particular emphasis on the relationship of marketing strategy to business and corporate strategy.

Even the most brilliant marketing strategy may fail if it is not executed properly. Marketing strategy, therefore, must take into ability of the organization to implement it. As we discuss throughout the text, and particularly in the chapter on communicating with customers, the individuals who are to be involved in executing marketing strategy should also be involved in its development, both for the knowledge they can bring to bear and to ensure a sense of ownership in the strategy.

Business Markets

It is estimated that half or more of manufactured goods are sold to organizations and that, in total, more goods and services are involved in sales to business buyers than to consumers. In the United States alone there are some 13 million organizations who buy good and services, many in a chain leading from raw materials to finished products. In the automotive industry, for instance, equipment manufacturers supply the steel industry with the necessary machinery to mine coal and iron ore and to convert the ore to steel. Steel suppliers supply their steel directly to car manufacturers and to a host of component manufacturers who also supply the car manufacturers. Suppliers of wide range of services, from accounting to medical insurance to specialized consulting, provide these services at all levels in this chain. In a world economy, it is clear that the market for business products and services is enormous.

While the sheer size of business markets makes the case for their importance, their diversity indicates the complexity of establishing appropriate marketing strategies to serve them. Organizations buy and sell an incredible array of goods and services; some familiar such as computers or architectural services, others less familiar such as insulation for spacecraft or remote diagnostics for maintaining sophisticated machine tools.

Business markets are frequently contrasted to consumer markets to make the point that there are fewer buyers, larger buyers and geographically concentrated buyers, with close relations between suppliers and customers. This tends to over simplify the nature of business markets. Some industries are, indeed, almost totally comprised of large players, as is the case for the tire manufacturing industry, dominated by Goodyear in the United States, Michelin in France and Bridgestone in Japan, the aircraft manufacturing industry, dominated by Boeing in the United States and Airbus in Europe, or the main frame computer industry, dominated by IBM worldwide. Others, however, are characterized by thousands of small firms with no one firm having more than a small share of the market, as is the case in the furniture manufacturing industry. Still, others are characterized by both large and small players, as is the case in the accounting industry with the Big 5 dominating the large corporation market, worldwide, but with countless small, sometimes individual, practices serving the needs of medium and small clients.

The General Motors' purchasing department spends more than $85 billion annually on industrial products and services—more than the gross domestic products f Ireland, Portugal, Turkey, or Greece. The 1,350 professional buyers at General Motors each spend more than $50 million annually.[1] Others, such as General Electric (GE), DuPont, and International Business Machines (IBM), spend more than $60 million per day on purchases to support their operations.[2]

In some industries, customers may be geographically concentrated, as in the steel industry with major clusters of customers near Pittsburgh in the United States and in the Ruhr region in Germany.

Others are widely dispersed, particularly service businesses and local governments.

This variation in industry composition, size of customers and their geographic location suggests the variety of options firms must consider as they select a particular target market, or elect to serve multiple markets.

Relations between suppliers and customers, and the nature of purchasing practices, display similar variability. Some customers prefer, and nurture, long-term relations with suppliers, on the premise that they have much more to offer than just availability and price. Others aggressively pursue low prices, using a wide variety of purchasing tactics, including a willingness to change suppliers frequently. Again, this variation suggests the variety of options available to a supplier. Some may elect to serve only customers who prefer long-term relations. Others may target just those who pursue low prices, because of volume considerations or favorable cost structures. Still others may target both segments, despite the additional complexity of doing so.

The nature of the contract and forms of payment also vary. Most exchanges in business markets involve purchases where payment is made in cash on receipt of the goods, but rentals and leases are common. GE, for instance, is the largest owner in the world of passenger aircraft that it, in turn, leases to airlines. In many instances, transactions involve some form of barter, where payment is made in goods, or offset, where payment may be made in cash but the supplier also guarantees to purchase a certain amount of other goods over some set period in the future. While rentals, leases or barter and offset may expand the firm's opportunity set, their pursuit cannot be undertaken without taking into account the requirement for special competencies.

Despite the variation in business markets, there is a common theme. Regardless of the size of the purchasing organization, its location, or its industry, it buys only in order to accomplish its objectives or strategy. This significantly influences the nature of demand in business markets. First, demand is derived. That is, demand for business products and services is ultimately derived from demand for consumer goods. If demand for consumer goods changes, so will demand for business products and services. The number of mufflers bought by automobile manufacturers, for instance, is dictated by the number of cars they make. Second, demand is relatively price inelastic for many product categories. Substantial cuts in the price of mufflers would not motivate automobile manufacturers to purchase more mufflers than needed for the cars produced. While this is true for mufflers, it should be noted that it might not be true when the cost of the component or raw material represents a substantial part of the cost of the finished product. A substantial reduction in the price of steel, for instance, if passed along to consumers in the form of lower car prices, might be expected to increase the sale of cars and, hence, of steel as well. Third, demand is highly price cross-elastic. Even though the automobile industry will not buy more mufflers than it needs, all else being equal the low priced supplier will enjoy the largest share of the available business. Fourth, demand for many products and services sold to organizations tends to be volatile. This is particularly the case for long delivery cycle equipment or in industries where capacity is added in large increments, as is the case for turbine generators or for heavy steel mill machinery. Orders for such equipment tend to dry up at the bottom of a business cycle, whereas many orders are placed when economic prospects are favorable. In broad terms, therefore, business marketing strategy must take into account not only the immediate customer but, as we discuss further in Chapter 4, must also take into account the customer's customer.

Historically, with the possible exception of tourism, international markets have been more important for industrial and commercial goods and services than for consumer products. There are exceptions, of course, but as a general rule, technical function has crossed national borders more easily than have features that must meet local consumer preferences. Edison's first commercial power plant, for instance, was installed in London in 1882, six months before one was installed in the United States. Many years later, Compaq Computer was building a plant in Scotland to serve the European market even before it had sold its first computer in the United States.

In recent years, world trade has been expanding at a greater rate than the growth in world economic output. In this environment of expanding trade, the U.S. trade deficits in recent years have tended to mask both the positive contribution of capital goods, industrial supplies, and services to the trade balance and their relative importance as components of international trade.

Even so, and until recently, many firms have treated international business markets as something outside of the mainstream of organizational activities. The last two decades, however, have been characterized by an unprecedented growth of world trade, which has expanded at a much greater rate than the growth of world product. With this expansion has come the increasing realization that for many firms consideration of international market opportunities should be on a par with consideration of domestic market opportunities.

As we will discuss in Chapters 2, 3, 4, and 5, understanding business markets requires a good understanding of marketing concepts, good situation analysis and a good marketing intelligence system. In this book, we take the view that the fundamentals with respect to marketing decisions are not restricted by national borders. While it is not imperative that every firm target markets in more than one country, we argue that decisions on market selection must be based on comprehensive understanding of market opportunities and this can only come from analysis that crosses country borders, both with respect to customers and competitors and with respect to industry trends and characteristics.

Business Products and Services

In the previous section, we described some of the characteristics of business markets that must be taken into account in the formulation of marketing strategy. Business marketing strategy is also influenced by the characteristics of the product or service itself, irrespective of the target market. A number of classification schemes have been developed to further identify the nature of these goods and services, as a basis for better understanding the nature of the purchasing process for them and thus developing marketing strategy. Most classification schemes include the following:

Raw Materials

This category includes farm products, mining and mineral products, coal and iron ore. These products tend to be commodities, with few opportunities to differentiate one product from another based on product characteristics. Supply, however, is critical and in many instances customers enter into long term contracts, both to insure supply and to protect against price fluctuations associated with commodities.

Manufactured Materials

As with raw materials, this category includes some manufactured products that are also essentially commodities, such as sulphuric acid or semi-finished food products, such as dough sold to bakeries. It also includes proprietary manufactured materials such as DuPont's Nylon®, GE's Lexan® or Elopak's Pure-Pak® containers for milk and fruit juices. For proprietary materials, there is significant opportunity to differentiate products. In many instances, market development is a major concern, both with the purchasing customer and the ultimate user and branding is an important element of marketing strategy.

Components

This category includes such products as small motors, used in appliances, and microprocessors, used in personal computers. In some instances, the component loses its identity in the finished product. Few buyers of appliances, for instance, are aware of the make of the electric motor used in an appliance. In such cases, product performance is important but product preference is almost totally determined by the appliance manufacturer. In other cases, the component may be well known, as with PCs, where Intel has extensively advertised its microprocessors to end users, with the expectation that end user preference for Intel products will influence the computer manufacturer to use them. In either situation, continuity of supply and quality are critical. Price, relative to competitors is important but less so in the situation where end user preference can be developed. Absolute price also may be important, if the component has a significant influence on the price of the end product in a price sensitive market.

Construction
This category includes buildings and other structures such as oil drilling rigs, processing plants or pipelines. These products are usually provided by heavy engineering contractors, either to a design of an architect or consulting engineer or, particularly in the case of processing plants or pipelines, to the design of the contractor. The contractor, of course, is also the purchaser of a wide variety of products necessary for the construction. Key considerations are the ability of the contractor to deliver a well performing facility, on time and within budget.

Capital Goods
This category includes a wide variety of products ranging from heavy or fixed equipment such as turbine-generators or mainframe computers to factory equipment such as lift trucks or hand-tools to office equipment such as typewriters or stand alone personal computers. Heavy or fixed equipment and some factory equipment will be carried on the books as plant and equipment and will be depreciated over a relatively long period of time. Price is important, but long-term functionality and service are critical, as these products become the heart of the manufacturing process. Less expensive or portable products are frequently expensed in the year of their purchase, reflecting their shorter lives. Functionality is still important but price and availability tend to dominate the purchasing decision.

Maintenance, Repair and Operating Supplies (MRO)
This product category includes the incredible variety of products needed to run offices and factories. Products include parts for capital goods, small tools for the manufacturing facility, paint for the buildings, stationary for the office; the list goes on and on. Inexpensive on an individual basis, total expenditures are significant. Price, therefore, is a major consideration, as is availability.

Services

Organizations purchase a broad range of services. Some are directly related to a product, and are provided either pre or post sale. These can be complex, as in the case of servicing of sophisticated machine tools or computers, or relatively simple, as in the case of typewriter repair. When products are first introduced, the service is usually packaged with the product. As the product matures, service may be separated from the product and is frequently sourced from an independent provider rather than the product manufacturer. Other services are essentially independent of a product. Again, these can be complex, as in the case of legal, architectural or consulting services, or simple, as in the case of janitorial services. For relatively mundane services, the service provider is usually chosen from a number of potential suppliers and price may well be the predominant selection criterion. For more sophisticated services, the selection process is usually complex, with decisions being made at high level in the organization, taking into account a number of criteria.

The Approach of the Book

This book is designed for the reader who has been exposed to broad fundamentals of marketing, either through previous course work or through extensive work experience. Our emphasis, therefore, is on improving the student's ability to analyze business-marketing situations and develop appropriate plans or courses of action. While the subject of business marketing can be studied in a number of ways, this text will rely heavily on textual coverage of major concepts and recommendations for further reading.

Textual Material

The textual material has been written to ensure good coverage of concepts fundamental to business marketing, without overwhelming the student with detail. It can be viewed as having three distinct sections, as shown in Figure 1.1. Chapters 1 and 2 are designed to provide the conceptual framework within which business marketing analysis and decision making take place. Chapters 3, 4 and 5 are designed to provide the necessary background for situation analysis, focusing on understanding the industry and the customers and understanding the process of acquiring information. Chapters 6 to 11 treat the five key areas of marketing decision-making. While the emphasis is on decisions that form the basis of strategy, implementation is a key theme that also runs through these chapters.

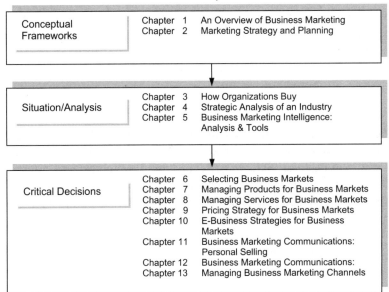

Figure 1.1: Plan of Text

Summary

All marketers are faced with certain fundamental issues, including target market selection, market segmentation, and decisions about product, price, promotion, and distribution. The nature of business marketing, however, with its emphasis on selling to organizations rather than to individual consumers, the size of business markets, and the wide variety of strategic choices available to business marketers, merits specialized consideration. Organizations buy only to accomplish their objectives or strategy, and the buying process is characterized by multiple influences. Business marketers must understand the forces that give rise to organizational demand and must be able to analyze complex organizational buying processes. The size of business markets is enormous, comprising more than half the world's economic activity. The diversity of these markets presents business marketers with a wide array of strategic choices with respect to both horizontal and vertical market selection, which should take into account international as well as domestic opportunities.

A variety of classification schemes have been developed to assist in the analysis of business markets. One scheme classifies business products in terms of raw materials; manufactured materials; components; construction material; capital goods; maintenance, repair, and operating supplies; and services. Each category suggests variations in marketing strategy and its implementation. Throughout the text, we introduce other classification schemes that suggest similar variations in marketing strategy. In the final analysis, however, marketing strategies and their implementation must take into account the unique situation of the firm with respect to its competencies, its opportunities, and the values of its management.

Further Reading

The suggestion for further reading has been selected to reinforce and elaborate important concepts and to expose the student to the current literature of business marketing. Beyond these two objectives, we hope this exposure to this literature will encourage the student to make its reading a permanent part of a life long approach to learning about this complex and ever changing subject.

B. Charles Ames, "Trappings vs. Substance in Industrial Marketing," *Harvard Business Review* (July-August 1970): 93-102.

Frank V. Cespedes, "Industrial Marketing: Managing New Requirements," *Sloan Management Review* 35 (spring 1994): 45-60.

James Carbone, "Reinventing Purchasing Wins the Medal for Big Blue," *Purchasing* (16 September 1999): 38-60.

George S. Day, "The Capabilities of Market-Driven Organizations," *Journal of Marketing* 58 (October 1994): 37-52.

Ajay K. Kohli and Bernard J. Jaworski, "Market Orientation: The Construct, Research Propositions, and Managerial Implications," *Journal of Marketing* 54 (April 1990): 1-18.

John C. Narver and Stanley F. Slater, "The Effect of a Market Orientation on Business Profitability," *Journal of Marketing* 54 (October 1990): 20-35.

---

[1]Gregory L. White, "How GM, Ford Think Web Can Make Splash on the Factory Floor," *Wall Street Journal* 3 (December 1999), p. A1.

[2]Ann Millen Porter, "Big Spenders: The Top 250," *Purchasing* 6 (November 1997), 40-51.

Chapter 2

Marketing Strategy and Planning

"There is only one valid definition of business purpose: to create a customer. Markets are not created by God, nature, or economic forces but by the people who manage a business. The want a business satisfies may have been felt by customers before they were offered the means of satisfying it....but it remained a potential want until the action of business people converted it into effective demand."[1]

The marketing concept holds that the purpose of a business is—or should be—to satisfy the wants and needs of its customers better than its competitors and at a profit. This requires the collective efforts of all those in the organization. Guiding these collective efforts is the role of business strategy. Marketing strategy may guide the development of business strategy but it must also support it and work in harmony with other functional strategies.

Typically, business strategies establish broad business objectives, indicate the scope of the business, in terms of products and markets, and identify the principal technologies and source of competitive advantage. The components of business strategy are usually the functional strategies. These include a marketing strategy, which deals with target markets and the actions necessary to reach them effectively; a manufacturing strategy, which deals with make or buy decisions, plant size and manufacturing processes; a research and development or engineering strategy, which addresses such issues as basic or applied research and fields of technology; a financial strategy, which deals with methods of financing, financial terms, credit risks, or working capital requirements; and a human resources strategy which addresses skill requirements, size and nature of the work force, and people management systems.

Depending on the nature of the business, the business strategy may include other dimensions as well. Marketing strategy, however, lies at the heart of business strategy. More than any other, it is concerned with the external environment and so is looked to provide guidance with regard to markets to be served and products to be produced; the fundamental business decisions. These business decisions can only be made in the context of the resources of the firm and its collective skills and abilities. Marketing strategy, therefore, must be as concerned with the capabilities of the firm as it is with customers, competitors, and other elements of the external environment.

This chapter is principally concerned with marketing strategy. Because of its relationship to business and corporate strategy, we first introduce a number of key strategy concepts and elaborate the relationship between marketing, business, and corporate strategy. We then describe the major planning concepts and tools that have been used to guide the formulation of corporate and business strategy and which establish the context within which marketing strategy is developed. We then focus on the specifics of marketing strategy and the marketing planning process.

Key Strategy Concepts

Strategy is an elusive term, used in host of ways. We have corporate strategies, business strategies, and functional strategies. We have growth strategies, diversification strategies, harvest strategies, turnaround strategies; the list could go on. Regardless of usage, three key concepts should be kept in mind. First, the concept of strategy implies a fit or match between opportunities and threats in the external environment and the capabilities of the firm. Unfortunately, examples abound of firms that failed to recognize the importance of fit. A major European manufacturer of expensive plumbing supplies, for instance, decided to introduce an inexpensive product line to compete more effectively in southern European markets. The new product line, however, turned out to be as expensive as existing products. Only after the fact was it concluded that the design and manufacturing skills required for inexpensive products were very different than those associated with its successful expensive products. Marketing strategy, therefore, must go beyond just taking account of customer wants and needs, competitor actions, and other elements of the external environment. It must also take into account the capabilities and resources of the firm in all functional areas.

Second, in some instances, the term strategy is used in a broad sense, to convey both objectives and courses of action. Andrews, in his classic work on strategy, defined it as "the pattern of major objectives, purpose, or goals and essential policies and plans for achievement of those goals, stated in such a way as to define what business the company is in, or is to be in, and the kind of company it is, or is to be." [2] Others separate courses of action from objectives. Corey, for instance, defines an objective as a desired end and strategy as a plan for achieving it. [3] We prefer the broader definition but, regardless of definition, it is important to recognize the linkage of objectives and action. Too fre-

12

quently, firms will establish objectives without identifying the specific action needed for their attainment. A major U.S. supplier of chemical analysis equipment, for instance, established a sales growth objective of fifteen per cent, in a market that was growing at the rate of ten percent. No provision, however, was made for either an increase in promotional expenditures or for specific direction of the sales force on ways to achieve such growth. Not surprisingly, the objective was not achieved. Beyond linking objectives and action, it is important to recognize that marketing objectives must also support business objectives. It makes little sense, for instance, to establish sales growth objectives that can only be achieved at the expense of profit objectives.[4]

Strategic Planning

Marketing strategy is normally developed in connection with the firm's strategic planning process. From one organization to another, this process is highly variable. In some organizations, strategies are the result of a very formal process, with well-defined planning structures and procedures, and extensive planning document. In others, they may be the result of ad hoc processes, with little or no effort to formally record the strategy in written documents. To the extent that strategic planning processes share a common characteristic, it is the frequency with which they are changed or modified. When strategic planning first became popular, in the early 1970s, the tendency was to set up separate planning components, charged with the responsibility for development of comprehensive strategic plans; plans which were then given to operating components for execution. Many planning components then evolved into large bureaucracies, isolated from the operating components. The tendency was also to do planning on an annual basis, geared to the development of an annual budget rather than to the strategic requirements of the firm. Plans tended to be inflexible, with opportunities for change considered only during the next annual planning cycle.

During the 1980s, growing disenchantment with the results of strategic planning led to a significant shift away from separate planning components. Planning, it was concluded, was better done by those line managers responsible for execution of the plans. Strategic planning components were either abolished or changed. At Intel, for instance, the principal responsibility of the vice president for strategic planning was not to develop strategic plans. Rather, it was to assist the planning process of line managers and to insure appropriate corporate reviews. Planning calendars were also changed. Firms in dynamic industries, particularly high tech businesses, reviewed strategies quarterly, semi-annually or as events dictated. Firms in less dynamic industries found that strategic plans could span longer time horizons. In either case, plans became more flexible. Changes in strategy did not have to wait for a formal planning review but could be modified as circumstances changed.

As the nature of strategic planning has changed, increasing importance has been attached to marketing planning and the marketing planning process. In a Conference Board survey, over 60% of the respondents indicated they expected more emphasis on marketing plans in the future. In fact, some 10% of the respondents indicated that formal marketing planning was new in their organizations within the last five years. The same study also found that one of the most significant changes in the planning process was a much more deliberate effort to have the marketing plan mesh with the overall plan for the business.

Strategy at Three Levels

Most firms originate with a single product or service, targeted at a single market. Some remain focused on just these original products and markets. Lincoln Electric, for example, has focused on manufacturing welding equipment for manufacturing industries and the construction industry for almost 100 years. In such a case, business and corporate strategy are synonymous. In these situations, marketing strategy is concerned with supporting just the business strategy. Other firms expand by offering new products or pursuing new markets, organically (i.e., through internal growth) or through merger and/or acquisitions. The result is a corporation made up of many businesses, generally designated as SBUs (strategic business units). Through the implementation of the SBU concept and the investment priority matrix, John F. Welch Jr., chairman and CEO of GE, spawned a strategic redirection that has provided GE with world market-share leadership in nearly all of its major businesses.[5] In multi-business corporations, marketing strategy also needs to take corporate strategy into account.

In broad terms, the relationships between corporate, business and marketing strategy are shown in Table 2.1.[6] The key question for corporate strategy is "what businesses should we be in?" During the 1960s and 1970s, the trend was toward broadly diversified businesses, or conglomerate corporations. Implicit in this trend was the view that management skills were generic; easily transferable from one business to another. In the 1980s, the trend reversed. Many found diversification into unrelated businesses was unprofitable. Many acquired businesses were divested. The new view of management skills was that firms should "stick to their knitting." In the broadly diversified corporation, the role for corporate level marketing was minimal, restricted primarily to identification of emerging market opportunities.

14

	Corporate Strategy	Business Strategy	Marketing Strategy
Scope:	Ultimate destiny of the firm.	Plans the war	Plans the battle.
Basic Questions:	What businesses should we be in, how do we allocate responsibility for results, how do we allocate resources, how do we organize?	What products, for what markets, with what competitive advantage?	What product variations, for what segments, at what prices, with what communications, and what distribution?
Objectives:	Current and future ROI and ROE,* earnings per share, stock price, contributions to other stakeholders.	Broad in terms of the total business, with specific $ profit or ROI targets.	Narrow in terms of segments, with specific volume and contribution targets.
Planning Horizon:	Longest tem.	Long term.	Medium term.
Resources Allocated to:	Business units.	Engineering, manufacturing, and marketing.	Product planning, promotion, and distribution.
External Focus:	Comprehensive macro in nature.	Comprehensive, essentially macro in nature, but in the context of business.	Sharply focused on customers, competitors, channels, and laws affecting marketing.
Major concerns:	Capitalizing on synergies, adding value.	Formulation of overall strategy, functional integration.	Formulation and implementation, management of marketing activities, and functional relations.

*ROI (return on investment), ROE (return on equity)

Source: Adapted with permission from *Journal of Marketing*, published by the American Marketing Association, Frederich E. Webster Jr., vol 56 (October 1992), 1-17.

Table 2.1: The Relationship of Corporate, Business, and Marketing Strategy

In corporations with more closely related businesses, the role for corporate level marketing expanded, with emphasis on coordination of the marketing efforts of the businesses and corporate positioning efforts. At Honeywell, for instance, corporate marketing led the effort to coordinate the work of Honeywell's several sales forces, many of which called on the same customers, and developed an overall positioning strategy for all the businesses, emphasizing partnerships with customers with an advertising theme "Together We Can Find the Answers."

The key questions for business strategy are "what products, for what markets and with what competitive advantage?" These decisions are made at the business level, based on inputs from all functional areas. While marketing strategy is at the heart of business strategy, in operational terms it must support business strategy and must direct the marketing efforts of the business to achieve business objectives. In multi-business firms, it must also support corporate marketing efforts.

As marketing strategy becomes more closely integrated with business and corporate strategy, it must take into account the planning tools and concepts which have been developed to assist in the their formulation. Many of these are also useful for the development of marketing strategy itself. In the following sections, we describe a number of these planning tools and concepts.

Corporate Strategy

As multi-business corporations emerged or grew, questions arose as to how corporate managers could understand diverse businesses with respect to a host of business decisions. Traditional measures of ROI (return on investment) and ROS (return on sales) were good indicators of past performance but were not necessarily good indicators of future potential. They did not, for instance, provide a basis for agreement as to future results. In particular, they did not indicate those businesses in which the corporation should continue to invest and those in which it was time to reap the rewards of past investment. What was needed was an approach which provided corporate managers with a better way to understand the strategic situation of each business, to assess its future potential on dimensions other than past profitability, and to have at least a generic sense of appropriate strategies for businesses with which they were not intimately familiar. This need led to the development of a number of planning approaches, based on the concept of managing the businesses as a portfolio in order to optimize the overall results of the corporation. We briefly describe the two most widely used portfolio approaches and their implications for marketing strategy.

The Growth-Share Matrix

First proposed by the Boston Consulting Group (BCG), this approach holds that the corporation should manage its portfolio of businesses in such a way as to optimize the firm's cash flow.[7] Graphically, the scheme is depicted in Figure 2.1. Businesses are positioned in the matrix on the basis of sales growth and market share. The general concept is that businesses in the high growth category are in the growth phase of the product life cycle and businesses in the low growth category can be considered mature. However, there is nothing sacred about the dividing line. In Figure 2.1, we show the dividing line as growth in GDP (gross domestic product) on the premise that markets growing faster than the growth in GDP are not yet saturated and so can be considered growth markets. Some early examples established the dividing line at 10%; roughly the sum of inflation at the time and growth in GDP. Many firms, however, establish their own dividing lines or omit a dividing line and merely use a continuous scale on which to array their businesses. The key point is that growth rate is an indicator of a particular businesses need for cash to fund continued growth.

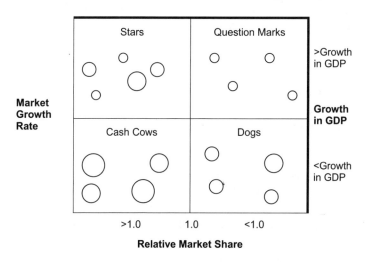

Source: Reprinted from Long Range Planning, February 1977, Barry H. Hedley, *Strategy and the Business Portforlio*, 12, Copyright 1977, with permission from Elsevier.

Figure 2.1: Growth-Share Matrix

Market share is generally considered relative to the firm's largest competitor. The dividing line between high and low share companies is usually placed at 1.0 or 1.5 but, again, there is nothing sacred about the dividing line and in many instances the dividing line will have a different value for high and low growth businesses, on the assumption that relative market share is less important when a business matures. The key point is to recognize the extent to which differences in market share have affected cumulative volume and, hence, costs. Finally, the size of each circle indicates the relative revenue of the business, to easily convey those impacts of the individual businesses on the cash flow of the firm.

Two basic premises underlie the Growth-Share approach. First, that high relative market share is the key to low relative costs and so is a source of competitive advantage. This is based on the concept of the experience or learning curve, which holds that cumulative volume leads to predictable decreases in cost. The firm that maintains a dominant market share will, therefore, have the greatest cumulative volume and the lowest cost. Second, that the portfolio of businesses should be managed in such a way as to optimize cash flow, using mature businesses to supply the cash needed to fund new ventures, which have the potential to generate surplus cash at some future date.

The widespread use of the Growth-Share approach attests to its many appealing characteristics. The notion of using cash flow as a way to manage a portfolio is intuitively appealing. The two-dimension classification scheme is easily learned and easy to apply. It quickly conveys the broad strategic situation of a business and suggests both the nature of the objectives for the business and the ways for their accomplishment, facilitating discussions between corporate and business management about future strategies. We briefly describe each of the four classifications and their associated generic marketing strategies.

Stars
These are high growth, high share businesses that produce high profit margins. Cash is needed for reinvestment in the business to sustain growth; hence, there is little cash flow in or out of the business.

Generic prescriptions for marketing strategy for Stars include:

- Protect or grow share
- Make constant product improvements
- Improve market coverage
- Consider price reductions
- Focus on sources of growth

Cash Cows
Low growth, high share businesses are also expected to produce high margins. Investment for growth is not necessary; hence there is a large cash flow above the needs of the business, which can be used to fund Question Marks, R&D, acquisitions, dividends, or other corporate purposes.

Generic prescriptions for marketing strategy for Cash Cows include:

- Maintain market share or dominance
- Maintain price leadership

Question Marks

Low share, high growth businesses have low profit margins and need externally supplied cash in order to grow. Future potential may justify an infusion of cash to fund continued growth.

Generic prescriptions for marketing strategy for Question Marks include:

- Invest to gain share
- Grow share in a niche with an eye on the whole market
- Abandon the business if potential returns are not attractive.

Dogs

Low share, low growth businesses have low profit margins. Cash is not needed as growth is not expected and the businesses have little likelihood of providing cash for other purposes.

Generic prescriptions for marketing strategy for Dogs include:

- Stay focused on a specialized niche
- Look for price improvement opportunities
- Position the business for sale or liquidation

Despite its widespread use, many concerns have been expressed about the Growth-Share approach. The dividing lines are somewhat arbitrary and can be used inappropriately. In addition, market share is frequently difficult to calculate and can be significantly influenced by the definition of the market. The experience effect is not uniformly applicable to all industries. In many instances, large portions of a manufacturer's costs may be determined by suppliers, and the manufacturer's own experience may only slightly affect total costs. Still further, empirical evidence indicates there is substantial performance variation within the various categories. Many businesses categorized as dogs, for example, have been found to perform very well. There are concerns about the unit of analysis. Many business units are, in fact, comprised of smaller businesses. Classification of business units that are composites may obscure very different situations for the smaller businesses that make them up. Consideration of just cash flow may fail to consider possible synergies between businesses. Finally, there is concern that the approach does not take into account the motivations of managers and that some of the labels may actually demotivate managers.

Overall, a major concern has been that the approach is simplistic and does not fully take into account the totality of a firm's strategic situation. This concern lead to the development of another approach by McKinsey and General Electric, variously described as the Stop Light matrix, the industry attractiveness-business position matrix or, to use GE terminology, the Investment Priority Matrix.[8]

Investment Priority Matrix

This approach focuses on establishing priorities for investment in the businesses that make up the corporation's portfolio. Graphically, the scheme is depicted in Figure 2.2. Businesses are positioned in the matrix on the basis of business position and industry attractiveness. As with the BCG approach, businesses are represented by circles whose size indicates the relative revenue of the businesses.

Industry Attractiveness

	High	Medium	Low	
Business Position	Aggressively invest for growth in market position, volume, and profit	Invest to protect market position and to improve profit-ability	Invest to exploit position and to improve profits	Strong
	Invest to improve market position and profitability	Invest to hold position and improve profitability	Invest only to harvest position, contain risk, and reduce drag	Medium
	Invest for profit improvement, not for better market position	Invest minimally, contain risk, and reduce drag on the company	Prepare for probable exit, divestiture, liquidation, or slow winddown	Weak

Source: Adapted from Analysis for Strategic Marketing Decisions 1st edition by DAY. © 1986. Reprinted with permission of South-Western, a division of Thomson Learning: www.thomsonrights.com. Fax +1 800 730-2215

Figure 2.2: The Investment Priority Mix

Business position is a composite assessment that takes into account market share but that also can take into account other factors such as size, profitability, and skills of the firm, customer relations, distributor relations, or patent positions. Industry attractiveness is a composite assessment that takes into account growth of the industry but that also can take into account other factors such as industry profitability, competitive intensity, ability of the industry to pass cost increases to customers, or government regulation.

To assign a business to a particular category, some firms establish weights for appropriate factors and then assess a particular business, using a Likert scale of 1-5, where 5 is very favorable and 1 is very unfavorable. The method is shown in the following example but it should be noted that only an illustrative set of factors is used. In actual practice, many more factors might be involved. These scores can then be used to assign a business to a particular cell in the matrix, as shown in Table 2.2.

	Weight	Rating = (1 – 5)	Value
Market Attractiveness			
Overall market size	0.20	4	0.80
Annual market growth rate	0.20	5	1.00
Historical profit margin	0.15	4	0.60
Competitive intensity	0.15	2	0.30
Technological requirements	0.15	4	0.60
Inflationary vulnerability	0.05	3	0.15
Energy requirements	0.05	2	0.10
Environmental impact	0.05	3	0.15
Social-political-legal	Must be acceptable		
Total Score	**1.00**		**3.70**
Industry Attractiveness			
Market share	0.10	4	0.40
Share growth	0.15	2	0.30
Product quality	0.10	4	0.40
Brand reputation	0.10	5	0.50
Distribution network	0.05	4	0.20
Promotional effectiveness	0.05	3	0.15
Productive capacity	0.05	3	0.15
Productive efficiency	0.05	2	0.10
Unit costs	0.15	3	0.45
Material supplies	0.05	5	0.25
R&D performance	0.10	3	0.30
Managerial personnel	0.05	4	0.20
Total Score	**1.00**		**3.40**

Source: Hosmer, Larue T., Strategic Management: Text & Cases on Business Policy, p. 310, 1st Edition, © 1982. Adapted by permission of Pearson Education, Inc., Upper Saddle River, NJ.

Table 2.2: Factors Underlying Market Attractiveness and Competitive Position in GE Multifactor Portfolio Model: Hydraulic-Pumps Market

Strategy prescriptions for the various cells of the Investment Priority matrix are generally couched in terms of investment objectives, as shown in Figure 2.2. Less prescriptive than the Growth-Share approach, the objectives do, however, provide an overall sense of direction for marketing strategy.

As with the Growth-Share approach, the widespread use of the Investment Priority approach also attests to its many appealing characteristics. It overcomes the objection that market share and growth do not fully capture the strategic situation of a business. It allows for assessment of the future attractiveness of an industry. Because it does not focus just on growth and market share, it is somewhat more flexible with respect to the unit of analysis. It avoids the use of demotivating labels. Once a business has been classified, corporate management or staff can track whether the business is, indeed, investing as its classification prescribes.

Despite its appealing characteristics, there are concerns about the Investment Priority approach. Choice of the dimensions on which industry attractiveness and business position are to be evaluated, as well as the evaluations themselves, are subjective decisions. Inevitably, there are arguments between the business unit and corporate as to how the business should be classified. While broad investment objectives are specified, there is little in the way of definitive prescriptions for strategy. Finally, the unit of analysis may be a problem. At GE, for instance, at a time when sales were in the neighborhood of $25 billion there were 39 SBUs. EG&G, on the other hand, a U.S. manufacturer of technical products, with sales of some $600 million had designated 101 components as business elements with responsibility for strategic planning.

Implications for Marketing

The foregoing was not intended to be a comprehensive description of portfolio approaches. Rather, it was intended to provide understanding of a key situational aspect that those in marketing must take into account as they formulate and implement marketing strategy. It should be understood that not all firms use portfolio approaches. Some have tried and then abandoned them, disappointed, for some of the reasons given. In other instances, large strategic planning staffs have been downsized, eliminating some of the expertise necessary to manage a portfolio approach. The key point is that in most corporations businesses are not free to choose their strategies, independent of the corporate situation. Those in one business may feel there are enormous opportunities, ready to exploit if only corporate managers would free them from the onerous burden of current profit responsibility. Those in another may feel that they deserve one more opportunity to turn the business around after several years of disappointing profit results. Finally, even if a business is classified as a Star, or in the upper left corner of the Investment Priority matrix, it should be recognized that the strategy prescriptions are only guides. It is still the corporate prerogative to decide on the level of investment or reinvestment in the business, taking into account other circumstances. In short, the objectives corporate assigns to the business become the strategic reality for marketing.

Although developed principally for use at the corporate level, it should be recognized that portfolio approaches also have applicability at the product level. Hence, they also can be directly used for marketing planning. As will be discussed in the Product Life Cycle (PLC) section, the Growth-Share matrix has much in common with the product life cycle. Using the Growth-Share matrix to visually display products quickly conveys the mix of products in the marketing portfolio and indicates if the balance in the various categories is appropriate. The Investment Priority matrix can be used to assess the strength of a product's position and its future market attractiveness and so make decisions on allocation of marketing resources.

Business Strategy

Interest in strategic planning has led to the development of a number of planning tools applicable at the business level as well as the corporate level. Three are of particular interest to those in marketing.

Product Market Expansion Matrix

For most firms, growth, in both sales and profits, is a basic objective. Fundamental to achieving this objective are decisions as to what markets to serve and what products to make. These decisions must be made in the context of the firm's strengths, weaknesses and competitive advantage. According to Ansoff, who first proposed what has come to be known as the Product Market Expansion Matrix, there are four fundamental choices, as shown in Figure 2.3.[9]

The firm can continue to serve existing markets with existing products. If these markets are growing at a rate that meets the firm's growth objective, then the growth objective is achieved by maintaining market share. Market growth rates below the firm's growth objective require the firm to increase its market share. Competitive position, with regard to cost, product features, or both is key to success. Monitoring the firm's position with respect to competitors is a critical activity.

Where the nature of competitive rivalry is such as to rule out a market share strategy, product development or market development strategies are the logical alternatives. The choice is a function of the skills of the firm and, particularly, the degree of change the firm is capable of managing. Product development strategies, focused on existing markets, require good understanding of existing market needs and the existence of product development processes that effectively link marketing to R&D and manufacturing. Market development strategies, which may lead the firm to entirely new markets, suggest an organization capable of considerable change. New markets require learning new purchasing practices or new uses for products and the establishment of new relations with distributors, customers, or both. Some market development strategies may require only modest changes, involving principally the field sales force. This was the case for the European subsidiary of a U.S. chemical manufacturer when it shifted its attention from large customers who bought on price to small customers for whom application service was more important. In other instances, extensive change is required, as was the case for MacTec, a Swedish manufacturer of water measurement equipment, when it was considering expansion from Europe to markets in the United States.

		Products	
		Existing	New
Markets	Existing	Market Share Strategy	Product Development Strategy
	New	Market Development Strategy	Diversification Strategy

Source: Adapted by permission of *Harvard Business Review*. From "Strategies for Diversification" by Igor Ansoff, *Harvard Business Review* (September-October 1957): 113–124. Copyright © 1957 by the Harvard Business School Publishing Corporation; all rights reserved.

Figure 2.3: Product-Market Expansion Matrix: Strategic Choices for Growth

Diversification is the most difficult growth strategy, combining, as it does, both the necessity to develop new products and learn new markets simultaneously. The degree of difficulty can be somewhat reduced through diversification that is closely related to existing products and markets, as was the case when Texas Instruments started producing personal computers. Nevertheless, most diversification strategies essentially start new businesses and should be viewed in that light.

The Profit Impact of Market Strategy (PIMS)

Despite similar positions on the portfolio matrixes or similar strategic choices for growth, profitability of firms varies enormously. In the

1960s, GE launched an investigation to determine if the variation in the performance results of its some 150 businesses was solely attributable to the skills of its managers or, alternatively, if some of the variation could be explained by situational variables or specific patterns of managerial decisions. Subsequently the investigation was moved to the Marketing Science Institute and then to the Strategic Planning Institute where investigations continue. The initial study, headed by Dr. Sidney Schoeffler, found that, indeed, there were certain factors that explained as much as 70% of the variation in ROI (return on investment), used as the principal measure of business performance. These are generally grouped in three main categories and are those associated with the following:

- The market environment (e.g., market growth rate, importance of the product to end users, marketing expenditures);
- Competitive position (e.g., relative quality, market share, patent protection);
- The capital and production structure (e.g., investment intensity, capacity utilization, vertical integration).

Beyond the businesses that have actually participated in PIMS, both by providing data and comparing their own business performance to the performance of other businesses in the PIMS database, the database has been used extensively by academic researchers. Their findings have been reported in numerous journals and have served as broad guidelines for many strategic decisions and have also served as the basis for many strategic planning models. Much of this research has been summarized in The PIMS Principles.[10]

Its extensive use notwithstanding, there has been considerable criticism of PIMS, both as to its methodology and its use. Businesses in the database, for instance, tend to be large and relatively sophisticated. While some of their products may be new, the overall mix of products is generally well beyond the introductory stage of the product life cycle. These characteristics have led to questions about the generalizability of the findings. Data are self reported and some of the data require subjective assessments, which may result in biased reporting. It has been pointed out that there are problems with some of the statistical analyses. Users of PIMS have been criticized for looking for simplistic answers to complex problems or for assuming that PIMS would, somehow, develop a complete business strategy.

Despite the criticisms as to its methodology and use, the fact remains that the PIMS database is the largest single strategic database available either to managers or to researchers. As with all other tools developed to assist in the formulation of strategy, used with care and understanding it has the possibility to provide valuable insights in the development of business and marketing strategies.

Product Life Cycle (PLC)

The concept of the PLC is familiar to most marketers. In brief, it holds that most products go through four stages. In the first stage the product is introduced. If the introduction is successful, the second stage sees rapid sales growth, up to the point that the market starts to saturate. Once saturation occurs, the product enters the mature stage where growth slows to parallel the overall growth of the economy. Finally, in the fourth stage, decline is expected, principally because new or different products are introduced that better meet customers' wants and needs.[11]

Marketing strategies that are appropriate in one stage of the PLC are not likely to be appropriate in another. In Table 2.3, we list some of the traditional prescriptions for marketing strategy over the PLC. Similarities will be noted between stages of the PLC and cells of the Growth-Share Matrix and between marketing strategy prescriptions for these stages or cells. These strategy prescriptions represent the average experiences of many firms. Hence, they are useful as guides for strategy. It should be noted, however, that they are generic. In a sense, they are prescriptions one might make if one knew nothing else about the situation.

Consider, for instance, the standard prescription to price high in the growth stage of the PLC. As we will see in Chapter 7, this is the standard skimming price strategy, which is appropriate in certain circumstances. There are other circumstances, however, when a low price or penetration strategy might be more appropriate. Similarly, the standard prescription is to cut back on promotion dollars in the decline stage of the PLC. In many instances, however, this action will accelerate the sales decline when higher expenditures on promotion would have extended the PLC. In short, as with the strategy prescriptions associated with the Growth-Share matrix, the PLC prescriptions for marketing strategy are starting points for strategy formulation. As with any other planning tool the PLC should be used to assist in formulating strategy, not to specify it.

	Stages of the PLC			
Element	**Introduction**	**Growth**	**Maturity**	**Decline**
Objective	Establishment	Penetration	Defense	Harvest
Customers	Innovators	Early adopters	Mass market	Laggards, specials
Competitors	Few	Many	Some	Few
Profits	Negative	Peak	Declining	Low
Price	High	High/medium	Medium	Low
Distribution	Exclusive	Selective	Intensive	Selective
Promotion focus	Concept/trial	Brand/ features	Value/ differentiation	Special applications
Promotion cost	Medium	Large	Moderate	Small
Service	Low	High	Moderate	Low

Source: Adapted with permission from *Journal of Marketing*, published by the American Marketing Association, George S. Day, Fall 1981, 60-67.

Table 2.3: Market(ing) Elements over the Product Life Cycle

International Product Cycle

In the mid-1960s, the international product cycle (IPC) was proposed as a way to explain firms' export activities.[12] According to the IPC, new products go through the introductory and growth stage of the PLC in countries with many scientists and engineers (i.e., inventors) and with affluent customers. As the country then with the most scientists and engineers and the highest per capita income, the IPC suggested the largest percentage of new products would be introduced in the United States. According to the IPC, following introduction and growth, mature products would then be exported to other countries; first to other developed countries and then to less developed countries. Finally, there would be a shift of manufacturing to less developed countries. The IPC is shown in Figure 2.4.

The IPC is useful in pointing out that marketing strategies need to take into account the stage of the PLC in a given market. It needs to be recognized, however, that in many instances producers of business products do not have the luxury of leisurely introducing the product in the home market, to be exported to other markets at some later date. Increasingly, the nature of global competition and global customers requires simultaneous introduction of new products in many markets. In addition, meeting the needs of increasingly demanding customers may favor locating manufacturing facilities close to customers rather than in a less developed country with the low labor costs.

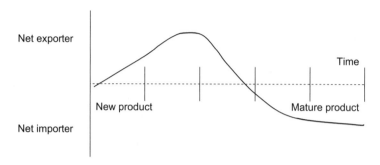

Phase I	Phase II	Phase III	Phase IV	Phase V
All production in United States	Production started in Europe	Europe exports to DCs*	Europe exports to United States	DCs export to United States
US exports to many countries	US exports mostly to DCs	US exports to DCs displaced		

*DCs = developing countries

Source: Adapted with permission from the *Quarterly Journal of Economics*, 80:2 (May 1966), Raymond Vernon, "International Investment and International Trade in the Product Cycle," pp. 199-207. © 1966 by the President and Fellows of Harvard College.

Figure 2.4: The Product Life Cycle Framework Applied t o International Markets: A U.S. Perspective

Marketing Strategy

Marketing strategy should have two purposes. First, to provide broad guidance to the development of business strategy and, second, to guide and direct marketing activities. We define marketing strategy as those customer focused objectives that guide and support the business strategy and those decisions and actions with respect to target customers, price, product, promotion and distribution necessary for their accomplishment. More comprehensively, marketing strategy should answer the following questions:

- What are our objectives? That is, what are we trying to accomplish?
- What customers should we target?
- What is our product, from the customer's perspective, what role does it play, and how should it be positioned?
- What price should we charge?

- How should we communicate about our product to targeted customers?
- How should we distribute our product?
- What information do we need about the external environment and reaction to our marketing efforts?
- What options did we consider in formulating our marketing strategy?
- What are the critical actions necessary for accomplishment of our strategy?
- What are the critical assumptions on which our strategy is predicated?
- How will we coordinate with the rest of the organization?

The answers to these questions should be found in the marketing plan. Good marketing plans are simply written statements of the marketing strategy for a given time period. The format of marketing plans can vary enormously. Some plans will be comprehensive and will include all the firm's products and all the served markets. Others will be more sharply focused, either on a limited set of products or on a specific market. In either case, the plan will usually include the situation analysis on which it is based.

Regardless of format, certain elements are common to most plans, as shown in Table 2.4. Without exception, the plan should convey a sense of the objectives to be accomplished and the way in which they are to be accomplished. Credibility of the plan is enhanced by a discussion of the various options that were considered before choosing the option selected. Credibility is also enhanced by stipulating key assumptions and critical actions.

The Marketing Planning Process
We define marketing planning as a flexible process, whose purpose is to develop or modify marketing strategies, which interacts with, or is integrated into, the processes by which business strategies and other functional strategies are developed.

External and internal situation analysis is essential to the marketing planning process. The customer is key but competitors, the industry and its structure, the nature of distribution channels, and the trends in the broader environment all shape the context within which marketing strategy is developed. The concept of strategy as a match between the external environment and the firm's capabilities emphasizes the need for internal analysis. In Table 2.5, we identify specific areas for analysis. In subsequent chapters, we will address these areas more extensively. The key to situation analysis, however, is to continually ask what the implications are for the marketing program. If, for instance, the buying decision is made by a group, how can promotion reach all the buying influences? Similarly, if customers vary extensively in their purchasing practices, will it be necessary to have more than one marketing program?

The analysis should lead to the development of key problems and opportunities facing the firm that relate to the specific issues or decision questions faced by management. These need to be considered in the context of the skills of the firm. The emergence of a corporate personal computer market was much more an opportunity for IBM, with its direct corporate contacts, than for Hewlett-Packard, with its strong commitment to sell through distributors, or Dell, with its strong direct marketing efforts. Such analysis enables assessment of the overall situation (i.e., is it very favorable, somewhat favorable, neutral, somewhat unfavorable or very unfavorable?) and should assist in identifying key issues that the marketing program needs to address.

Design of the planning process involves consideration of a number of questions. Particularly:

- Who is responsible for the plan?
- Who should review or approve the plan?
- How should the marketing planning relate to the strategic planning process?
- What are the major deficiencies of marketing plans?

In most industrial firms, marketing planning is a team effort. Primary responsibility for the marketing plan usually falls on one person; most frequently the marketing manager, the vice president of marketing or a product manager. Development of the plan can be carried out by one person, with inputs from others. Alternatively, it can be carried out by a task force or standing planning committee.

An interesting aspect of planning is the location of responsibility for planning information. Responsibility can be centralized, either in a formal market research or marketing management information system (MMIS) function. Alternatively, it can be decentralized to the various product or market managers. As businesses expand, the skill required to manage large databases and information systems argues for centralization. On the other hand, managers of centralized functions frequently are remote from the daily information needs of product or market managers and may be remote from the field sales force, a prime source of information. Hence, the information gathering processes they develop and their analysis of data may not adequately respond to the realities of the market situation.

Objectives
The volume to be sold (in dollar amounts and/or in units) and market share.
Profit contribution (in dollar amounts or in margins).
Non-financial objectives (e.g., image, key relations, new accounts etc.).

Target Customers
Who they are.
Where they are.
What their characteristics are.
What segments are served.

Product
A description of the basic product plus service, packaging, warranties, etc.
Position. What the product is expected to do for the customer. How it relates to competitive products.
Role. What the product is expected to do for the firm, beyond simply contributing to profit (e.g., cash cow, lead into new markets, defend against a competitive attack).
The branding strategy.

Distribution
Direct or through distribution.
Use and role of agents or wholesalers.
If through distribution, then:
Types of wholesalers.
Channel length or number of levels.
Exclusive or selective.
Role for each type and level of wholesaler.
Key functions or activities.
Margins and other motivating mechanisms.

Promotion
The nature of the promotional effort, with particular attention to role of the sales force.
The targets of the promotional effort.
The promotional mix: relationship between personal selling, advertising, sales promotion, and publicity.
The role of distribution (if used) in the promotional effort.
The promotional target.

Price
The overall price policy including relationship to competition, variation in prices, responsibility for setting prices, etc.).
Specific price to end-users.
Discount structure to end-users and intermediaries.

Contingencies
Contingencies that might occur.
Action to be taken
Event(s) that will trigger contingency actions.

Market Research
Additional market research needed before the plan is implemented.
Research needed after the plan is implemented to ensure it is on track.

Other Options Considered
The plan should identify critical assumptions and actions critical to success.

Note: Many plans also include the situation analysis, which is the foundation on which the plan is developed. Here we only list the objectives of the plan and their principal means of achievement.

Table 2.4: Contents of a Comprehensive Marketing Plan

External Analysis

The Customer
It is important to develop an explicit view of the motivations of the customer(s), the nature of the purchase decision process for the goods or services under investigation, and the degree to which these vary between customers or groups of customers. Often it will also be important to extend analysis to the customer's customers.

The Market
Here we are concerned with the overall size of the market, both current and future, and with the size of segments that vary in motivations, the nature of the buying processes, or other dimensions that would either rule out some customers or require modifications in marketing strategy.

The Industry
Marketing strategy must take into account the salient characteristics of the industry in which the firm will compete. It must, for instance, take into account the extent of competition, positions of competitors, their current strategies or possible initiatives, and possible reaction(s) to the firm's strategic or tactical moves. It must also consider how the industry fits in the business system, where value is added, and trends in the industry.

Distribution Structure
Few aspects of the external situation are more critical to the success of a marketing plan than good distribution. Analysis needs to take into account the structure of distribution channels, the likelihood of availability of distributors to the firm, the nature of relations with distributors, and so on.

Product Life Cycle
Marketing strategies should change over the product life cycle. While the exact state of the PLC cannot be estimated with certainty, it is useful to compare proposed changes in strategy with generic prescriptions for various stages of the PLC.

Environmental Climate
A wide variety of external events can influence customer or competitor behavior or the firm's own situation. Categories for analysis include technology, the political situation, the economic situation, and social trends. Events need to be classified as favorable, thus providing additional opportunities; or unfavorable, thus representing threats to be defended against.

Internal Analysis

Skills of the Firm
Marketing strategy must take into account the ability of the firm to implement the chosen strategy and to defend itself against initiatives of competitors. This goes beyond the marketing skills of the firm; it also includes engineering skills, manufacturing skills, overall management skills, and other organizational capabilities.

Financial Resources of the Firm
Marketing strategies must be financed. Most often, funds must be committed to marketing activities considerably in advance of revenues. Marketing strategy must assess the extent of resources and the degree to which they will be made available to fund marketing expenses.

Corporate or Business Strategy
Marketing strategy must take into account and support overall business strategy. Business strategy, in turn, must take into account and support overall corporate strategy. Overall objectives, sources of competitive advantage, and the assigned role of the business within the corporate portfolio can significantly influence marketing strategy.

This table draws heavily on the Marketing Planning Outline developed by Professor James R. Taylor and his colleagues at the University of Michigan Business School, and his work in this area is gratefully acknowledged.

Table 2.5: Situation Analysis for Marketing Planning: Areas for Investigation

Increasingly, marketing plan approval takes place at the level of the SBU general manager or higher. In some instances, the marketing plan is reviewed as part of the SBU plan at several reviewing levels. In other instances, advisory boards with specialized knowledge of selected target markets may review and comment on plans before they are submitted for approval. The extent to which marketing planning is part of the business planning process varies considerably. An example of extensive involvement is shown in Illustration 2.1.

The marketing manager is the most significant functional contributor to the strategic planning process, with leadership roles in defining the business mission; analysis of the environmental, competitive, and business situation; developing objectives, goals, and strategies; and defining product, market, distribution, and quality plans to implement the business's strategies. This involvement extends to the development of programs and operating plans that are fully linked with the strategic plan.

Source: From a speech by Steve Harrell, a GE strategic planning manager, presented at the American Marketing Association's Summer Educators' Meeting, Chicago, August 5, 1980.

Illustration 2.1: Strategic Planning at GE

Where this degree of involvement exists, it is usually the result of a top-down, bottoms-up planning process. With many exceptions, this is done on an annual basis. Early in the planning year, planning assumptions and broad objectives are given the businesses or functions. Planning assumptions might include economic forecasts, exchange rate forecasts, or political risk assessments. For some businesses, assumptions might be more specific. Objectives invariably include profit expectations and may also include productivity targets or other performance measures. Of particular interest to marketing may be the identification of new and potentially attractive target markets.

In the context of established corporate objectives and planning assumptions, business objectives and assumptions are then established by the SBU manager. Depending on how the SBU is organized, functional or other managers then initiate the planning process within their components. Key to this planning effort is development of plans that support the business objectives and that coordinate with other components.

Where planning is done on an annual basis, component plans are usually integrated into a business plan in the middle of the planning year. Subsequent steps in the planning process will include a higher-level review, with either approval or modification. The approved strategic plan then becomes the basis for establishing the financial plan for the business. Depending on the degree to which combined financial plans of all the SBUs meet corporate objectives, there is either approval or renegotiation of financial objectives for individual SBUs. The final combination of financial plans becomes the corporate budget for the forthcoming year.

Summary

Marketing Planning is not isolated from other activities of the organization. Rather, it takes place within the context of corporate and business planning and objectives. In broad terms, marketing planning needs to recognize three key concepts: the importance of the match between opportunities and organizational competence, the importance or linking actions to objectives, and the need for marketing objectives that support business objectives.

A number of tools or analytical frameworks have been developed to assist corporate planning. Two frequently used tools are the growth-share matrix and the Investment Priority matrix. Marketers should understand how these and other planning tools are used and how their use may influence marketing plans. Additional tools developed to assist business and marketing planning include the product-market expansion matrix, PIMS, the PLC, and the IPC. Marketers can use these tools as guides to assist in the planning process, which also must take into account the unique situation of the individual firm.

Although marketing planning needs to consider corporate and business planning and objectives, its principal focus must be on understanding the external situation—customers, the competitors, and the industry within which the firm competes. Good situation analysis is imperative, starting with how and why customers buy. The marketing plan can take many forms, but all plans should clearly convey the marketing objectives, the target market, and the critical decisions or policies on product, price, promotion, and distribution, as well as key assumptions and anticipated contingencies.

In subsequent chapters, we will address more extensively, areas for analysis and options for market selection, price, promotion, product, and distribution strategies.

Further Reading

George S. Day, "The Capabilities of Market-Driven Organizations, " *Journal of Marketing* 58 (October 1994): 37–52.

George S. Day, *Market Driven Strategy: Processes for Creating Value* (New York: The Free Press, 1990).

Further Reading

Rohit Deshpande, John U. Farley, and Frederick E. Webster Jr. "Corporate Culture, Customer Orientation, and Innovativeness in Japanese Firms: A Quadrad Analysis," *Journal of Marketing* 57 (January 1993): 23–37.

Kathleen M. Eisenhardt and Shona L. Brown, "Time Pacing: Competing in Markets that Won't Stand Still," *Harvard Business Review* 76 (March/April 1998): 59–69.

Gary Hamel, "Bring Silicon Valley Inside," *Harvard Business Review* 77 (September/October 1999): 70–84.

Eric von Hippel, Stefan Thomke, and Mary Sonnack, "Creating Breakthroughs at 3M," *Harvard Business Review* 77 (September/October 1999): 47–57.

Robert S. Kaplan and David P. Norton, "Using the Balanced Scorecard as a Strategic Management System," *Harvard Business Review* 74 (January/February 1996): 75–85.

Soren M. Kaplan, "Discontinuous Innovation and the Growth Paradox," *Strategy & Leadership* 28 (March-April 1999): 16–21.

David L. McCabe and V. K. Narayanan, "The Life Cycle of the PIMS and BCG Models," *Industrial Marketing Management* 20 (1991): 347–352.

---

[1] Peter F. Drucker, *People and Performance: The Best of Peter Drucker on Management* (New York: Harper & Row, Publishers, Inc., 1977), 89–90.

[2] Kenneth R. Andrews, *The Concept of Corporate Strategy* (Homewood, IL: Dow Jones-Irwin, Inc. 1971), 28.

[3] E. Raymond Corey, *Industrial Marketing: Cases and Concepts* (Englewood Cliffs, NJ: Prentice-Hall, Inc., 1983), 2.

[4] William A. Sahlman, "How to Write a Great Business Plan," *Harvard Business Review* (July-August, 1997): 98–108.

[5] John a Byrne, "How Jack Welch Runs GE," *Business Week* (8 June 1998): 88–95.

[6] The discussion in this section draws on Ferderich E. Webster Jr., "The Changing Role of Marketing in the Corporation," *Journal of Marketing* 56 (October 1992): 1–17.

[7] Barry D. Hedley, "Strategy and the Business Portfolio," *Long Range Planning* (February 1977): 12.

[8] George S. Day, *Analysis for Strategies Marketing Decisions* (Mason, OH: Southwestern College Publishing, a division of International Thompson Publishing, 1986), 204.

[9] Igor Ansoff, "Strategies for Diversification," *Harvard Business Review* (September-October 1957): 113–124.

[10] For a comprehensive review of the PIMS studies, see Robert D. Buzzell and Bradley T. Gale, *The PIMS Principles* (New York: The Free Press, 1987).

[11]George S. Day, "The Product Life Cycle: Analysis and Applications Issues," *Journal of Marketing* (fall 1981): 60–67.

[12]Raymond Vernon, "International Investment and International Trade in the Product Cycle," *Quarterly Journal of Economics* (May 1966), 191–202.

Chapter 3

How Organizations Buy

Why do organizations buy, and how? Answers to these questions are fundamental prerequisites to market selection and to the development and implementation of marketing strategy. In this chapter, we identify the key aspects of organizational buying and describe the nature of professional purchasing. We next discuss approaches that have been developed for analyzing organizational buying. Finally, we develop implications for marketing strategy.

Buyer Behavior: An Overview

In most organizations, the signed purchase order is the culmination of a complex process. This process usually involves a number of individuals. Their individual and collective decisions are influenced by organizational factors, such as the nature and purpose of the organization, its policies and organization structure; and by personal factors, such as individual values, perceptions, skills and interpersonal relations, both within and without the organization. Marketing strategy needs to take into account the following key characteristics of this process.

Derived Demand

The starting point for understanding organizational buying is to recognize that an organization's demand for products and services derives from its activities supplying its customers. That is, businesses buy only as required to meet the needs of their customers. For raw materials, or components that directly enter the product, demand will closely parallel fluctuations in demand in the final market. Demand for MRO (maintenance, repair, and operating) items and some services, particularly those closely associated with the production process, will also closely track demand in the final market. For suppliers it is important to be able to forecast short term demand for their customers' products or services, as determined both by short term economic activity and competitive position. In some instances, there will be opportunities to work with customers to stimulate demand in the final market. Aluminum manufacturers and beverage firms, for example, have jointly promoted the benefits of aluminum as a can material to consumers. In other instances, a supplier may work exclusively with one customer, and so give that customer an advantage over competitors.

For capital goods and more complex services, demand is more likely to be based on customer requirements determined by long term demand, replacement needs or other circumstances not related to immediate levels of economic activity. Demand for machine tools or consulting engineering services, for example, is tied to plant expansions or modernization. In many instances, capacity expansion is made in large increments, lengthening the period between purchases of associated goods and services. For suppliers this may emphasize forecasting long-term requirements, in order to justify maintenance of readiness to serve or maintenance of customer relations in the absence of orders for long periods of time. Demand for some services, such as investment banking or consulting services associated with mergers and acquisitions, may be determined by strategic moves of the firm, not directly related to economic activity. Difficult to forecast, it is still important for providers of such services to maintain relations so as to be positioned to capitalize on opportunities as they may arise.

While the extent of demand for products and services is determined by the demand for the customers' products, the nature of demand is shaped by the customer's overall business strategy. A customer's decision to enter foreign markets, for instance, may significantly change requirements for the supplier's product. When U.S. manufacturers of large refrigerant compressors established plants in Europe, A.O. Smith, a U.S. manufacturer of electric motor components for compressors, established a manufacturing plant in Ireland to shorten the supply line, facilitate customer contact, and better meet European voltage and frequency requirements. Similarly, the customer's decision to change the technological base of a product may have profound implications for a component supplier, as was the case when the radar business at GE decided to change from analog to digital electronics. Monitoring strategies, particularly of key customers, is of critical importance to suppliers.

Multiple Buying Influences
We have previously identified multiple buying influences as a key aspect of business buying. Functional requirements for products are usually determined by individuals in engineering, R&D or manufacturing, but may also be determined by those in marketing. Delivery requirements are usually determined by individuals in manufacturing but also may be determined by those in marketing. Policies regarding relations with suppliers and the nature of the purchase decision-making process

are usually determined by individuals in the purchasing department but are frequently influenced by those in other functions and by upper management.

Although multiple buying influences exist, it is important to recognize that the degree of influence exerted, and the involvement of various individuals in specific purchasing decisions, can vary enormously. As we will subsequently consider in more detail, some purchases are relatively routine, as might be the case with highly standardized components purchased repetitively, and the purchase decision may be made by one individual at relatively low level. Other decisions may be the culmination of long and extensive investigations, as might be the case for the acquisition of a large computer or for the selection of an architect for a major building, with the CEO making the final decision.

Consideration of multiple influences needs to recognize that, in many instances, those outside of the buying organization may influence the purchasing decision. Architects or consulting engineers involved in plant expansions usually specify equipment characteristics and have at least some say in equipment approval. Specialists may be hired to assist the firm in purchases that are beyond its normal area of competence. In the paper industry, the printer's purchasing decision may be influenced by the advertising agency or by the printer's customer.

Long Term Relationships[1]
A key characteristic of business marketing is the recognition by both buyers and sellers of their mutual dependency. From the seller's standpoint, with relatively few customers, this emphasizes the importance of repeat orders. How well the supplier performs on current orders is a major determinant of future business. But the relation goes beyond merely ensuring repeat business. Customers, for instance, can be a major source of new product ideas and buyers and sellers can collaborate in joint market development activities.[2] From the buyer's standpoint, the existence of highly qualified suppliers, capable of supplying the firm's current and future requirements, economically and reliably, is critical.

The exact nature of the relationship between buyer and seller will, of course, vary. In some instances, it may be close, with a high degree of trust and information sharing. In others, it may be arms-length, with formal processes and rules to guide it. With many exceptions, the norm in the United States leans more toward reliance on rules and contractual terms whereas in much of the rest of the world, particularly Japan, southern Europe and Latin America, there is more reliance on personal relations, developed over long periods of time.

A recent interest has developed in the study of industrial networks, which recognizes that firms operate in the context of interconnected business relationships, forming networks. As described by Gadde, Huemer, and Hakansson, "these relationships affect the nature and the outcome of the firms' actions and are their potential sources of efficiency and effectiveness."[3]

While the interdependency of buyers and sellers may be apparent, what may not be apparent is the extent of attention by those in purchasing to the management of buyer-seller relations. In fact, its management is generally held to be one of the major objectives of the purchasing function.[4] In most firms, development of comprehensive purchasing strategies, including searching for and qualifying suppliers, is a highly active process, usually led by hose in the purchasing function.

Make versus Buy or Outsourcing

In many instances, organizations have the option to make rather than buy, with regard to both products and services. A classic example is found in the beverage can industry, where large beverage firms can make some or all of their cans and so are able to use the credible threat of self-manufacture to put extreme price pressure on can suppliers. Services, with their relatively low capital requirements, are even more vulnerable to the threat of self-provision. Except for the most specialized services, such as investment banking, or some accounting services required by law to be externally provided, even small firms can elect to provide a host of services internally.

Historically, firms have elected to make, or provide internally, in order to ensure continuity of supply, to achieve cost savings, to ensure quality or some combination of all three. Today there is a definite trend to higher levels of external sourcing, both for products and services. GE, for instance, in equipping its new washing machine manufacturing plant in Kentucky, established a policy that the only certain in-house manufacturing activity would be final assembly. All other manufacturing activities had to be justified on a value-added basis or they were to be purchased externally. More broadly, this trend is encouraged by concepts of the "hollow corporation," envisioned as a small core of activities, surrounded by a network of external suppliers or the "virtual corporation." envisioned as an organization that constantly changes its form as it responds to changes in its external environment.

A number of factors are responsible for this trend. Carefully qualified suppliers are demonstrating they can ensure continuity of supply and quality of product or service, at least at the same level as those produced internally. Specialized suppliers not only may have cost advantages over internally produced components or services, but also their use may free up capital needed for the core business. For instance, Emery Worldwide's new operation, Global Logistics, has expanded its transportation services to include warehousing of both raw materials and finished goods for its customers, taking material into inventory, maintaining inventory records, and re-ordering when inventory gets too low. Federal Express has provided a similar global logistics process for National Semiconductor Corporation that will give National a two business-day delivery service to all its customers worldwide. Finally, external suppliers are frequently more responsive to the needs of the business than an internal component.

Reciprocity
Many businesses do business with each other. Raw material suppliers, for instance, may buy capital goods from those who buy their raw materials. Equipment manufacturers may buy components from those to whom they then attempt to sell their equipment. This has the potential of setting up agreements where, "You buy from me, I'll buy from you." In the United States, reciprocity is legal, as long as it is not enforced through coercive power by one of the parties and as long as it does not substantially lessen competition. Even where it may be legal, however, there is concern that purchasing decisions involving reciprocity may fail to take into account quality of product, reliability of supply or other important attributes. Efforts to use reciprocity as a selling tool have the potential to alienate those in the customer's organization for whom product performance or price are of prime importance.

Competing With Customers
In many instances, suppliers may find themselves competing with their customers. Aluminum companies sell aluminum to can manufacturers and also make cans in direct competition with them. Similarly, Siemens, a large manufacturer of electrical switchboards which use internally produced components also sells these components to switchboard manufacturers with whom it competes. Multi-product business can compete with customers less directly. At GE, one business sells equipment used for testing jet engines to Pratt and Whitney. Another competes with Pratt and Whitney to sell jet engines to the aircraft industry. For suppliers and buyers this raises a number of interesting questions. To what extent, for instance, can the supplier's representa-

tives be taken into the buyer's confidence with regard to future requirements? And, which customer, internal or external, is favored in
times of short supply?

For Lucent Technologies, the part of AT&T, which manufactured telecommunication systems, the potential conflicts were sufficiently large as to be one of the factors in the decision to spin Lucent
off as a separate company. Since the spin-off, Lucent has developed
much stronger relationships with the regional Bell operating companies who formerly may not have wanted to do business with Lucent, as
AT&T was one of their major competitors.

Organization of the Purchasing Function
In large enterprises, the option exists for centralized or decentralized
purchasing, or some combination of both. The electronic businesses of
GTE, for instance, with plants scattered throughout the U.S., established local purchasing departments for needs unique to the particular
plant. Requirements common to several plants, however, were combined and annual negotiations were held with suppliers, to establish
blanket-purchasing contracts against which local plants could draw. In
such situations, the blanket-purchasing contracts involving the local
plants become an issue, as we will see in Chapter 9.

International Aspects
Closely related to growth in exports and world trade has been the
growth in international sourcing. According to Monczka and Trent, international sourcing strategy progresses through four phases: (1) domestic sourcing, (2) foreign sourcing based on competitive need, (3)
foreign sourcing as part of a sourcing strategy, and (4) coordinated
global sourcing for competitive advantage.[5] Many of the aspects of a
coordinated global sourcing strategy are simply logical extensions of a
domestic strategy that looks for qualified suppliers who can reliably
supply goods and services at the lowest possible price. For marketing
strategy it is important to recognize both the similarities and differences of domestic and international sourcing.

The principal factors influencing the buying decision remain
constant. Quality, availability, price, assurance of supply and service
are key considerations, regardless of country of manufacture. On the
other hand, the nature of buyer-seller relations, product standards, language, country laws, and currency denomination may vary. The very
formal relations between buyers and sellers in the German speaking
countries of Germany, Austria and parts of Switzerland are in sharp
contrast to the relatively relaxed relations found in the Scandinavian
countries. Except in the U.S. the metric system is the world standard.
The International Organization for Standards (ISO) is attempting to

coordinate technical standards on a worldwide basis, but many still vary by country or region. English, frequently described as the language of business, is not the language customers in non-English speaking countries prefer for business discussions. In France, for instance, the regional manager for ALCOA, having made an initial contact with an important customer who was totally fluent in English, was told that all future conversations must be in French if ALCOA expected to do any business with the firm. The reliance on legal contract language in the United States is in sharp contrast with the reliance on personal relations in Japan, countries in the Middle East, southern Europe, and Latin America. The legal system in the United States, the United Kingdom and other common law countries is substantially different from the system in France, Germany and other code law countries, significantly influencing contract formation and the location for resolution of disputes, should they arise. Finally, currency denomination for payment is always a contentious issue, raising as it does questions both of convenience and exposure to risks associated with currency fluctuation.[6]

Professional Buyers
With some firms spending as much as half or more of sales revenues on purchase of materials and services, it should be clear that purchasing decisions have a major impact on the firm's performance, both in operational and financial terms. There has been concern, however, that firms have not assigned professional buyers an appropriate role in the purchasing process.[7] In many instances, decisions regarding capital equipment may be made by those in engineering or manufacturing, based principally on functionality, with inadequate attention to price, terms or other considerations. Similarly, decisions regarding raw materials, components or services may be made by those in manufacturing, based principally on reliability of supply; again with inadequate attention to price, terms or other considerations. Although there is considerable basis for these concerns, there is no question that there is a long term trend toward according professional buyers in the purchasing department a more influential role in defining the purchasing process and making the purchasing decision. At least in part this is due to the efforts, in the United States, of the education programs of the Institute of Supply Management (ISM), formerly the National Association of Purchasing Management (NAPM); designed to improve the competence of purchasing professionals. In 1975, NAPM inaugurated a certification program and to date has qualified some 23,000 Certified Purchasing Managers (C.P.M.s). Similar organizations operate in most other industrial countries, linked together by the International Federation of

Purchasing and Material Management (IFPMM). In Japan, for instance the counterpart of NAPM is the Japan Material Management Association (JMMA). In the following section we more fully address the role of professional purchasing.

Professional Purchasing

Most organizations have a professional purchasing function staffed by well-trained, experienced individuals whose responsibility is to ensure the organization buys wisely. Once assigned primary responsibility for relatively mundane purchases, increasingly those in purchasing are playing a significant role in purchases of a wide variety of equipment. An extreme example is the 1992 appointment by General Motors of José Ignacio López de Arriortúa as its purchasing czar. Backed by GM's new CEO John F. Smith, Jr., López combined 27 separate purchasing divisions into one to increase the leverage of GM's enormous purchasing clout. Despite concerns about buyer-seller relationships, López demanded double-digit percentage price cuts from suppliers, shared proprietary supplier information with competitors, and shaved some $4 billion from the cost of GM's purchases.

As the scope of purchasing has increased, the influence of those in purchasing on the overall purchasing process has also increased. A leading purchasing textbook identifies the following objectives for purchasing management:[8]

1. To support company operations with an uninterrupted flow of materials and services.
2. To buy competitively.
3. To buy wisely.
4. To keep inventory investment and inventory losses at a practical minimum.
5. To develop reliable and effective sources of supply.
6. To develop good relationships with the vendor community and good continuing relationship with suppliers.
7. To achieve maximum integration with the other departments of the firm.
8. To administer the purchasing function in a professional, cost-effective manner.

To meet these objectives, the purchasing function is becoming increasingly proactive in both its internal and external relations. Of particular interest to those in marketing are the policies promulgated by purchasing departments with respect to acquisition and evaluation of proposals and, more generally, buyer-seller relations.

Acquisition and Evaluation of Proposals

The normative or commonly prescribed approach to the acquisition of proposals is to describe requirements in sufficient detail such that qualified suppliers can respond with quotes or bids that can be evaluated, with the award going to the lowest or best bidder. Subject to meeting certain constraints, it is generally felt that this competitive bidding process is efficient and results in competitive prices for the buyer. The constraints are that the dollar value of the purchase must be large enough to justify the bidding expense; that specifications must be clear; that there must be an adequate number of sellers willing to quote; that sellers must be qualified and want the order; and that there is sufficient time for obtaining and evaluating quotes or bids.

Evaluation processes are becoming more formal and sophisticated. Prospective suppliers may be evaluated with respect to technical or production capability, quality control, managerial capability, financial condition, and service capacity. For relatively standard products, or low dollar volume purchases, this evaluation may be based on catalogs, financial reports, or other readily available data. For complex or high dollar value purchases the evaluation may include visits to the facilities of two or three suppliers. Table 3.1 illustrates how potential suppliers might be evaluated.

Factor	Maximum Score	Score Supplier A	Score Supplier B
Technical competence	15	12	10
Production capacity	20	15	12
Quality control	20	15	18
Managerial capability	10	7	8
Financial condition	10	8	7
Prepurchase service	10	7	9
Postpurchase service	15	7	11
Total	100	71	75

Table 3.1: Evaluating Prospective Suppliers

Current suppliers may also be evaluated, either for continuation or for making a particular purchasing decision. Table 3.2 shows how Chrysler Corporation grades suppliers of electronic components.

When actual bids or quotations are being evaluated, factors used to evaluate prospective suppliers or the performance of existing suppliers can be combined with factors specific to the individual transaction to assist in making the purchase award. In many instances, the purchasing department will ask the engineering or operating departments to make an economic evaluation of competing proposals, which will then be used in combination with the price and evaluation of other factors, to make the final determination as to the best proposal.

Supplier Rating Chart:

Supplier Name: _____ Commodity: _____

Shipping Locations: _____ Annual Sales Dollars: _____

	5 Excellent	4 Good	3 Satisfactory	2 Fair	1 Poor	0 N/A
Quality 40%						
Supplier defect rates						
SCQ program conformance						
Sample approval performance						
Responsiveness to quality problems						
Overall rating						
Delivery 25%						
Avoidance of late or overshipments						
Ability to expand production capacity						
Engineering sample delivery performance						
Response to fluctuating supply demands						
Overall delivery rating						
Price 25%						
Price competitiveness						
Absorption of economic price						
Submission of cost savings plans						
Payment terms						
Overall price rating						
Technology 10%						
State-of-the-art component technology						
Sharing research development capability						
Capable and willing to provide circuit design services						
Responsiveness to engineering problems						
Overall technology rating						

Buyer: _____ Date: _____

Comments: _____

Source: Adapted from information provided courtesy of Daimler Chrysler AG.

Table 3.2: How Daimler Chrysler Grades Suppliers

Suppliers, it is held, must perceive competitive bidding, as fair. Two policies are prescribed to achieve fairness. First, buyers must be willing to do business with every vendor from whom a bid is solicited and, second, to give a reasonable explanation to unsuccessful bidders as to why they did not receive the award. Simple as these requirements may seem, they are difficult to put into practice. Suppliers are not all equal. Buyers may have favorites, frequently for legitimate reasons. Some evaluation criteria are subjective in nature and sellers may not accept the buyer's evaluation. Discussion of price, even after the fact, may be seen as closely related to negotiation. As a result, many buyers avoid disclosure of details of either their evaluation criteria or of their bid analyses.

While competitive bidding is the normative approach, there are extensive variations in purchasing approaches. In those instances where there is only one supplier, some form of negotiation is required. Many buyers insist on receiving cost information from the supplier and this, itself, may well become a matter for negotiation. When the value of the order is small, or time to place the order is of the essence, buyers may elect to place the order non-competitively or on the basis of informal quotations. Even in instances where there are many suppliers, a firm may elect to do business with only one, as is frequently the case where the firm has adopted just-in-time manufacturing (JIT). In this situation, the firm may establish stringent performance expectations of the supplier. Hewlett-Packard, for instance, told its prospective JIT suppliers that one of their expectations of the chosen suppliers would be continuing price reductions.

When there are many potential suppliers, some firms elect to split their business between two or more of the lowest bidders, generally in order to ensure continuity of supply. Still another approach is what has been called stimulated competition. Just short of an auction, the buyer uses the original bids as a starting point for extensive discussions with suppliers on ways for them to reduce costs and so reduce their bid price. Finally, even within the firm, purchasing approaches may vary. Sole source may be the approach for some purchases. Normal competitive bids or stimulated competition may be the approach for others.

Buyer-Seller Relationships
We have previously described the long-term relationships that typify business-to-business marketing, sometimes stretching over decades. A simplistic view of the relations between buyers and sellers assumes that the principal, and sometimes only, contact between firms is by those in sales and purchasing. In fact, in many situations, there is extensive contact between various members of buying and selling organizations. Specifying engineers, for example, frequently talk directly to design engineers. Management representatives in both organizations

may interact in business and social situations. Order expediters talk to order processors or production staff.

This suggests the need for formalizing the relationships between the two organizations and many firms have established written purchasing policies that attempt to describe the nature of the desired relationship. Given the complexities of most relationships, however, many policies governing relationships between buyers and sellers are informal and represent the views not only of those in purchasing but also other functions as well as top management. Recognizing these complexities is key to both the development and implementation of marketing strategy.

Just-In-Time (JIT) Manufacturing

JIT is an approach to manufacturing, relying on the concept of achieving quality improvement and cost reduction by delivering parts and materials to the production process at just the moment they are needed. Originated in Japan by the Toyota Manufacturing Company, the 1980s saw firms throughout the world adopting the concept. With it have come significant changes in purchasing and buyer-seller relations.

At the core of the JIT concept is the reduction or elimination of parts and materials inventories, and significant improvements in quality. For purchasing this has meant a major change in approach to suppliers. At the heart of this change is the closer integration of production of the buyer and suppliers, usually accompanied by a switch from several suppliers to one, or at most a few. Extensive sharing of information is required to facilitate rapid adjustment by suppliers to precisely meet the buyer's schedule of requirements. Suppliers are held to higher quality standards, to eliminate the requirement for incoming material inspections. JIT suppliers are generally chosen for long periods of time as the degree of required integration militates against frequent changes in suppliers. In many instances this closer integration leads to a partnership in which the supplier assumes much of the burden for innovations in design, based on greater insight as to buyer needs. As previously indicated, it is usually expected that suppliers' costs will improve due to increased volume and increased certainty of orders, leading to the requirement that suppliers continually reduce prices.

For those in purchasing, the move to JIT presents several challenges. Dependency on fewer suppliers makes supplier selection and management of the relationship more critical than ever. Even carefully selected suppliers may be more interested in the increased volume than in the changes necessary to operate as effective JIT suppliers. As one industry representative said, "The easy one-half of the job of implementing JIT is doing it inside. The tough one-half is doing it with suppliers."[9] Supplier training, therefore, is a required part of the move to JIT and the primary responsibility for this training rests with the purchasing department.

Not all firms will successfully convert to JIT manufacturing. A major GE facility, which had moved to JIT and close partnerships with a number of its suppliers, concluded that further reductions in the price of materials and components could only be achieved by going back to many suppliers competing vigorously for each order. Many suppliers are unwilling, themselves, to adopt the JIT philosophy necessary to be a successful JIT supplier. Others find it difficult to simultaneously supply both JIT and non-JIT customers. It is clear, however, that good understanding of how JIT works and what customers expect of a JIT supplier is becoming important for an increasing number of firms.

The Battle of the Forms
Most of the discussion leading up to placing an order focuses on matters of product specification, price and delivery. Frequently overlooked are the general terms and conditions stipulated by buyers and sellers. Contained on the back of most purchase orders or quotation letters, these may state some relatively mundane requirements, such as the number of copies of invoices, but they also address the matter of responsibility in the event of failure of either party to perform. Inevitably, there is conflict between these terms and conditions. Sellers attempt to limit their risk, particularly with regard to warranty provisions and possible failure to live up to all aspects of the contract. Buyers, on the other hand, seek to hold sellers to the highest possible level of responsibility. The most contentious issues are *fitness for purpose and merchantability*, dealing with the question of what is warranted; *cover*, dealing with the rights of the buyer to procure a product from an alternative source in the event of late delivery, and *damages*, dealing with the obligations of the seller to reimburse the buyer for costs raising out of failure of the product.

In the United States, this has given rise to a phenomenon unique to business marketing, usually referred to as the "Battle of the Forms" in which buyers and sellers strive to make their terms and conditions the basis for the contract. In the exchange of quotation letters, purchase orders and order acknowledgements, each party insists on its terms and conditions. In previous years, this resulted in what was called the "Last Shot Doctrine," which held that, unless objected to, the terms in the last document to be sent formed the basis of the contract. The Uniform Commercial Code (UCC), adopted by most states during the 1950s, negates the Last Shot Doctrine and provides that in the event of conflict between the party's terms, the basis for the contract shall be those terms on which there is agreement *plus* the provisions of the Code on those matters where there is silence or disagreement. In general, these provisions tend to favor the buyer. In particular, the Code's treatment of fitness for purpose, merchantability, cover and damages is unacceptable to most suppliers.

The situation becomes more complicated when doing business across national borders. Not only are desires of the contracting parties likely to differ substantially, but there is the question of legal jurisdiction in case of dispute. To address this matter, the United Nations developed the Convention on Contracts for the International Sale of Goods (CISG), which has many similarities to the UCC. If the buyer and seller are located in countries that have ratified the convention (now including the United States and many countries in Europe and Asia), then most contracts involving the sale and purchase of goods will be governed by provisions of the CISG.

Inasmuch as the vast majority of contracts are completed without significant problem, the importance of terms and conditions is frequently ignored. Few in marketing are expert in matters of contract law. Trying to reach agreement on specific terms may be contentious and time consuming. As a result, sellers tend to give them little attention unless some event has occurred to expose them to unanticipated liability. Purchasing agents, however, are constantly reminded of their importance, through seminars and the considerable attention they are given in the trade press, and are likely to give them relatively high priority. While it is beyond the scope of this text to deal with all the complexities of either the UCC or the CISG, it is important for business marketers to recognize their importance and to take appropriate steps to ensure that they can live with the legal provisions of contracts as well as with the more familiar matters of product specifications, price and delivery.

Purchasing Trends
There is little question that the role of the purchasing function is changing. The introduction to a recent book on purchasing asserted "the revolution in purchasing is challenging the traditional thinking that has dominated business for the last twenty years. The adversarial relationship between buyers and suppliers is evolving into a new partnership, based on long-term business goals. Companies are now leveraging the role of purchasing to achieve competitive advantage in supplier quality, product delivery and new product development."[10] Its importance to the organization is indicated in a recent survey that found that two-thirds of CEOs and presidents now view the function as

very important to the overall success of their firms.[11] More recently there has been a trend to enlarge the scope of the purchasing function. In the U.S. the National Association of Purchasing Management changed its name to the Institute of Supply Management and many organizations have similarly retitled the purchasing function. In their new role, supply managers are increasingly assigned the responsibility for supply chain management, an assignment which is challenging the profession to determine its future responsibilities.[12, 13]

The exact nature of change will be determined both by those in purchasing and by the strategic situation of the firm. Growing professionalism of those in purchasing has the potential to expand their role and enable those in purchasing to become involved in quality and customer satisfaction efforts and, more generally, in strategic planning. Partnership relations with suppliers will be pursued in situations where they can make unique contributions in areas such as product development or JIT manufacturing. In other instances, purchase price considerations will be predominant, as at General Motors, and suppliers can expect to face extreme bidding or negotiation pressure. While individual firms will differ in their approaches, the common theme will be one of increased proactivity on the part of those in purchasing.

Perhaps the most significant current trend in purchasing is toward the increased use of electronic means to communicate with suppliers, place orders, and otherwise manage transactions with suppliers. As long ago as 1978 a working party, functioning under the guidance of the United Nations Economic Commission for Europe, had decided on a number of principles for data transmission, including a set of interchange rules to govern interchange of data between trade partners by means other than paper documents, i.e., by teletransmission methods including direct exchange between computer systems. A first set of interchange rules was published in 1981 in the form of "Guidelines for Trade Data Interchange" which offered potential users a basis for developing their systems.[14] For many organizations, EDI became an efficient, economical, and effective way to place orders, verify order status, and otherwise communicate with suppliers.

The advent of the Internet has increased the use of electronic means to conduct business with suppliers. It offers professional purchasers a diverse range of online buying forums, with varying levels of features, complexity, and cost. The most basic tool for a business buyer is the use of suppliers' websites, which provide information and sometimes provide a means to place an order. Many suppliers, particularly of MRO items, offer on-line catalogs, which, in some instances, provide the opportunity to negotiate prices.

The Internet has also facilitated the development of electronic market places, which are aggregations of buyers and sellers in vertical and functional markets. Vertical market places serve specific industries whereas functional, or horizontal, market places serve a variety of industries.

Related to the development of electronic market places are web-based auction sites.[15] Such auction sites are highly varied, both with respect to the nature of goods at auction and the responsibility for managing the auction site. In general, and as with market places, auction sites are categorized either as horizontal, focusing on specific products for a wide variety of industries, or vertical, focusing on a wide variety of products for a specific industry such as automotive or semiconductor. In some instances, an auction site may be managed by the buying firm. In others, a third party may manage the auction site.

Buyer Behavior: Analytical Frameworks

The foregoing suggests the complexity of the organizational buying process. In this section, we introduce two models that are particularly useful in its analysis and the development of marketing strategy.

The BUYGRID Model

To fully understand organizational buying behavior requires identification of the steps in the buying process, and recognition of how these steps may vary, depending on the specific buying situation. A widely used study has identified eight steps, or Buy Phases, as shown in Table 3.3, with three categories of buying situations, or Buy Classes; New Task, Modified Rebuy and Straight Rebuy.[16]

The New Task situation involves a requirement or problem that has not arisen before. There is little past experience to draw on and a great deal of information is needed. The buyer seeks alternative ways of solving the problem and considers alternative suppliers. Such needs occur relatively infrequently but represent an opportunity for suppliers to get in on the ground floor and establish a position for subsequent purchases. In New Task situations, all Buy Phases are involved. Problem recognition can come from within or without the firm. Determining and describing the characteristics and required quantity of the needed item involves many individuals in the firm. Opportunities may exist for suppliers to assist the process. The search for suppliers, and their qualification, is extensive. This is usually the last opportunity for a supplier to become established as a prospective bidder. Proposal solicitation and supplier selection involves many buying influences in the firm, all of whom need to be contacted by the supplier. The order routine goes beyond merely placing an order and involves a wide variety of follow-up activities. Finally, some kind of assessment of supplier performance is made, as a basis for placing future orders.

| Buy Phases | New Task | Buy Classes | |
		Modified Rebuy	Straight Rebuy
Anticipation or recognition of a problem (need) and a general solution	Yes	Maybe	No
Determination of characteristics and quantity of needed item	Yes	Maybe	No
Description of characteristics and quantity of needed item	Yes	Yes	No
Search for and qualification of potential sources	Yes	Maybe	No
Acquisition and analysis of proposals	Yes	Maybe	Maybe
Evaluation of proposals and selection of suppliers	Yes	Maybe	Maybe
Selection of an order routine	Yes	Yes	Yes
Performance feedback and evaluation	Yes	Yes	Yes

Source: From Patrick J. Robinson: Industrial Buying And Creative Marketing. Published by Allyn and Bacon, Boston, MA. Copyright © 1967 by Pearson Education. Reprinted/adapted by permission of the publisher.

Table 3.3: The BUYGRID Framework

In the Straight Rebuy situation the routine is far simpler. The product has been specified, and suppliers qualified. All that is required is solicitation of proposals that focus on price and delivery, with some form of performance review following the receipt of the product or service. The objective of qualified suppliers is to stay qualified. The objective of non-qualified suppliers is to provide evidence to the buyer to justify moving to a Modified Rebuy situation.

Modified Rebuy situations can arise out of either New Task or Straight Rebuy situations. Following a New Task purchase, it may develop that some modifications need to be made with respect to future purchases. The objective of qualified suppliers is to stay qualified and, perhaps, influence specifications so as to achieve competitive advantage. In some instances, previously non-qualified suppliers may have the opportunity for reconsideration. Alternatively, poor performance by suppliers in Straight Rebuy situations, or evidence of special qualifications of new suppliers, may also lead to Modified Rebuy situations.

An Organizational Model of Buying Behavior[17]

Although the BUYGRID Framework identifies the phases in the buying process, and indicates how these phases may vary depending on the buying situation, it does not address the interrelationship of organizational factors and individual factors that influence the decision making process. Webster and Wind have developed an excellent framework for better understanding and analyzing these interrelationships.

They propose thinking about the individuals involved in any buying decision as belonging *to a buying center.*[18] They further propose that buying behavior is a function of the individual characteristics of those who make up the particular center, plus what they call *group factors, organization factors* and *environmental factors*. Finally, they propose that each of these four factors can influence the buying decision through a set of variables relating to the buying *task* and through a set of variables not directly related to the task at hand (*non-task*). Insights into the decision making process within a particular buying center can be developed by identifying each of its determinants, for both task and non-task variables. A brief example of such use is shown in Table 3.4.

The starting point for analysis is to identify the individuals in the buying center. Webster and Wind define the buying center as that group of individuals who collectively interact in order to accomplish the objectives of the specific buying task. Roles within the center vary. Purchasing agents may select suppliers within certain parameters of delegated authority. Specifiers define required features and characteristics. Users influence specifications and supplier selection based on projected needs and past experience. Gatekeepers (e.g., receptionists, secretaries, librarians and, sometimes, purchasing agents) control the flow of information or access to others in the center.

Within the center, the locus of influence may vary substantially. In some instances, all members of the center will have equal say and influence. Increased product complexity, however, may shift the influence to individuals in the engineering function. Strong personalities may exercise influence disproportionate to their functional expertise as in the case where the purchasing manager overrules an engineering recommendation despite product complexity. Political aspects can shift the locus of influence, as in the case where top management takes special interest in a large purchase, perceived to have implications outside the organization. Finally, the number of individuals in the center will vary. In New Buy situations, the center will include many influences. In the case of a Straight Rebuy, the center may include only individuals in purchasing.

Source of Influence	Task Variables	Non-task Variables
Individual factors	Desire for low price, short delivery, total cost, etc.	Desire for close personal relations, ego enhancement, cost, etc.
Group factors	Procedures to set specifications, buying committee processes	Off-the-job interactions among group members
Organizational factors	Policies with respect to quality, bidding procedures	Policies regarding community relations
Environmental factors	Expected trends in business conditions	Political factors in an election year

Source: Wind, Y.; Webster, JR., Frederick E, Organizational Buying Behavior, 1st edition, © 1972. Adapted by permission of Pearson Education, Inc., Upper Saddle River, NJ.

Table 3.4: A Classification of Determinants of Organizational Buying Behavior

Many have characterized business purchasing as rational and, hence, unemotional. In fact, the behavior of individuals in the buying center is very much influenced by their personal needs, goals, habits, past experience, information and attitudes. Those in the buying center form a group whose previous interactions and social experiences establish a set of shared values and patterns of communication, which direct and constrain the behavior of individuals in the group. Organizational factors such as objectives, policies, procedures, and structure and reward systems define the formal organization as an entity and significantly influence the buying process at all stages. Finally, environmental factors, including the influence of market stimuli and technical, political and economic characteristics of our society, influence the organization, its members and its patterns of interaction.

These four factors are, in turn, influenced by task and non-task variables. Task variables are those that directly relate to the objectives of the buying task. Examples might include an individual's desire to obtain the lowest price, meetings to set product specifications, company policies with respect to product quality and expected trends in business conditions. Non-task variables might include personal values of a religious nature, off the job interactions among company employees, company policies regarding community relations and social or political trends.

Implications for Marketing

We conclude this chapter by reiterating the importance of understanding organizational buyer behavior. Marketing strategy must take into account the wide variation in customer situations and purchasing practices. In many instances, sales representatives may have the opportunity to influence the nature of purchasing practices, particularly with respect to evaluation approaches. As we will discuss in Chapter 6, the nature of purchasing practices is usually a key segmentation variable. In many cases, market research will focus on just a few customers but must ensure inclusion of the views of the many individuals who make up a particular buying center or decision-making unit. Product, price and distribution decisions and overall promotion strategy will be determined, in large part, by the purchasing practices of the targeted market segment (s.). The customer's strategic situation may indicate opportunities for joint market development activities.

While formulation of marketing strategy needs to take into account a variety of customer situations, implementation of strategy, usually the responsibility of the field sales force, needs to be based on in-depth understanding of each assigned account. As we will discuss in Chapter 9, the ability of individual salespersons to diagnose and comprehensively understand the decision making process for each account is critical to sales success.

Summary

Understanding how organizations buy is a fundamental prerequisite to the development of marketing plans and their implementation. Such understanding must take into account the key aspects of organizational buying behavior: derived demand, multiple buying influences, long-term relationships, the customer's ability to make or buy, the possibility of competing with one's customers, the various ways in which the purchasing function may be organized, and the growth in international sourcing. It must also consider the growth in professionalism of the purchasing function and the increasing influence of those in purchasing or buying decisions. A number of models have been developed to assist in analyzing organizational buying behavior. Two models particularly useful for marketers in developing marketing plans for understanding how individual customers buy are the BUYGRID model and the organizational model of buying behavior developed by Webster and Wind.

Further Reading

James Anderson and Jim Narus, "Partnering as a Focused Market Strategy," *California Management Review* (spring 1991): 95–113.

Further Reading

Michele D. Bunn, "Taxonomy of Buying Decision Approaches," *Journal of Marketing* 57 (January 1993): 33–56.

Richard N. Cardozo, Shannon H. Shipp and Kenneth J. Roering, "Proactive Strategic Partnerships: A New Business Markets Strategy," *The Journal of Business and Industrial Marketing* 7, no. 1 (winter 1992): 51–63

David Ford, ed., *Understanding Business Marketing and Purchasing* (London: International Thomson, 2001), especially readings 4.1–4.9.

David Ford and others, *Managing Business Relationships* (Chichester, England, John Wiley, 1998).

Michael E. Heberling, "The Rediscovery of Modern Purchasing," *International Journal of Purchasing and Materials Management* (fall 1993): 47–53.

Jan B. Heide and Allen M. Weiss, "Vendor Considerations and Switching Behavior in High-Technology Markets," *Journal of Marketing* 59 (July 1995): 30–43.

Wesley J. Johnston and Jeffrey E. Lewin, "Organizational Buying Behavior Toward an Integrative Framework," *Journal of Business Research* 35 (January 1996): 1–15.

N. Kumar, "The Power of Trust in Manufacturer-Retailer Relationships, *Harvard Business Review* (November-December 1996): 92–106.

Robert D. McWilliams, Earl Naumann and Stan Scott, "Determining Buying Center Size," *Industrial Marketing Management* 21 (1992): 43–49.

Glen D Souza, "Designing a Customer Retention Plan," *The Journal of Business Strategy* (March-April 1992): 24–28.

Robert E. Speckman, David W. Stewart, and Wesley J. Johnston, "An Empirical Investigation of the Organizational Buyer's Strategic and Tactical Roles," *Journal of Business-to-Business Marketing* 2, No. 4 (1995): 37–63.

Frederick Webster, "The Changing Role of Marketing in the Corporation," *Journal of Marketing* 56 (October 1992): 1–17.

Brent M. Wren and James T. Simpson, "A Dyadic Model of Relationships in Organizational Buying: A Synthesis of Research Results," *Journal of Business & Industrial Marketing* 11, No. 3/4 (1996): 68–79.

---

[1]In the readings, we have included "The Development of Buyer-Seller Relationships in Industrial Markets" by David Ford, which discusses some of the basic concepts developed by the IMP (Industrial Marketing and Purchasing) group in Europe. An outstanding collection of work of this group is contained in *Understanding Business Markets: Interaction, Relationships and Networks*, ed. David Ford, (San Diego, CA: Academic Press, Inc. 1990).

[2]See, for instance, Cornelius Herstatt and Eric von Hippel, "FROM EXPERIENCE: Developing New Product Concepts Via the Lead User Method: A Case Study in a "Low-Tech" Field," *Journal of Product Innovation Management*, 9 (1992): 213–221

[3]Lars-Erik Gadde, Lars Huemer, Hakan Hakansson, "Strategizing in industrial networks" *Industrial Marketing Management* 32 (2003): 357–364

[4]See, for instance, Lars-Erik Gadde and Hakan Hakansson, *Professional Purchasing* (New York: Routledge, 1993).

[5]R. M. Monczka and R. J. Trent, "Global Sourcing: A Development Approach," *International Journal of Purchasing and Materials Management*, (spring 1991): 2–7

[6]See, for instance, Lutz Kaufmann and Craig R. Carter "International Supply Management Systems—The Impact of Price vs. Non-Price Driven Motives in the United States and Germany," *The Journal of Supply Chain Management*, (summer 2002): 4–17

[7]Michael E. Heberling, "The Rediscovery of Modern Purchasing," *International Journal of Purchasing and Materials Management* (fall 1993): 47–53.

[8]Donald W. Dobler et al, *Purchasing and Materials Management: Text and Cases* (New York: McGraw-Hill, Inc., 1990).

[9]Charles O'Neal and Kate Bertrand, *Developing a Winning J.I.T. Marketing Strategy: The Industrial Marketer's Guide* (Englewood Cliffs, NJ: Prentice-Hall, Inc., 1991), 13.

[10]John E. Schorr, *Purchasing in the 21st Century* (Essex Junction, VT: Oliver Wight Publications, Inc., 1992).

[11]William A. Bales and Harold E. Fearon, "CEOs'/Presidents' Perceptions and Expectation of the Purchasing Function," *Center for Advanced Purchasing Studies*, (May 1993): 33–34.

[12]Andrew Cox "Is Supply Chain Management Best Practice?" *Inside Supply Management,* (May 2003): 6–8.

[13]Keah Choon Tan "Supply Chain Management: Practices, Concerns, and Performance Issues" *The Journal of Supply Chain Management,* (winter 2002): 42–53.

[14]See www.unece.org/trade/untdid/texts/d100 for United Nations Directories for Electronic Data Interchange for Administration, Commerce and Transport (UN/EDIFACT).

[15]See Sashi, C.M. and Bay O'Leary, "The role of Internet auctions in the expansion of B2B markets," *Industrial Marketing Management* 31 (2002): 103–110 for a more comprehensive discussion of auctions on the Internet.

[16]Patrick J. Robinson and Charles W. Faris, *Industrial Buying and Creative Marketing* (Boston: Allyn & Bacon, Inc., 1967).

[17]This section draws heavily on Frederick E. Webster, Jr. and Yoram Wind, *Organizational Buying Behavior* (Englewood Cliffs, NJ: Prentice-Hall, Inc., 1972).

[18]Most other models refer to the buying center as the decision-making unit (DMU) and elsewhere we will use this terminology.

58

Chapter 4

Strategic Analysis of an Industry

The focus of marketing strategy is on effectively meeting the wants and needs of carefully selected customers. But this is not enough. To be successful, a firm's marketing strategy must meet these wants and needs more effectively than those of its competitors. In other words, one of the goals of marketing strategy must be to develop or exploit the firm's competitive advantage. It must, therefore, not only know how organizations buy. It must also take into account strategies of competitors; strategies which are the result of a complex interaction of competitive rivalry, influenced by a host of external events. Understanding this complex interaction, and developing inferences for the development of marketing strategies, is the goal of industry analysis.

The conventional approach to industry analysis is to consider those firms that compete with each other, and to consider how this competition, or rivalry, is influenced by external forces. Another approach is to consider the principal activities required to produce a good or service in its final form and then develop an understanding as to the role of each activity Alderson, a pioneering marketing academic, argued for this approach through analysis of what he called the transvection chain; that is, all the transactions and transformations that take place going from raw materials to the ultimate product or service purchased by the final customer.[1] More recently, concepts such as "deconstructed" firms, "value-adding partnerships" and "virtual corporations" have been introduced, focusing attention on subsets of value adding functions and the coordinated relationships necessary between firms to provide the total value-chain activities needed for a market offering.[2] Many of these concepts are included in what has come to be called business system analysis.

In this chapter, we will first provide the conceptual underpinnings of industry and business system analysis. We will then outline a multi-step approach to a marketing strategy oriented analysis that combines concepts of industry and business system analysis.

Industry Analysis

Market and industry analysis are closely related. In fact, some economists use the term market to include both buyers and sellers. For business marketers, however, it is important to distinguish between the two. Market analysis is concerned with discerning wants and needs of customers and how they buy to satisfy those needs. Industry analysis, on the other hand, is concerned with how to satisfy these needs better than competitors do.

The term industry tends to be used in many ways. Used broadly, it might include a variety of firms providing a wide array of goods and services. The telecommunications industry, for instance, includes local providers of voice and data service, long distance providers of voice and data service, hardware suppliers of such products as digital switches for central office use or commercial institutions, hardware suppliers of a wide variety of other products such as fiber optic cables, handsets, and, increasingly, wireless phones, personal computers and software. In some instances these products and services are provided exclusively to organizations, in others they are provided exclusively to individual consumers, and in still others they are provided to both. Surrounding these products and services which one would automatically associate with the telecommunications industry is a host of other firms who are major suppliers to the industry such as contractors or providers of vehicles or maintenance equipment.

For some purposes, it is useful to analyze an industry defined in such broad terms. Growth of the overall industry, for instance, influences the available business for all firms and so may determine significant investment decisions. Technology developments in one segment may have implications for those in another, even if the two segments do not compete with one another. Data compression techniques, for instance, are of interest to both providers of data transmission services and manufacturers of digital switches and other forms of computers. Defining an industry in such broad terms, however, does not focus on immediate competitors; those with whom a given firm may compete for patronage of customers.

For this purpose we borrow, with modification, from Kotler[3] and Porter[4] and define an industry as a group of firms that offers products or services that are reasonably close substitutes for one another. It should be noted here that the analysis should focus on competitors at the business level. General Electric, for instance, does not compete in the market place as a corporate entity. Rather, its medical equipment business competes with the medical equipment business of Siemens, its light bulb business competes with Phillips' light bulb business, and so forth. Similarly, IBM's personal computer business competes most directly with firms such as Dell, Compaq and Apple whereas its mainframe business competes most directly with firms such as Amdahl, Bull or Cray Research. The precise definition of the group will vary as a function of the purpose of the analysis, which might include:

- Identification of potential competitors.
- Identification of market niches not currently being served by other players
- Anticipation of attacks by competitors on customer positions.
- Identification of competitors' weaknesses for potential attack
- Learning from competitors as to successful strategies or skills
- Identification of opportunities to cooperate with competitors

In the accounting industry, for instance, the Big Five seldom compete with the small local firms. They might, however, feel it important to identify and follow medium size firms which either have the potential to grow to a national or international scale or who otherwise might have the capability to attack certain Big Five firm customers. Similarly, manufacturers of electro-mechanical calculators such as Marchant would have been well advised to include manufacturers of electronic calculators, such as Sharp, as potential competitors. It is interesting to note that apparently they did not, in part because Sharp did not have the extensive service facilities. What was not recognized was that electronic calculators would not require nearly the level of service required by electro-mechanical calculators.

Definition of the group may also depend on the circumstances of the firm. At one time, a U.S. manufacturer of turbine generators might have identified just U.S. manufacturers of turbine generators (such as GE, Westinghouse, and Allis-Chalmers) as comprising the turbine generator industry, although non-U.S. manufacturers might have been included if it was felt they were credible potential competitors. Today, the industry is truly global and any industry definition must include Asea Brown Boveri (ABB) of Switzerland, Siemens of Germany, and Hitachi of Japan.

Complete industry analysis, then, and the accompanying examination of competitive behavior, allows managers to gain a better understanding of the playing field on which a group of firms compete. Without such analysis, it is impossible to explain performance differences or discover opportunities for advantage between firms competing in the same industry. In addition, without such analysis accurate assessment of one's own strengths and weaknesses is impossible, as these strengths and weaknesses have meaning only in relationship to competitors.

Approaches to Industry Analysis

A number of frameworks have been developed to facilitate industry analysis. Scherer, for instance, has developed a model of industrial organization analysis designed to facilitate understanding of the basic conditions underlying demand and supply which influence industry structure which, in turn, influences industry conduct.[5] Perhaps most popular is the five forces model developed by Porter which examines rivals and how their strategies interact, influenced by the power of buyers and suppliers, the threat of substitutes and the potential entry of others into the industry.[6]

Rivalry

At the heart of Porter's model are the firms that compete with one another for customer patronage. As we describe in Chapter 5, a major objective of marketing intelligence is to develop an understanding of these competitors, their strategies, their strengths and weaknesses, their possible aggressive moves or their vulnerability to attack. Within the industry, we may find competitors with significantly different strategies. Some may concentrate on cost reductions, making possible aggressive pricing strategies. Texas Instruments, for instance, long-favored this approach to its semi-conductor business. Others, such as Intel, may emphasize functionality, with relatively higher prices. For analytical purposes it is useful to identify those competitors who appear to be following similar strategies directed to a given target market. We do this using what is called strategic group mapping.

Strategy Mapping

The purpose of strategy mapping is to facilitate making strategic decisions, taking into account how the firm's strategy interacts with the strategies of rivals. In some industries, all or most competitors may follow the same strategy. In commodity businesses, for instance, there may be little opportunity for product differentiation and economies of scale may require that all firms pursue all possible markets. In such cases all the firms will be in one strategic group. In most instances, however, there are considerable degrees of freedom with respect to strategic decisions and competitors will follow different strategies. While each strategy is ultimately unique, competitors may be evaluated on major dimensions and then assigned to a strategic group consisting of firms following generally similar strategies. The balanced scorecard strategy can be constructed, as shown in Figure 4.1.[7] Once constructed, the map can be used to visualize the consequences of actual or potential strategic moves of various players or to visualize potential strategic opportunities for building shareholder value. Depending on the strategic question, maps can be constructed using other dimensions.

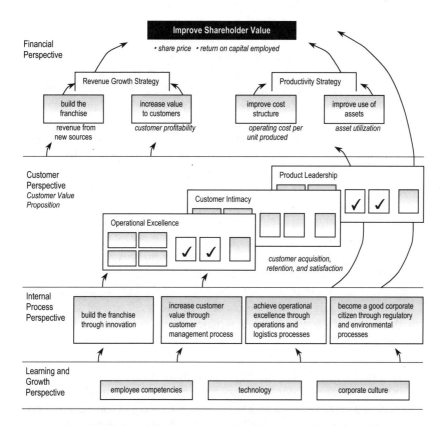

Figure 4.1: The Balanced Scorecard Strategy Map

Beyond the general insights this approach develops, such maps can be used to consider how rivalry might change, depending on strategic choices made by various players. In some instances, significant barriers may exist between strategic groups. Distribution patterns, in particular, are difficult to change, at least in the short run. Other barriers may exist as a result of required key success factors, as we will subsequently discuss. In other instances, changing strategy may be less difficult, suggesting opportunities for offensive moves or the need to prepare for defenses against the offensive moves of competitors.

Bargaining Power of Buyers and Suppliers

In some industries, such as can manufacturing, large buyers and suppliers are the norm. Beverage producers can, and do, easily move to self-manufacture of cans, putting severe constraints on a can manufacturer's ability to increase prices. Can manufacturers usually need the steel or aluminum supplier more than the supplier needs the firm and large suppliers may have the capability to forward integrate, as in the case of aluminum cans, making them less responsive to the needs of the firm. Industries where there is such homogeneity of suppliers and buyers severely limit the strategic choices the firm can make. On the other hand, in many industries buyers and suppliers are heterogeneous, facilitating a much greater range of strategic options. Some firms may elect to sell to large powerful buyers because the volume of available business is sufficiently attractive to offset the ability to the buyer to negotiate low prices, as is the case in the steel manufacturers supplying the automobile industry. Others may elect to serve only customers for whom their product represents a small percentage of total purchases, thus reducing the incentive for the buyer to aggressively negotiate for low prices. The Dexter Corporation, for instance, produces highly specialized materials such as a film used to coat the interior of beer cans. Representing only a small percentage of the total cost of a can, yet with important functional characteristics, price increases can be passed on relatively easily.

Potential New Entrants and Possible Substitutes

While the fundamental attention of the firm is most focused on its customers and competitors it must also take into account the potential entry of new competitors as well as the possibility of substitutes. Industries with high profit margins and low barriers to entry are obviously attractive targets for new players. For the firms within the industry, therefore, this requires consideration of the extent to which barriers to entry can be created and the extent to which opportunities to raise prices should be foregone. Some barriers are structural, such as capital requirements, and cannot easily be influenced by the firm. Others, such as patents and switching costs, are under control of the firm and so are potential elements of the firm's strategy. Pricing decisions not only need to take into account their deterrent effect on potential entrants but also must take into account potential substitutes for the firm's product. Engineered plastics producers, for instance, supplying material for automobile bumpers must take into account the cost of potential substitute materials such as steel or aluminum.

The Business System

Porter's approach considers the industry in terms of firms that compete with one another and how their rivalry, and thus firm profitability, is influenced by four external forces. Business system analysis takes a different perspective. As Gilbert and Strebel have argued, "Many definitions of a company's business, or of its industry, have been too narrow: there is more to its business than a product, a process, and a market; there is in fact an entire chain of activities, from product design to product utilization by the final customer, that must be mobilized to meet certain market expectations."[8]

Mintzberg et al. suggest a model based on Porter's value chain, in which a second level of strategy can encompass functional level strategies. As shown in Figure 4.2, they may include "sourcing," strategies throughout "processing" strategies, and output "delivery" strategies, all reinforced by a set of "supporting" strategies.[9]

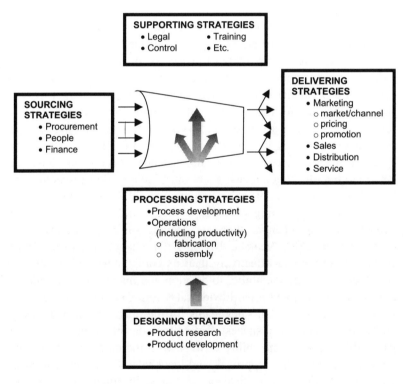

Figure 4.2: Functional Areas in System Terms

The logic of business system analysis is based on the notion that competitive advantage is derived from offering higher perceived valued, lower delivered cost, or both, than ones competitors. To achieve these objectives requires that all the activities in the chain be coordinated. If, for instance, low delivered cost is viewed as the critical competitive parameter, then all the activities in the value chain, including selling and distribution, must be managed toward this aim; even if the firm itself does not have direct control of a particular activity. Dell Corporation, with its direct marketing, is a classic example of matching low cost manufacturing (through its strategic alliances with suppliers who provide "just in time" inventory for assembly) with its low cost selling and distribution.

Key Success Factors and Competitive Advantage

Of the many understandings developed through industry and business system analysis, few are more important than key success factors and sources of competitive advantage. These are often misunderstood and frequently used interchangeably. Although related they are, in fact, two very different things.

Key success factors are those activities that must be done well, or resources which must be thoroughly controlled, to insure that a particular strategy has the potential to succeed. In other words, they are those activities or resources that are necessary for any and all firms that elect a particular strategy focusing on a particular target market. As such, they do not necessarily lead to competitive advantages. Still further, because they are associated with a particular strategy, key success factors will vary from one strategic group or one industry to another. In the fragrances industry, for instance, players who have targeted large multi-national customers must have market research capability to assess how a particular fragrance might enhance a customer's product offering. Lacking such a capability would preclude them from consideration as potential suppliers. Having such a capability might confer competitive advantage, but only if it enabled the firm to meet customer needs more effectively than its competitors. Other key success factors include the ability to develop and manufacture a wide variety of fragrances and a worldwide sales force, staffed with salespersons who can operate in sales teams. In the pharmaceutical industry, on the other hand, key success factors include the ability to develop patentable products, the ability to work with the medical industry and regulators to gain their approval, and local sales forces that can introduce new products to medical practitioners. In either situation other capabilities, advertising, for instance, might be desirable. Their lack, however, would not preclude a player from participating in the industry. In short, in identifying key success factors for particular strategies, it is important to keep in mind that the activities assessed be industry-relevant and that the key success factors be strategy-relevant.

As opposed to a key success factor, which is mandatory to be a player in a particular industry, competitive advantage refers to some aspect of the firm's situation which enables it to meet customers' wants and needs better than its competitors. It can derive from a key success factor, as might be the case with a pharmaceutical firm whose sales force can introduce new products more quickly than can competitors and so establish preemptive positions, or whose research and development efforts lead to products with strong patent positions. It can also derive from some aspect of the firm's position, developed over time. For many years, its name gave IBM a competitive advantage over smaller and less known rivals who, in many instances, offered more functionality than did IBM, with equal service and reliability.

Although competitive advantage is frequently described in terms of a particular activity, resource, or position, such as new product development capability, access to financing, or a highly regarded brand name, it takes on meaning only if it is translated into superior performance in the market place, as perceived by the customer. Hewlett Packard, for instance, established an enviable record on college campuses, which enabled it to recruit some of the best and brightest engineering graduates. As a result, Hewlett Packard developed an outstanding engineering competence. Even so, this is a competitive advantage only if it provides the customer with demonstrably superior products or services. Similarly, while many firms pursue, and achieve, low cost in order to develop competitive advantage, it is, in fact, a competitive advantage only if customers actually see lower prices, or favorably evaluate the firm for its past pricing moves, or if it dissuades competitors from aggressive pricing moves.

Two important aspects of competitive advantage need to be kept in mind. First, is the need for realistic appraisal of the firm's situation. It is the authors' experience that competitive advantage is frequently overestimated, either through failure to think in customer terms or because of lack of good marketing intelligence. Second, and increasingly, is the difficulty of sustaining a particular competitive advantage. Experience effects, for instance, which are associated with low cost, tend to erode in mature industries and, in any event, can frequently be avoided. Broad product lines, which make it easier for the customer to do business with one rather than several firms, may be difficult for one sales force to represent, particularly as products become more complex. Favorable evaluation of brand names, associated with past service or products, can erode, even with careful nurturing. This is not to suggest that firms should not pursue competitive advantage. Rather it is to emphasize the importance of realistically appraising how the firm compares to its competitors and the need to pursue competitive advantage on an ongoing basis.

Industry Life Cycle

The concept of industry life cycle is closely related to the notion of product life cycle, as discussed in Chapter 2. Porter points out that the product life cycle is the grandfather of concepts for predicting the probable course of industry evolution.[10] There are, however, some important differences; particularly with respect to time horizons and focus. As with products, industries go through stages of introduction, growth, maturity and decline. Generally, they do so at a slower rate than is the case with individual products. The personal computer industry, for instance, is now some 25 years old and is still in the growth stage. However, within the industry, product life cycles are shortening dramatically. Some products have, in fact, already gone through all four stages and are no longer produced. As discussed in Chapter 2, the principal focus of product life cycle analysis is on the market and its response to marketing strategy. On the other hand, the principal focus of industry life cycle analysis is on competitors and their behavior. In terms of the five forces, Hussey and Jenster argue that industry evolution has major implications with respect to potential competitors and rivalry, as shown in Figure 4.3.[11]

Their behavior, of course, is influenced by characteristics of the market. It is also influenced by structural shifts such as changes in capital intensity, on technological changes which may impact product designs, on changes in manufacturing processes, and so forth. In analyzing an industry from a life cycle standpoint, the focus of the analysis is on the basis of competition and how it is changing and on the development of opportunities for competitive advantage.

Conducting the Analysis

We have previously indicated the importance of identifying the purpose of a particular industry analysis. We believe, however, that all analyses should answer three general sets of questions:

1. Is the industry attractive and why, or why not? Attractive industries tend to be high growth, with high barriers to entry, capacity added in small increments, high profit margins, and suppliers and buyers with relatively low bargaining power.
2. If the industry is attractive, what are the economic structures of the different activities in the industry; and how might

changes threaten the attractiveness of each? If the industry is not attractive, what opportunities exist to improve attractiveness? What changes are likely to occur?

3. What are the main competitors' strategies now, and what are they likely to be in the future? Are there different groupings of companies that seem to be competing in a similar way? What are the differences, if any, in the profitability between strategic groups and between firms within the groups, and why? What are the key success-factors associated with each strategic group?

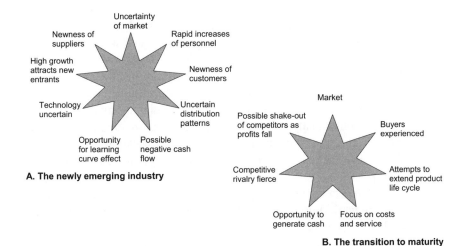

Figure 4.3: The Effect of the Product Life Cycle on Industries

Structuring the Industry Analysis Process

When conducting a complete industry analysis we suggest a six-step process, as follows:

1. Establish the purpose and scope of the analysis
2. Profile the industry
3. Map the business system, both in terms of strategic groups and an activity chain.
4. Analyze strategic groups
5. Analyze key activities
6. Develop implications for marketing strategy

Establishing the Purpose and Scope of the Analysis

The starting point for analysis is often a business issue or challenge, such as declining margins, unsatisfactory asset turnover, market share deterioration, changing technology, emergence of new competitors or novel moves by old foes into new markets or segments, changing customer needs, environmental threats or regulatory modifications. As with any other analytical exercise, the analysis should start by specifying the exact purpose of the task. The clarification of the purpose should also include attention to whom and in what form the analysis is to be presented.

The statement of purpose is a necessary step in that it aids in the subsequent definition of scope of the analysis. As often is the case, an analysis of this type is conducted by a team of people, and it is therefore necessary to specify what should and should not be included in the analytical task. We have found it useful to define the scope in terms of the four broad dimensions given in Figure 4.4.

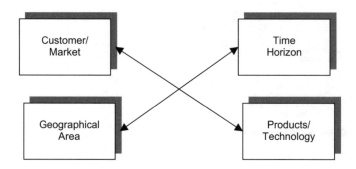

Figure 4.4: Defining the Scope of the Analysis

The following are illustrations of how the dimensions may be used to focus the scope of the analysis.

Whom	Customer Needs/ Market Served:	Hotel, restaurant and catering market (end user groups/end users served)
What	Product/ Technology/Services:	Cooking stoves and ventilation systems
Where	Geographic Area:	Nordic counties
When	Time horizon:	Analysis to cover period 2000 to 2010

Profiling the Industry
We profile the industry by first answering two sets of questions. Using the Porter five forces model as a starting point:

- Who are the competitors? This should include both those that compete directly as well as those who are sufficiently close competitors that their strategies need to be taken into account as the firm formulates its marketing strategy.
- Who are the buyers, suppliers, potential entrants and possible substitutes and what are their major characteristics?
- What is the overall size of the industry and what is its growth rate, in terms of both physical units and dollar value?
- What are the key characteristics of the industry, in terms of its technologies, its capital structure, its manufacturing processes and its position in the industry life cycle?

Then, using the business systems approach:

- What are the key activities that define the industry, regardless of who performs them, and what are the key cost elements?

It is often useful to think about an industry in a historical context. This enhances understanding of the changes, which have occurred in the past, and provide a basis for anticipating possible changes in the future. Through plotting historic data, such as growth rates, cyclical volume changes, seasonal fluctuations, profit margin changes, asset turnover fluctuations, technological breakthroughs, degree of vertical integration, acquisition and merger patterns, one can find clues to changes which have driven industry performance. Possible questions to ask might include:

- What have been the key developments in production (e.g., have manufacturing patterns shifted by volume or value or by country of trade area)?
- How have patterns of international trade changed (e.g., with respect to imports, exports, or balance of trade)?
- How have patterns of distribution changed (e.g., what about the structure of distribution, logistics, inventory levels, etc)?
- How have consumption patterns changed (e.g., what categories have increase or decreased, what about country or regional variations)?
- What about the number of industry participants (e.g., increased, decreased, and why)?

Mapping the Strategic Groups and the Business System
One or more maps of strategic groups should be developed, plotting the firms that have been identified as competitors on appropriate dimensions. Generally, these dimensions will represent major possible strategic choices or options on which firms in the industry can build their strategies. These will generally include options with regard to competing on cost or features, targeting domestic or multi-national markets, selling direct or going through distribution, and broad or narrow product lines. For multi-national firms they might also include options with regard to standardized or differentiated products and home country or dispersed manufacturing facilities.

The business system should be mapped, on the basis of the five or six key activities necessary to meet expectations of the final customer. This map should take into account that some players will be involved in many activities, integrating either forward or backward. Others may be involved in only one, or few.

Analyzing the Strategic Groups and the Individual Players
The purpose of mapping competitors into strategic groups is to develop insights into the broad positions of the various players, the key success factors, the possible sources of competitive advantage, potential moves of the players and barriers to mobility. For individual competitors the analysis needs to evaluate their strengths and weaknesses, their sources of competitive advantage, their vulnerability and likely responses to attack, and possible aggressive moves.

Analyzing the Key Activities
Key activities are considered in detail for three reasons. First, to develop an understanding of how and where value is added in the business system. Second, to provide a detailed framework within which to assess a firm's strengths and weaknesses relative to its competitors' activities. Third, to develop insights for appropriate coordination of key activities in ways that will provide customers with the greatest value at the lowest possible cost. For each activity, opportunities to decrease costs and increase value need to be evaluated. Similarly, it is necessary to examine threats, which may increase costs and decrease value. These opportunities and threats should be consolidated into an integrated view, which gives a full picture of the industry. Starting the analysis with the most downstream activity ensures that the analysis takes place from the perspective of both the customer and the customer's customer.

Developing Implications for Marketing Strategy
The key purpose of the previous steps is to develop insights that will guide the formulation of marketing strategy and reveal opportunities for improving the internal operations of the firm. At a minimum, such analysis should sharpen insights with respect to:

- Key success factor requirements for a particular strategy
- Sources of competitive advantage
- Unserved, or underserved, market segments
- Implications of market selection with regard to negotiating power of buyers
- Feasibility of various strategic options
- Profit potential of various strategic options
- Strengths and weaknesses of competitors and their offensive and defensive profiles
- Strengths and weaknesses of the firm
- Opportunities for integration or divestiture of key activities
- Potential competitors.

Summary

Good marketing strategies require understanding of the industry within which the firm competes, with particular emphasis on immediate competitors and the forces that may influence their behavior. They also require understanding of where in the business system value is added, and how. As mentioned in the beginning of this chapter, industry analysis is a fundamental part of a strategic marketing decision making. It is closely related to market analysis and, in many instances, the two will overlap. It is, nevertheless, a very different form of analysis, with different questions and approaches. The specific issues or problems, which dictate the nature of the analysis, are related to the specific company situation. The analysis itself will often uncover additional important issues the company needs to address in selecting and implementing a certain market strategy.

Further Reading

Kathleen M Eisenhardt and Shona L. Brown, "Time Pacing: Competing in Markets that Won't Stand Still," *Harvard Business Review* 76 (March/April 1998): 59-69.

Xavier Gilbert and Paul Strebel, "Developing Competitive Advantage." in *The Strategy Process,* eds. James Brian Quinn and Henry Mintzberg (Englewood Cliffs, NJ: Prentice Hall, 1987).

Gary Hamel, "Bring Silicon Valley Inside," *Harvard Business Review* 77 (September/October 1999): 70–84.

Eric von Hippel, Stefan Thomke, and Mary Sonnack, "Creating Breakthroughs at 3M," *Harvard Business Review* 77 (September/October 1999): 47–57.

Per V. Jenster and Peter Barklin "The Nobel Art and Practice of Industry Analysis," *Journal of Strategic Change* 3 (1994): 107–118.

Michael E. Porter, "How Competitive Forces Shape Strategy," *Harvard Business Review* (March-April 1979).

---

[1]Wroe Anderson, *Marketing Behavior and Executive Action* (Homewood, IL: Richard D. Irwin, Inc., 1957).

[2]See, for instance, James C. Anderson, Håkan Håkansson, and Jan Johanson, "Dyadic Business Relationships within a Business Network Context," *Journal of Marketing* (October 1994): 1–15, who argue that analysis of dyadic relationships must take into account suppliers, customers' customers, and a host of other ancillary firms.

[3]Philip Kotler, *Marketing Management, Planning, Implementation and Control,* 11th ed. (Englewood Cliffs, NJ: Prentice-Hall, Inc., 2003), 245.

[4]Michael E. Porter, *Competitive Strategy* (New York: The Free Press, 1998), 5.

[5]F. M. Scherer, *Industrial Market Structure and Economic Performance*, 2d ed. (Boston: Houghton Mifflin, 1989), 4.

[6]Porter, *Competitive Strategy*, 4.

[7]Robert S. Kaplan and David P. Norton, "Having Trouble with Your Strategy? Then Map it," *Harvard Business Review 78* (September/October 200): 168.

[8]Xavier Gilbert and Paul Strebel, "Developing Competitive Advantage," in *The Strategy Process*, 2d. ed., eds. Henry Mitzberg and James Brian Quinn (Englewood Cliffs, NJ: Prentice-Hall, Inc., 1991), 82.

Further Reading

[9]Henry Mintzberg and others, *Strategy Process: Concepts, Contexts, Cases*, 4th ed. (Englewood Cliffs, NJ: Pearson Education, 2003), 118.

[10]Porter, *Competitive Strategy*, 157.

[11]David Hussey and Per Jenster, *Competitor Intelligence: Turning Analysis into Success* (New York: John Wiley, 1999), 56.

Chapter 5

Business Marketing Intelligence: Analysis and Tools

This chapter discusses business marketing intelligence (BMI), an important activity because it links an organization to its external environment and makes it possible for management to develop informed and rational decisions about markets, competitors, and strategy. We first introduce BMI and explain why it is important. We distinguish BMI from marketing research and argue that BMI is much more than traditional marketing research. We then discuss different types of marketing intelligence; continuous and problem related. New technology is continuously changing the nature of BMI. We analyze the state of the art intelligence software, define principles for how to search for information effectively on the Internet and build integrated business intelligence systems on the Intranet. Then we address issues related to BMI system design, benchmarking, and sources of intelligence. The impacts of demand-analysis are highlighted, and we explain customer satisfaction analysis, customer requirements analysis, and sales forecasting. We conclude the chapter with discussions about how to organize and manage intelligence efforts.

Intelligence and Information

The Importance of Business Marketing Intelligence

Intelligence is one of the most important business marketing functions. Intelligence activities of collecting and analyzing internal and environmental conditions are important to strategy formulations and operational conduct. The literature on Business Intelligence (BI),[1] of which BMI is a part, has increased tremendously in the past five years. Other terms found are Competitor Intelligence and Competitive Intelligence (CI), which are narrower types of intelligence activities. BMI may be seen as the part of the larger BI activity that is limited to the concern of business marketing.

BMI includes the gathering and understanding of market trends; customer needs, perceptions, attitudes, beliefs, and behavior; competitors' thinking, strengths and weaknesses; and all factors that influence business-to-business relationships. We view BMI intelligence as a broad set of activities, because success as a business marketer requires understanding the broader context of the market and the customers' strategic and operating environment.

BMI has three unique characteristics:

1. Business marketers usually deal with a smaller set of customers than consumer marketers do. Most business customers (and potential customers) are usually known to the business marketer. Therefore, intelligence activities often involve either the entire relevant customer population or much smaller samples than in consumer marketing.
2. How organizations buy, as outlined in Chapter 3, involves multiple buying influences. These influences impact the reliability of the intelligence obtained from customers. Business intelligence information is often dependent on who is talking to the customer and who in the customer organization responds. To get a response that depicts a customer's organizational viewpoint, several customer sample points may be required.
3. The business marketing sales force usually has a close relationship with customers. This relationship represents a tremendous source of both customer and competitive information. A key issue in BMI is how to capitalize on the information the sales force has or can get.

The globalization of business has increased the need for broad-based intelligence systems. Even companies that consider themselves primarily local or regional find that an intelligence system based on a much broader geographical base is necessary. Technology often forces organizations to do extensive intelligence. For example, when new laser technology is developed and announced in Colorado, it does not take many hours before competing firms in Japan have all publicly available information reported to them by local consultants.

Entrepreneurial firms and firms in early stages of a product life cycle often need entirely different types of intelligence than firms in mature stages of the life cycle. A young entrepreneurial firm often needs market, product, and customer intelligence, while a firm operating in a mature oligopoly may need price and cost intelligence.

Broadly speaking, there are two types of intelligence processes related to the product life cycle which demand quite different competencies; intelligence related to the planning, production, and adjustment of products; and marketing intelligence related to the phase when the product has conquered the market whether on an up-going or a down-going sales curve. The first type is often considered more strategic or tactical in nature, whereas the second is more operational in nature, as shown in Figure 5.1.[2] The first type of intelligence is more technical and marketing related, whereas the second more sales related. For a company to be successful in its overall business intelligence efforts, it is important that the two different types of intelligence activities be synchronized so that the one knows when the other is taking over.

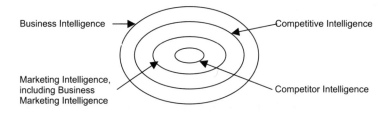

Figure 5.1: The Types of Intelligence in a Company

Business Marketing Intelligence Defined

Business marketing intelligence is the collection, analysis, and interpretation of relevant internal and external marketing information. It is a process that makes it possible for a firm to learn about, understand, and deal with new challenges. Marketing intelligence is therefore a future-oriented activity that helps an organization cope in the market. It includes all ways an organization acquires and uses information. It is comprised of all kinds of market and marketing research; the collection and analysis of internal data, competitive analysis; analysis and reverse engineering of competitor's products; understanding how and where to add value for customers; and the process of synthesizing large amounts of informally gathered information about the industry and business environment. This environment can be divided into a number of areas of study; economic, political, social, technological, infrastructural, ecological, legal, and demographic, which together illustrate the interdisciplinary nature of the subject. Marketing intelligence can be as comprehensive or as narrow as a company may want it to be. The business intelligence process is often illustrated by a number of specific business intelligence working tasks in a circle where the company gains experience each time a new intelligence process is started. In real life a company may be working on several assignments at the same time, or it may go back and forth between the specific working tasks in the circle, but it still serves as an illustration of the kind of working processes, which occur within the intelligence unit. The Business Intelligence Cycle may be said to consist of five distinct tasks or phases, as shown in Figure 5.2.[3]

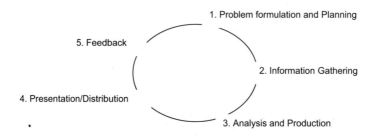

Figure 5.2: The Business Intelligence Cycle

From these tasks, BMI consists of three important management activities. These activities are:

- Gathering internal and external data. The gathering of BMI data is a comprehensive task that includes activities ranging from collecting objective empirical market research data to recording subjective statements from salespersons. It may include activities such as periodic, detailed analysis of current data about customer sales gains and losses; recording employees' attitudes towards a particular customer or competitor; and scanning the trade press to assess events in the industry.
- Coding and interpreting the data collected. It is often very difficult to code and to provide valid and reliable interpretation of the broader dimensions of BMI. Over the last few decades, many firms have made substantial efforts to create centralized marketing information systems. Most of these efforts have failed due to the variety of data usually collected through BMI activities, to the lack of appropriate management and technology required to handle the complexity or due to the lack of commitment by higher management.
- Application of knowledge to produce useful information from data to be used in developing marketing strategy. An essential ingredient of BMI is the application of manage-

ment knowledge and experience to marketing data collected. Only managers with the appropriate industry experience can assess the validity of BMI, translate it into a proper strategic context, and convert the knowledge into appropriate operating activities.

Business marketing intelligence activities (BMI) includes continuous, problem-related, and integrated activities. Continuous BMI activities consist primarily of collection of data from secondary information sources and input from internal resources such as accounting, sales and cost data, technical standards, as well as customer sales gains and loss data. Specific problem-related activities include market research, research related to product development, establishment of target customer profiles, and specific assessment of market potential. Integrated activities use a variety of tools to assistant in interpreting problem-related and continuous research.

The Society of Competitive Intelligence professionals (SCIP) asked its members what methods of analyzing CI information were most used, and which were rated most effective. These survey results are shown in Table 5.1.[4, 5]
From the evaluations about the analytical methods used we see that it is often the simpler methods, which are considered most effective. From the evaluations of the role of competitor intelligence in support of sales and marketing, research suggests that see that most importance contributions are in guiding decisions at the strategic level of the organization.

The Increasingly Important Role of New Technology to BMI
With the continuous development of new efficient computer- and software technology, more managers are implementing Marketing Decision Support Systems (MDSS). MDSS are formally structured computerized information systems that help managers make routine decisions. With current information systems technology this is possible. An MDSS can vary from sophisticated expert systems to simple sales variance analysis. MDSS is usually best applied to repetitive and routine decision-making activities: for example, decisions related to order scheduling, field service, or order quantity discounts. MDSS is also used in sales reporting, customer service, and variance analysis related to product shipment. In general, the major portion of strategic marketing intelligence tends to be manual, and it maybe difficult to get good financial returns on very sophisticated MDSS in business marketing.

According to a survey conducted by Fuld & Company, Inc., 48% of companies have an organized CI effort, and 72% plan to either develop or purchase CI software tools.[6] There may be said to exist four major categories of software, which give support to business intelligence activities today: Intelligence software, Knowledge Management solutions, Search engines/agents and Data Warehouse/OLAP solutions.[7] Only the first category actually supports information analysis from other Business Intelligence software, as shown in Table 5.2. The other three present useful and valuable software solutions, but no real analytical support.

Tools for Analyzing Information [Percent using each tool]	Effectiveness of Analysis Tools [Percent rating each tool extremely or very effective]	CI Effectiveness in Support of Marketing [Percent Rating CI Extremely or Very Effective]	Objectives of Sales and Marketing Intelligence [Percent Rating Objective Extremely or Very Important]
Competitor profiles: 88.9%	SWOT analysis: 63.1%	Decision support: 67.4	Develop marketing strategies: 76.2
Financial analysis: 72.1%	Competitor profiles: 52.4%	Market monitoring: 66.7	Anticipate change / Market monitoring: 74.5
SWOT analysis: 55.2%	Financial analysis: 45.5%	Identify market opportunities: 66.3	Identify new opportunities: 67.2
Scenario development: 53.8%	Win/loss analysis: 31.4%	Market plan development: 63	Identify new sources of advantage: 64.8
Win/loss analysis: 40.4%	War gaming: 21.9%	Market plan input: 57.4	Help sales win business: 58.4
War gaming: 27.5%	Scenario development: 19.2%	Investigating market rumors: 51.9	Develop marketing programs: 43
Cojoint analysis: 25.5%	Cojoint analysis: 15.8%	New product development: 50.3	Prioritize R&D spending: 23.5
Simulation/modeling: 25%	Simulation/modeling: 15.4%	Anticipating competitor initiatives: 48.1	
		Identify alliance partners: 36.9	
		Anticipating technology changes: 35.6	
		Investment prioritization: 33.6	
		Identifying competitor intangibles: 33.1	
		Understanding competitor costs: 27.4	
		Promotion/advertising changes: 26.4	
		Anticipating changes in distribution: 15.1	
		Anticipating supplier changes: 6.4	

Source: The study was conducted for SCIP by The Pine Ridge Group, Inc. and the T.W. Powell Company, 1998. Reprinted with permission from Pine Ridge Group and Knowledgeagency.

Table 5.1: Methods of Analyzing CI Information

The major types of analysis presented in Intelligence software may be divided into three broad groups:

1. *Relationship analysis* help the user analyze relationships between variables such as companies and people.
2. *Analysis of structured text* help the user structure and find important information in unstructured text (such as text documents).
3. *Comparative analysis* helps the user compare information in the system and has a wide range of application areas. It can focus on quantitative data, qualitative data, or help use existing models such as SWOT analysis and Porter's Five Forces model.

Support categories	Search engines/ agents	Intelligence software	Data Ware-House/OLAP	Knowledge Management
Information gathering	Yes	Yes	No (from internal Databases only)	Yes
Analytical support	No	Yes	No (only numerical Quantitative analysis)	No
Information distribution and reporting	No	Yes	Yes	Yes
Examples of software	Autonomy	Brimstone Intelligence	Cognos, Business Objects	Comitell

Source: Primary research, Fuld & Company, 2002.

Table 5.2: Different Business Intelligence Software & Characteristics

Together with the other phases in the intelligence cycle, these types of analysis give what we call degree of comprehensiveness in an intelligence software, and which is placed on the x-axis. Another important criteria for users of intelligence software is the degree of visualization, which is placed on the y-axis, as shown in Figure 5.3. This does not mean that a software which scores poorly on both criteria is not worth buying. It may be good for a specific operation in the BI cycle, like data-gathering from news sources. However, the quality of this kind of software will always depend on the quality of the data sources subscribed to, according to the proverbial "garbage-in garbage-out" concept.

Even though we have seen tremendous advances in the development of software for business intelligence support over the last decade, the types of analysis offered up to this point do by no means replace human analysis, and the importance of technology in the analysis process should not be overestimated. Instead, the intelligence software does help in increasing effectiveness and efficiency by gathering, reporting, sending, and sharing information over great distances.

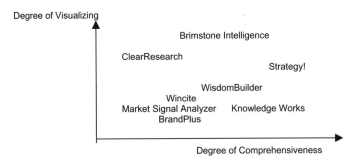

Source: Various sources and primary research, Fuld & Company 2002.

Figure 5.3: Degree of Support in Intelligence Software.

Principles for Using the Internet Effectively

The use of Internet in the BMI process has become increasingly important over the last decade, and it seems that this development has just started. Today there are very few companies in the industrialized world which do not have their own homepage or which you cannot find important business marketing data about on the Internet. Other important technological support for business intelligence systems include the development of Intranet systems and the extensive use of databases, which is often accessed through the Internet. Some companies have also developed Extranet systems together with competitors, clients, or suppliers, where some, but not necessarily all, information is shared.

The chances of finding useful information about a competitor on the Internet normally starts through a search engine. A main principle in search technique is that you would like to start with broader searches and then move closer to the targeted information as to decrease the chances of loosing out on important information. Even though many database services charge a fee, like http://www.lexisnexis.com/, there is a wide variety of free information available, and many ways of going around the extra costs, e.g. by borrowing the material through the library instead of paying for an expensive subscription to the same information over the Internet. The library is in all cases a natural first step for the information gathering stage of the intelligence cycle, preferably all through the Internet. But in most cases, a physical visit is still required, at least to pick up the books and documents requested.

When searching on the Internet, it is often best to start with an Internet address which leaves you with several possibilities, so called Multi Access Pages. For search engines, this could be http://www.allsearchengines.com/. In the same way, if you are looking for library databases you may want to start with a page that collects several databases, like http://sunsite.berkeley.edu/. Instead of looking at the selection of one bookstore, you may want to search in several bookstores at the same time, e.g. by http://www.bookfinder.com/ or http://www.abebooks.com/, or if you are looking only at newspapers http://www.onlinenewspapers.com/. For business magazines, you may find http://www.bpubs.com/ useful. A weakness with many free article databases is that the journals and magazines from where the articles are collected are not the best on the market as these cost more and less likely to occur in a free database. If you are looking for an encyclopedia service you may try http://www.encyclopedia.com. Or if you are looking for a dictionary try http://www.yourdictionary.com/, which claims to have 1800 dictionaries in more than 250 languages.

Another useful principle is to search by country, sector, branch, or academic discipline. Thus, if you are looking at only US government databases, you may want to try http://www.access.gpo. gov/su_docs/databases.html or http://www.sec.gov/index.html. About the EU, try http://europa.eu.int/geninfo/info-en.htm. Many countries have excellent Multi Access Pages. Thus, if you are looking for information in Norway, try http://www.kildene.com. There are also more specialized country search engines, like if you are looking for US businesses http://www.bigbook.com/, or people http://www.people search.net.

There are also pages divided by branch, for instance for business-to-business marketing, http://www.business2business.on.ca/businesslinks.html. Kompass gives you a wide variety of business-to-business marketing links in addition to its more known products at http://www.kompass.com/kintl/cgi-bin/KI_PROaction.cgi. Online Inc. at http://www.onlineinc.com/about.html is a B2B media and event producer for the digital media and electronic research community. If you are looking at general information on marketing and sales, try http://www.agencycompile.com/. For a Multi Access Page on Marketing see http://www.looksmart.com/. To look at different services offered by a BMI company see http://www.kae.com.

Many academic institutions have their own search pages where they gather a large number of valuable links (which are not always updated, but still), like e.g. if you are looking for issues related to Economic Intelligence you may want to start by looking at http://www.loyola.edu/dept/politics/ecintel.html or for Competitive Intelligence at SCIP's homepage at http://www.scip.org or http://CIseek.com. For more security related CI, it is difficult to avoid http://intelweb.janes.com/, Defense News and Aviation week & Space Technology. There are several CI magazines on the net, like http://www.intelligententerprise.com/. And at the end, if you cannot find something, there are companies for that too, like http://www.kirktyson.info who specialize in hard-to-find information.

It is not the purpose of this chapter to tell you about all the useful pages (which depend on the business you are in, and risk being outdated when your read this), but about the principles, which will help you find them by yourself. By following these principles, you should be able to reduce the overall time spent searching for information on the Internet and improve your information searching capabilities. You should also be able to compare prices for information thus lowering the cost of the BMI effort to your company.

Intranet: The Integration of Business Intelligence and Knowledge Management

If your company has developed an Intranet system the above mentioned addresses may be the sort of links you want to find there. In modern organizations, the CI function is often directed and controlled through an Intranet system which serves as an integrated location for the company's Knowledge Management Program.

The process may start with a manager who wants to find some information. She logs herself into the Competitive Intranet Intelligence System (CIIS), and chooses between searching for the information herself, or having the CI Team (CIT) search the information for her. If she decides that it may be more convenient to search for the information herself she proceeds to a large number of links to homepages, databases and search engines. If the company is using BI software, this could also be available here. If the manager chooses to have the CIT search for her, she answers an electronic questionnaire asking what she wants to know, why (as to help the CIT understand the problem), and how fast she needs the information. There might also be a box to check if the information can circulate freely on the Intranet or if it should be sent directly to her. The information requests can be divided into proactive and reactive. Reactive requests focus on what has happened and normally implies the support of secondary sources, while as proactive requests normally implies some sort of primary research and takes longer time. A CIT should of course be able to do both. A CIIS should be a place were managers and employees can search for all kinds of information, including searching in databases the company subscribes to, borrowing and buying books, and reading electronic newspapers.

The CIT serves both a pull and a push function. The pull function we have already described. The Push function can be in terms of general and specific News-To-Go Letters, which the manager can print out before leaving the office and read in the taxi on the way to a client. A danger with push information is that the CIT delivers nice-to-know information. The best system is one in which the whole management is engaged in asking questions. This is only possible through the development of trust, and is often connected with a slow development of the CIT, adding one person at the time.

The Value of Business Marketing Intelligence
Marketing intelligence and the information it produces tends to create change. Marketing intelligence is driven by the marketplace and by competitors. As competitors change strategy and introduce new products, customers respond to these changes by changing their preferences and purchase behavior. Competing firms must therefore engage in intelligence work to understand exactly what is happening. As new intelligence emerges, competing firms find new ways of providing additional value to customers. They then deliver this new value to customers, which again produces change. This market-oriented information gathering is an ongoing process. Firms capable of learning by uncovering new information, and that can create knowledge through intelligence, are usually those that maintain their competitive position.

Marketing intelligence, like many other corporate functions, has changed dramatically over the last few years. Today marketing intelligence is global and very much influenced by changing customer behavior and new technology. Not only large multinational corporations, but also small- and medium-size firms are sourcing goods and services to a much greater extent across borders. The extent of sourcing varies from product to product and industry to industry. Sourcing is used extensively in the technology-related areas; for example, in electronics it is very common for smaller firms to establish alliances and source products, components, or assistance worldwide. This substantially increases the need for intelligence activities. It also influences the resources required to do intelligence work and the organization of such efforts. Even for small- and medium-size firms there is substantial negative opportunity cost if such efforts are not conducted satisfactory. Many small- and medium-size firms' existence is threatened by developments taking place thousands of miles away. Failure to know about such developments, and to act appropriately, can have serious consequences for business performance.

Often the benefits and the use of business intelligence are not recognized or fail because top management does not appreciate its value. Management often does not give this function the priority and/or resources that are required. The function is often staffed with low-level, inexperienced managers rather than experienced ones. Experienced managers who can help operations managers translate business intelligence into strategy and implementations are often a scarce resource in an organization.

The Size of the BMI Activity

It is very difficult to estimate how important marketing intelligence is across world markets. However, it is clear that it tends to vary from industry to industry and across markets. BMI is growing in importance. One type of intelligence is market research. Table 5.3 shows market research revenue estimates for research agencies operating in all major regions of the world.

These agencies estimate that approximately $15,3 billion was spent on market research worldwide in 2000. Fifteen of the top 25 firms conducted research via the Internet in a significant way in 2000, accounting for 46% of global Internet market research, web site research and audience research spending. Three firms were fully engaged in Internet research: Jupiter Media Metrix, Harris Interactive, and NetRatings, Inc., a part of VNU.

Region	Market Research Turnover (In Mill. USD)	Region	Market Research Turnover (In Mill. USD)
Europe		Asia Pacific	
United Kingdom	1623	Japan	1206
Germany	1290	Australia	273
France	958	China	181
Italy	415	Other Asia Pacific	439
Other Europe	1658	Total Asia Pacific	2099
Total Europe	5944		
Americas		Other countries	136
United States	5922	Total World	15232
Canada	434		
Other Americas	697		
Total Americas	7053		

Source: © Copyright 2000 by ESOMAR ® - The World Association of Research Professionals. Published by ESOMAR.

Table 5.3: Marketing Research Turnover in World Markets, 2000.

Traditionally business-to-business market research has accounted for a smaller part, but includes predominately traditional qualitative and quantitative research. If the value of the broader definition of business intelligence is included, the resources used on business marketing intelligence are substantial. We estimate that between 60 and 90 percent of all business-to-business marketing intelligence is acquired through internal company resources. It is very difficult to estimate the size of this activity because it is conducted by company employees, and the amount of resources used on marketing intelligence are never publicly disclosed. However, the value of efforts could be in excess of $ 9 billion worldwide. BMI is often conducted by managers in different functions, at several organizational levels and as a part-time endeavor. Therefore, many companies may not know themselves what resources are committed to marketing intelligence. Also, the cost and complexity of collecting and managing marketing intelligence influences the degree to which it is conducted. For example, in Europe, Japan, and the United States, extensive electronic information resources are available at modest costs. In many developing countries this is not so. Hence, the nature of marketing intelligence differs across world markets.

Culture and Business Marketing Intelligence
Culture influences the nature and role of marketing intelligence. For example, it is estimated that in Japan market research spending through agencies in 2000 was $1,206 million. This is a very small amount compared to the size of the Japanese economy and their economic and global success, despite difficulties which hit the country in 1997. Market research often has a different role in Japanese firms that in U.S. or German firms. Japanese marketing intelligence is primarily an internal company function involving many employees at all levels. When a Japanese company wants to learn about a particular aspect of business in Europe or the United States, it often sends someone to live in that country for a period of time. Extensive, but often informal analysis is conducted, and all knowledge and raw data is forwarded to the main organization in Japan. Much information on foreign companies and activities ends up at METI[8] (The Ministry of Economy, Trade and Industry) through JETRO[9] (METI's technology information collection service) who distribute the information to companies who they think may need it. This provides excellent insight and a broad base for the corporate staff to develop an effective marketing strategy.

Swedish managers approach marketing intelligence differently. A study of Swedish and Japanese subsidiary managers in the United States showed that the Swedish managers were more self-confident than Japanese managers. Swedish managers did not view BMI as important as Japanese managers did. Swedish managers also tended to screen information more extensively, forwarding only those facts they believed their superiors needed. Swedish managers seemed to have a completely different approach to marketing intelligence and the dissemination of results from that of the Japanese managers. This implies that the focus, organizational structure, and reliance on BMI varies across cultures and that cultural norms may indicate management's use, willingness, and ability to use BMI in business development, as shown in Table 5.3.

Business Intelligence and Opportunity Cost
Marketing intelligence provides some firms with significantly potential market and competitive opportunities. But information is useless and the cost of collecting data is wasted if firms are not able to take advantage of intelligence. Few companies make conscious efforts to include systematic approaches to marketing intelligence. In many firms marketing intelligence is an ad hoc and occasional activity. Only when a particular problem arises or a plan needs to be developed does marketing intelligence become an issue.

Several Nordic companies have developed highly organized business intelligence systems over the past several years.[10] Ericsson have an excellent approach to the issue with their EBIN network (Ericsson Business Intelligence Network), their BIAP (Ericsson Business Analyst Program, which is a training program that all their analysts go through in order to get to know each other and to share methods) and the BIC (Business Information Center: the information portal containing thousands and thousands of industry reports and market studies. The troublesome situation, the company has encountered during the last couple of years, has lead to a reduction both in the number of analysts as well as the concepts described above, but the knowledge is there. The Internet portal at Ericsson is an excellent example of how to structure large amount of information such as industry analysis, reports, newsfeeds, internally generated reports, etc. The portal also provides the possibility to create individual newsfeeds about specific issues or companies that one needs to monitor.

Ericsson's Finnish counterpart, Nokia, has a more decentralized approach to business intelligence. Nokia is advocating a "virtual intelligence approach", which means that they rely heavily on non-professional analysts such as product managers, marketing managers and other personnel. Nokia argue that this is a very powerful method since the intelligence issue is viewed from many perspectives and the brainpower of large groups of people can be utilized. Nokia's strong corporate culture is a key reason behind the success of the company. Nokia's employees are a part of a very successful and relatively young company, and possess a team spirit and curiosity that few companies can match.

Tetra Pak is another highly successful global company that has used business intelligence as a key issue regarding business development and market planning. "Intelligence activities is integrated in every part of the business development process", says Thomas Stridsberg, Business Intelligence manager at Tetra Pak.

Tetra Pak also tries to use the intelligence activities in customer activities. A new potential client often gets an intelligence briefing/market analysis concerning his major markets. This shows the potential client that Tetra Pak can also be a partner in future planning and that they have a thorough understanding of the clients markets. This, in addition to a very competitive product, can sometimes be the thing that determines that they get the business.

Volvo has for a very long time had a coordinated approach to their market analysis and competitor intelligence activities. Understanding today's and tomorrows consumer trends as well as the potential maneuvers of the competitors has always been an important part of the automotive industry. The other automotive players like SAAB and Scania are also very active in this area.

One of the companies in the insurance/finance sector that has reached very far is Länsförsäkringar ("countyinsurances"), a Swedish company. The company has taken a clear strategic approach to their intelligence activities. A number of internal intelligence networks have been established in a way so that each look at a force in the business environment (e.g. customers, competitors, politics, technology, etc). Supported by intelligent agent technology as well as intelligence analysis software their goal is to identify and foresee important events in their environment. This knowledge is then reported to Peter Lööf and Ingemar Åkesson who is in charge of the intelligence activities at the corporate level.

Another insurance company, Alecta, is also active in developing business intelligence systems. "We have created Alecta Alert in order for all our employees to be aware of our situation", says Mats Falk, responsible for the system. Alecta Alert is an intelligent agent that monitors selected information sources on the Internet and other sources. "Thus, it was possible for everyone to create his own agent in order to monitor exactly the things that are relevant". This is an activity that otherwise would take up a large portion of the time the intelligence function has to it's disposition, Mr. Falk concludes.

Decentralized models of business intelligence are by many Nordic companies considered to be less costly and reduce the time for the information to reach the users. Many of these companies have made the costly experience that the hardest part of the BI cycle can be to get the information out to the right person at the right time. This part of the intelligence process, which corresponds to stage 4 in the BI cycle[11] – presentation/distribution – has as of yet received little attention in the BI literature.

Types of Marketing Intelligence

Business marketing intelligence can be divided into three broad categories: (1) continuous intelligence that picks up signals, symptoms, and the fact that can be used to assess performance or alert management to future problems, and (2) intelligence that focuses on solving a particular problem, and (3) integrated activities use a variety of tools to assist in interpreting continuous and problem-related research Table 5.4 shows examples of business marketing activities. All three types are important to a firm's total intelligence effort.

Continuous Marketing Intelligence

Continuous marketing intelligence efforts are broad activities often conducted by many people in the organization. This type of intelligence has an industry focus and often try to identify unknown threats. The entire marketing, sales, and field service staff usually supports this effort in various ways. A market-oriented and inquisitive management culture often influences the effectiveness and quality of this type of intelligence and what can be done with it. In marketing oriented organizations, non-marketing employees are also involved in intelligence activity. This is particularly true for business organizations where engineers and R&D personnel are in frequent contact with customers. Continuous BMI efforts include market assessments and trend analysis, market potential analysis, customer gain-and-loss analysis, competitor assessment, competitive cost and pricing assessments, market share analysis, new technology assessment, and product and customer satisfaction analysis. In Table 5.4 are listed a number of information items useful in conducting industry analysis.

Much of the data for ongoing intelligence usually comes from secondary published sources. This activity, referred to as desk research, is often overlooked in many companies. This type of BMI is particularly useful due to systems such as the North American Industry Classification System (NAICS) and standardized electronic databases. Several industrial classification systems exist. The North American Industry Classification System (NAICS) replaced the U.S. Standard Industrial Classification (SIC) system and is updated every five years.[12] The system divides economic activity into broad categories. The NAICS codes consist of up to 6 digits. The first two digits refer to a major product group such as "Food and Kindred Products" (Code 31). The next four digits refer to an industry subgroup. For example, the code for "Fruit and Vegetable Canning" is 311421. Over time, these codes have become a consistent way of classifying data. Many private industrial research and intelligence organizations use the NAICS code system. For example, American Business Information, Inc. in Omaha, Nebraska, provides prospect and mailing lists according to NAICS codes. One of the advantages with the NAICS system is that it has been developed in cooperation with Statistics Canada and Mexico's INEGI. NAICS also provides for comparable statistics among the three NAFTA trading partners.

Continuous	Problem-related	Integrated
Sales forecasting	Market potential analysis	Scenario analysis
Competitor analysis	Concept testing	Trend analysis
Market Pricing analysis	Alpha- and beta testing	Game theoretical approach
Customer satisfaction surveys	Focus groups	Industry analysis
	Ratio analysis	Pro/con analysis
	SWOT analysis	
	Benchmarking	
	Cost analysis	
	Delphi analysis	
	Network analysis	

Source: The study was conducted for SCIP by The Pine Ridge Group, Inc. and the T.W. Powell Company, 1998. Reprinted with permission from Pine Ridge Group and Knowledgeagency.

Table 5.4: Examples of Business Marketing Intelligence Analysis

Key sources of data for continuous marketing intelligence are financial reports, press releases, and trade magazines. Often firms subscribe to clipping services or newsletters that contain focused industry news or summaries of technology innovations, a large part of which are available electronically. Other data sources include electronic data bases and electronic mail, and services available over Dialog and Dun and Bradstreet; internal accounting information; trade shows; reports from sales and service field forces; suppliers and customers; multi-client industry studies; omnibus and syndicated research; and industry experts. Marketing intelligence work may also include periodic customer satisfaction surveys and specific audit activities of suppliers and distributors. Availability and access to data vary from region to region. For example, In Europe multi-client industry studies, omnibus, and syndicated research are popular sources of information, while in Latin America multi-client studies are poorly developed.

Managing the continuous marketing intelligence effort is difficult. First, many managers do not understand the real value of this kind of intelligence work. Therefore, they tend to request it in spurts or when special projects require attention, requiring that employees and outside marketing intelligence effort is usually placed relatively low in the organizational hierarchy and is staffed with relatively young and inexperienced employees. Younger employees may know how to use the Internet, but often have a disadvantage in knowing what information is relevant. Analysis and interpretation of intelligence data often require extensive industry experience.

Problem-Related Intelligence
The second type of intelligence is problem related. This type of intelligence is often initiated when a firm has a specific problem or need. The most common type of marketing intelligence is market research that collects primary data using qualitative or quantitative methods. Focus group and in-depth interviews are typical qualitative methods, and profiling target customers and defining the relative importance of product attributes are examples of quantitative intelligence. This ad hoc intelligence also includes such activities as benchmarking, reverse engineering, beta testing, and test marketing. Benchmarking is a systematic approach to comparing products and processes to the best firms in an industry. Later in this chapter, we discuss some of the issues related to benchmarking. Reverse engineering is a technical laboratory study of competitive products. Beta testing is the testing of a prototype product in a customer's operating environment. In Chapter 7, beta testing is discussed in some detail.

Problem-related intelligence gathering is common, and it is easier to manage for several reasons. First, it is related to a particular problem, the answer to which leads directly to some concrete action by management. It is therefore easier for a manager to assess the value of the research work. Second, this kind of work is often perceived as essential and can therefore be more easily justified. It tends to reduce a manager's perceived risk, and reflects a *due-diligence* approach to top managers. Many middle managers, therefore, use market research to cover their bases before a decision is made. Third, this type of research is easier to manage because usually business firms hire a research manager who coordinates the work. This involves writing the research briefs, requesting bids, selecting a contractor, and presenting the results. Results from this ad hoc effort usually are produced quickly, and if managers are satisfied with the turnaround, quality, and results, problem-related intelligence is often easy to justify.

Integrated Activities

A final activity is the integration of management inputs through informal observations, reports from meetings with external sources and management, opinions and experiences. Common to all this information is competitive data. The central component of the intelligence system is a function that conducts analysis of the data collected and provides integration. This includes synthesizing the information and preparing reports and recommendations to management. The intelligence is then integrated into strategy, planning, and implementation.

Benchmarking

Benchmarking is a concept that has become popular during the past two decades. In competitive benchmarking a firm's performance is measured against that of "the best-in-class" companies to determine how to achieve desired performance levels. Business functions are analyzed as processes that produce a good or service. Benchmarking can be applied to strategy, operations, and management support functions. Customers are the primary source for market and competitive benchmarking. Benchmarking should be a continuous process and should aim not just to match, but also to beat the competition.

By outsourcing the benchmarking function, as shown in Figure 5.4 for an example) the companies in the automotive industry can help each other, by splitting costs, gathering expertise, and by trying to find objective criteria for Benchmarking analysis, those that are likely to have the greatest impact on sales on the global market.

Mavel is a French automotive consulting company and research firm, which provide its members with quantitative and qualitative information, expert analysis and data on the global automotive industry by dismantling recent vehicles for benchmarking purposes. Its potential customers are part suppliers, carmakers, material manufacturers, machine and toolmakers, etc. The members, among them the French car manufacturer Renault, do not only benefit from the analysis, but participate actively in all steering committees deciding which cars are to be analyzed and which criteria are to be used in the Benchmarking.

The company has two operational facilities, one in Lyon and the other in Detroit. Their AUTOBENCH program is devoted to the design analysis of vehicles that have recently been launched on to the automotive market. Twenty-seven vehicles have been fully torn down and analyzed since the company started in 2000. In Europe, one vehicle is dismantled per month.

Figure 5.4: The AUTOBENCH Case.

In benchmarking, a firm compares it's own performance with products and processes of world leaders. Nonetheless, many Western firms are wary of looking too closely at companies they admire, fearing accusations of plagiarism or using competitors' or other leading firms' proprietary information or processes. Most firms take apart the products of firms they admire in the hope of discovering their manufacturing secrets. To supplement reverse engineering, firms use benchmarking. The technique involves several stages:

1. Determine which aspects of products, technology, or marketing the company may need to improve.
2. Identify a firm that is a world leader in performing the process.
3, Contact the company to find out exactly why it performs so well.

Often the ideal benchmark is a company in a different industry. Unlike the process of gathering competitive intelligence, benchmarking often involves the sharing of information about internal processes and then improving the process. It is important to distinguish benchmarking, which is a formal and rigorous process, from competitive intelligence. The difference is that benchmarking is entirely based on mutual agreement between two firms. The information sharing is confidential and cooperative. For international companies, good benchmarking partners may or perhaps should be firms outside one's home market. For example, European and U.S. automakers conduct extensive comparisons with Japanese auto makers to reduce their product development cycle time.

Some companies refuse benchmarking requests because their superb internal processes are sources of competitive advantage. As the popularity of benchmarking increases, obtaining good benchmarking data is becoming increasingly difficult. However, as indicated earlier in this chapter, there are legal and ethical ways to obtaining non-confidential information that will enable effective benchmarks to be performed without the target company's direct knowledge. The objective of competitive benchmarking is to obtain as much valuable information as possible while giving away as little as possible about a company's own strengths and weaknesses.

If a company has not implemented it's own Code of Ethics for gathering information there exists ready-made solutions, e.g. does the Society of Competitive Intelligence Professional (SCIP) present one for it's members available at www.scip.org/ci/ethics.html. (2002-08-08). An advantage with ready-made Codes of Ethics is that competitors know what to expect, which again may increase confidence among competitors and the likelihood of cooperation.

Intelligence Sources

For organizations committed to establishing an intelligence system, there are many sources of information available.

It is beyond the scope of this chapter to discuss each of these information sources. They are included merely as a checklist and to trigger thinking related to where firms may look to find symptoms of changes, competitive moves, price increases, and so on or answers to specific questions. Each company has specific needs and may find that some sources work better than others.

One source of intelligence data that deserves some attention is related to the intellectual property or patents of another company. Gathering patent information is primarily used by companies as a defensive mechanism to determine competitor's positions with regards to technology and product development strategy. Searches of patent, trademark, and copyright databases are easy, and often help businesses avoid legal trouble from violating a competitor's intellectual property rights. But intelligence property files can also be used in a company's offensive strategy. The use of patent databases for competitive intelligence and other business applications is growing in importance. It is particularly easy for non-U.S. firms to access U.S. patent information. In contrast, it is more difficult (and expensive) for non-Japanese companies to access similar data in Japan. Creative uses of these files enable firms to analyze technology, identify new business licensing opportunities, establish what the competition is doing, identify potential new competitors, and protect one's own intellectual property. Some sources are listed in Table 5.5.

Patents also have several advantages as a technology indicator. Patents provide a wealth of detailed information and comprehensive coverage of technologies. Some firms conduct statistical analysis of international records to assess and forecast technological activities of competitors. The results are often validated by comparison with expert opinion. Such analysis appears to be a valuable tool for corporate technology analysis and planning. Overall, results of patent analysis conform to the opinion of technology experts. This is particularly useful when such forecasts are combined with industry or product life cycle analysis.

Establishing an Intelligence and Information System

Much has been written about establishing marketing intelligence and marketing information systems. Proposals vary from formal computerized systems to informal manual systems. The system designed by FCM Limited described in Figure 5.5 indicates that effective marketing intelligence should contain both formal and informal components.

Internal sources:	Research Related:	Periodical, Reports, Journals and Books:
Accounting records	Bankers	Business periodicals index
E-mail hotlines	Competitor's product	General Press
Financial records	Competitor's customers	Handbooks
Intranet	Consultants	Industry reports
Internet	Focus groups	Marketing journals
	In-depth interviews	Moody's manuals
	Industry gurus	Standard and Poor's Industry
	Internet discussion groups	
	Investment companies	Trade directories
	Multi client studies'	University/academic case studies
	Original market research	Yellow Pages
	Own customers	
	Public activities	
	Stock market data	
	Suppliers	
	Unions	

Government and NPO Data:	Commercial Data:
Census Data	Advertising agencies
Country export councils	Advertising
Country trade commissions	Annual reports
Court documents	Business intelligence agencies
Federal Procurement Centers	Classified advertisements
Government statistics	Corporate directories
International trade statistics	Country surveys
Patent and trademark office	Credit records
State or country economic development offices	Industry associations
Tax records	Industry surveys
	Mailing list providers
	Marketing research agencies
	Security analyst research reports

Table 5.5: Sources of Information for Business Marketing Intelligence.

FCM Limited, a wholly owned subsidiary of Sherer International is one of the world's largest suppliers of flavors and fragrances. FMC consists of many business units that operate as profit centers and are responsible for their own strategies and plans, and regional organization that interface with customers. Customers range in size from small manufacturers of perfume to large manufacturers of detergent and food products. Some customers operate locally; other customers operate worldwide. Flavor and fragrance manufacturers are expected to work closely with customers to develop and supply flavors and fragrance that enhance customers' products. This requires active MI by FMC. The marketing research function was a corporate-level activity.

When FMC reviewed its approach to MI it identified a number of issues and obstacles that needed to be addressed:

- The business units felt that the centralized marketing research function was bureaucratic and excessively costly. Those in the function were perceived to feel that that they "owned" the data and that it was to be carefully doled out to the "less than bright" individuals in the business units.
- There was a "kingdom of Information" attitude, as individuals used possession of information to achieve power in the organization.
- Timeliness was a problem, and in an effort to do all things, no one thing was done well.
- It was perceived that the system required the user to do all the work and that data were not available in the way information was used.
- Much of the research seemed to be interesting rather than relevant, raising questions in terms of value added.

In broad terms it was felt that its was important to make MI data available to the business units and the regions in a standardized form, to continuously update the data, to offer tools and templates to facilitate its use by the business units and regions, and to restrict analysis done centrally for "big picture" issues. Specifically FMC identified the following categories of MI data/information:

Competitive information, with data on more than 100 competitors.

Market information, with information on market volume growth rates, and so on.

Key customer information.

A key objective was to design a system that would accept data from many sources. The system, which is under development, also had to be designed to handle both structured and unstructured data. Structured data would include market, competitor, and financial information. Unstructured data would include a variety of information, including "comments" and input by members of the sales force and other employees.

A major source of the structured market data would be a market research firm in the United Kingdom, which agreed to provide information on volume and growth rates of food and other household products in some 40 categories from some 140 countries, together with population and gross domestic product figures. By applying appropriate conversion factors, FMC can translate these numbers into market potential for FMC products, calculated market share by country, and identify potential opportunities. The contract provided that the research company would bill FMC £120,000 per year for three years, and for this amount the company would continually update the information. Other structured data would come from company reports, industry reports, market research reports, and so on.

FMC would use special software to access the various databases. Several members of the FMC's central marketing staff had been trained in writing computer software, and they had started a major effort to develop a comprehensive and user-friendly system. It is estimated that the users of the system would be able to generate some 600,000 tables of analysis. In addition, the system would provide for ways to search for "comments" section using key words.

As with any MI system of this kind that contains proprietary information, there is the risk that the data may be used inappropriately. Restricting the access to the data however, would limit its use and seem to defeat the purpose of the system. The present plan, therefore, would allow essentially unlimited access, but patterns of use would be monitored for possible abuse.

Source: Company records. Company name and some data have been disguised.

Figure 5.5: Management of MI and FMC Limited

The creation of a marketing intelligence system can be viewed as a strategic institutional change tool. Strategic and competitive intelligence systems should include management information systems, conventional decision support systems, and knowledge-based systems.

The literature known as Knowledge management may be taken to mean comparing information collected about employees with information about the external environment. Many companies have such systems and substantial amounts of internal intelligence information. What makes MI a significant competitor at the beginning of the 21st Century is the continuous development of easy-to-use data base tools. Most firms have the necessary operating functions to integrate their own intelligence activities. In such cases, all that is needed is to organize the effort following a well-designed set of information- and intelligence-handling procedures. This requires a company culture that supports marketing intelligence as well as broad-based management commitment and use that can best be accomplished through senior management example and leadership.

The nature of and need for intelligence varies by company, market, and industry. Therefore, characteristics of intelligence systems also vary. Some factors that influence the design of the intelligence system include:

- The complexity of the environment.
- Organizational environment and culture.
- The complexity of the business (products/markets).
- Cultural "transportability" of products across international markets.
- The rate of technological change.
- Stage in the product life cycle and growth rates.
- Competitive structure and market share.

The lesson corporate leaders must heed from the history of intelligence in business organizations is that, as the complexity of the environment and their own organizations increases, their current intelligence activities may no longer suffice. With high business and environmental uncertainty, complexity increases and the need for a marketing intelligence system becomes vital. For example, changing customer demographics, industry innovation, the potential availability of product substitutes, the availability and new uses of technology, value changes, political instability, and shifts in public policy are factors that increase complexity and thus require marketing intelligence. Also, firms with many different product/markets must design their intelligence systems in such a way that relevant data are collected for each product/market combination.

Organizational structure impacts how and to what degree an organization conducts intelligence. Information flows from one organizational level to another and across organizational units. The organizational hierarchy and structure tend to influence the quality of intelligence and how intelligence information flows and is used throughout the organization. For example, in functionally organized companies, the integration and use of intelligence may be difficult across functions such as production, finance, and marketing because of entrenched cultures. This can particularly be true when marketing, rather than top management, initiates the intelligence efforts. On the other hand, when each function gathers and interprets intelligence data from different perspectives, the quality of the information gathered and how it is interpreted and converted into intelligence can be enhanced. Consequently, intelligence based on functional specialization provides depth of knowledge not found in organizations where all intelligence gathering and interpretation is conducted exclusively within the marketing department.

Different levels in the organization have the need for different kinds of intelligence. Strategic decisions are first of all the concern of the top-level management. The company is in need of tactics at the middle level management, smaller steps that will lead the company to any defined strategy. To make tactical moves the company is in the need of information, but of another kind. A third kind is operative intelligence, information to secure the day-to-day operations among front line managers. All three kinds of intelligence depend on each other for their combined success, as shown in Figure 5.6.

Figure 5.6: The Different Kinds of Intelligence Requested.

The aim of strategic intelligence is to alert senior management to events and developments, which may provide opportunities or threats which may have a significant impact on the value of the firm. The aim of tactical intelligence is provide information which can aid the implementation of strategic objectives. Operative intelligence is concerned with information which can be used in the daily business, such as in developing propositions, negotiations with customers and customer relationship.

Organizing Intelligence Work

One of the most important but difficult aspects of business marketing intelligence is how BMI efforts are organized and managed. Often this important function only receives a half-hearted commitment by senior executives and it becomes a periodic task in the marketing organization. The lack of commitment from senior management is often seen as the single most important reason that intelligence work fails. Others reasons for failure include trying to serve too many employees with too many intelligence topics, creating databases before the intelligence process and procedures have been proven, not establishing legal and ethical guidelines or separating the analysis from the collection unit. In this era of globalization, organizations need to incorporate new approaches in managing their intelligence processes. Several important factors include:

1. All key managers must agree that marketing intelligence is important and be committed to it. Managers must provide key strategic questions to guide the intelligence efforts and sufficient resources to accomplish required intelligence tasks.

2. Management must develop a company culture that encourages employees to search for intelligence and to question the validity and reliability of facts, assumptions, and conclusions in the spirit of organizational learning. In some of the most successful companies at implementing marketing intelligence systems, among them many Japanese, all employees have an understanding for and contribute in the information gathering effort.

3. Management must assign the intelligence function to a visible position in the organization. By doing so it signals the importance of BMI to all managers. Management must also require the BMI function to produce and widely distribute useful documents.

4. Management must provide a communication climate that facilitates horizontal and vertical dissemination of intelligence. This flow should be from the bottom up and from the top down.

5. Management must select executives with substantial industry experience. This provides maturity and credibility to intelligence interpretation tasks. Good intelligence briefings require positioning to organizational context. Senior managers are more likely to listen to a manager they know has significant experience than to a manager with little industry ex-

perience. This prevents irrelevant recommendations and predictions sometimes provided by inexperienced employees.

As shown in Figure 5.7, there is substantial variation in the degree of analytical thinking involved in the five different processes or phases of the Intelligence Cycle. Analytical thinking is not only important in the analytical phase of the Intelligence process, but also in the planning- and evaluation phase. It also illustrates in which parts of the process where top management involvement is most important; in the planning-, presentation- and evaluation phases. Information gathering involves less analytical thinking and is often delegated. This does not mean that analytical work is the only critical part in the BI cycle. The Nordic cases presented earlier in the chapter showed distribution and presentation is often where companies fail, either because they don't know who needs the information, information is produced for people who don't need it or the information arrives too late.

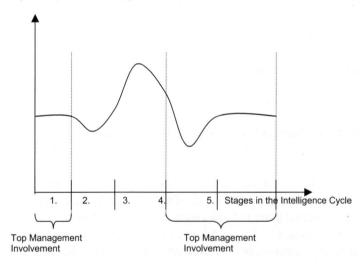

Figure 5.7: The Types of Competencies Related to the Five Stages of the Intelligence Cycle.

It is difficult to recommend exactly how the marketing intelligence function should be organized and where it should be located. However, the function commonly reports to a marketing manager or vice president of marketing. The advantage of this approach is that the marketing function has this resource at its immediate disposal. Market and customer data can easily be collected and interpreted. The disadvantage of this approach is that it is often viewed as an exclusive tool for the marketing function. Other functions or departments may receive intelligence only on a need-to-know basis. This makes it difficult for other functions to become equal partners in intelligence gathering. As we stated previously, other functions such as research and development, engineering, filed service, and manufacturing should be included as essential players in the intelligence gathering activities.

Another approach that appears to work is to disassociate the BMI activities somewhat from the day-to-day marketing operative activities. This can be done by establishing a marketing service organization that provides information and intelligence services to all departments. In practice this means that all functions receive intelligence and can request intelligence from this unit. Often when the marketing intelligence unit has such independent status, it also works closely with corporate and business management.

The broader intelligence effort of which MI is a part may be linked to Business Intelligence which does not only include information gathering about competitors and the narrower markets, but also technical competencies, possible partners, all kinds of influencers - organizations and individuals – all laws and regulations that define and limit business activities; in one term all that goes into keeping or making a business organization competitive.

Demand Analysis

Defining the Market Potential and Its Components

One of the most common BI activities is the determination of a company's potential in a particular market segment for a specific product. Figure 5.8 shows the various components of market potential. By understanding the nature and the size of thee components, it is possible to determine market potential in a company-specific context.

The top line in Figure 5.8 represents the total theoretical potential market according to a Trajectory Forecasting, where there is a definite trend upwards or downwards and we assume the curve will continue in the same direction for the period of the forecast. A similar potential can also be mapped by other types of forecasts, like Cyclic Forecasting, which is based on the assumption that history repeats itself.

The theoretical market size is the size of the market if all customers would purchase a specific solution to solve their functional needs. For example, consider the business office market for personal computers. One could argue that all employees could use a personal computer. However, it is not realistic to expect that this will happen in all offices worldwide, as there will always be those companies who cannot afford to buy a personal computer to all its employees or where all do not need one. Therefore, the number we get by counting all office workers is just a theoretical number. This theoretical number is the theoretical market size for personal computers. Therefore, the question we need to answer is how many firms are likely to purchase personal computers within a given period?

The answer to this question helps determine the size of the potential market, which needs to be broken down into smaller components. The next question is, what proportion of the potential market is available? Even though the market potential exists, the market infrastructure may be such that all potential customers may not be reachable. Many countries may have limited distribution or communications channels that restrict market penetration. Therefore, only a certain proportion of the potential market is available. This proportion is the available market or the level of likely penetration. The available market can be broken down into several components: the qualified market, the served market, and the penetrated market. The qualified market is the portion of the market for which a company with a given technology can qualify to compete. The served market is the portion of the market that the firm specifically targets. The penetrated market is that portion of the served market that the firm expects to reach with a particular marketing program.

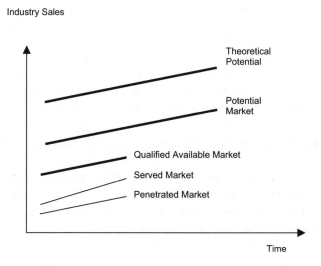

Figure 5.8: What is Market Potential?

It is very important for firms to go through an exercise similar to the one described above. It helps define what portion of the market is potential for the company. It may also reveal when a market potential represents an opportunity for a specific firm with a given solution.

Using Satisfaction Surveys to Understand Current Market Position

Many firms, particularly small- and medium-size companies, do not have a good understanding of their market position. In many international markets, market shares and market share growth figures are crude and inaccurate, which limits a firm's ability to accurately determine its competitive position. It is particularly important to obtain relative figures because they are the true measures of performance. A firm can have substantial aggregate growth but experience loss of its relative market position.

For this reason some business marketing firms conduct regular customer satisfaction studies. For example, the Diagnostics Division of Abbott Laboratories tracks customer satisfaction in 46 countries, a complex task that requires commitment and resources. To convince management that this was the appropriate intelligence approach, the MI group at Abbott used the arguments shown in Table 5.6.

- If you do not measure it, you cannot improve it.
- Do not mistake silence for satisfaction.
- If you are not keeping score, you are only practicing.
- It costs five times more to get a new customer than it costs to keep a current customer.
- Increase in customer satisfaction = $ XXX increase in sales = $ XXX in company profits.
- More than 90% of unsatisfied customers do not complain.
- Satisfied customers tend to buy more and are more willing to pay premium prices.
- Satisfied customers are loyal customers, less likely to switch to competitive products.
- Companies can boot profits by 100% by retaining just 5 percent of their customers.

Table 5.6: Arguments in Support of Customer Satisfaction Research.

For many of the reasons listed in the table, customer satisfaction measurement has become a popular intelligence activity. Although international customer satisfaction research is difficult to do, firms that can link satisfaction data to performance and evaluation may design customer satisfaction into their reward systems.

Understanding Customer Requirements

Another essential BMI activity is gaining an understanding of customer needs. Many firms give "lip service" to this requirement; they push what they know best (are product oriented) without attempting to understand what the customer really needs. Business marketers that are market oriented know the customer requirements better than the customer. In such situations, selling is less important and persuasion becomes unnecessary. In Chapter 3 we discussed in detail the needs and motivation of business customers. Below are some of the key marketing intelligence aspects of customer requirements:

- Know the customer's operations and product in detail.
- Understand the customer's cost structure.
- Identify how the initial purchase enhances the customer's value versus its customers and how it impact cost.
- Understand operating implications related to installation and startup.
- Understand the role of operating costs versus up-front investment.
- Find out how important product life cycle costs or cost of ownership are to the customer.
- Identify the customer's understanding of your product's relative benefits and the impact on the customer's cost structure and performance.

To determine customer requirements, business marketers must communicate directly with their clients. Much of the responsibility for intelligence gathering in many companies is given to the sales force. If used extensively, this can be an ineffective approach unless it is properly managed. Because salespeople may be biased toward the sale, they may not be objective assessors of what is in the best interest of the customer and the company in the long run. Consequently, it is important that other company employees such as marketing staff, product managers, engineers, researchers, and planners, communicate with the client organization. It is also common to use objective third parties, such as consultants and market research firms, to assist in the evaluation. Formal, problem-oriented market research is commonly used to identify customer requirements in addition to sales force recommendations. The nature of the research may vary from a survey to in-depth executive interviews. In Chapter 7, we discuss in more detail how a business marketer can use beta tests and conjoint analysis to determine and refine customers' product requirements.

Knowledge of the end consumer's needs is often overlooked in Business-to-business marketing. The idea of derived demand explains how vulnerable an end supplier can be to actual consumer demand in today's world market. A producer of steel pipes to the shipping industry is affected by the changes in demand in the cruise industry through a series of links, as shown in Figure 5.9.

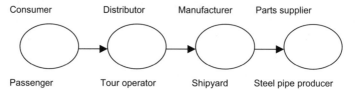

Figure 5.9: Derived demand in the Shipping Industry

Assessing Market Demand

In Chapter 3, we discussed how aggregate business market behavior often is a result of events in consumer or government markets. Business market behavior can therefore often be traced directly to changed behavior in these markets. Business market demand is often a derived demand. There is often a lag factor between changes in consumer demand and the impact that it has on business demand. Thus, an extremely important intelligence activity for business marketers is to identify and monitor factors that influence changes and periodic fluctuations in demand.

Another important factor in analyzing demand for business products is demand elasticity. Commonly discussed in relationship to pricing, demand elasticity reflects the positive and negative changes in demand as prices are reduced or increased. When the business marketer is selling a substitute product, in some markets and situations, this can result in quick changes in a firm's demand. However, it is not always that simple. In business marketing, relationships are important, and there may be substantial resistance to change even though there are economic incentives to use alternative suppliers. Personal relationships, service level, loyalty, and organizational culture are other important influences.

Product characteristics are another factor that influence demand fluctuations. Firms may use simple but effective guidelines: From the customer's point of view, does the product we provide contain attributes that are "like to haves" or are they "must haves"? If the firm provides a product with many of "like to haves" features, it would expect that demand would fall as price increased. If the firm provides a product that has many "must haves" features, it could expect demand to remain stable with price increases. From a marketing intelligence point of view, it is essential to determine the "must have" criteria. Failure to understand the difference between the two may have serious consequences. Many international companies through product development and delivery have incorporated a large number of "like to haves". But these efforts have had no influence on demand. They have only increased the firm's product and delivery costs.

Sales Forecasting
One of the primary objectives of BMI is to provide the basis for the forecast. It is thus directly linked to intelligence efforts. The better the market intelligence, the better the forecast. We include a description of forecasting here because it is essential to the economic performance of any business organization. Forecasts are directly linked to company budgets and plans. Figure 5.10 shows the relationships between the forecast and various company budgets. The forecast requires extensive external inputs, and most of the activities conducted by BMI are directly linked to the quality of the forecast.

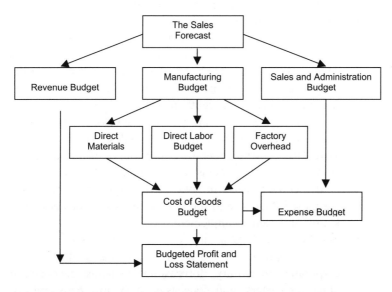

Figure 5.10: Why the Sales Forecast is So Important

Forecasting is important because it directs the planning, allocation, and use of a business organization's resources. If a forecast is to high, a firm has over-allocated resources and must go through the painful process of making cuts. If the forecast is too low, the firm usually has not allocated enough resources to satisfy the demand. This, of course, is also a problem, but a more pleasant one, because the firm may have to rush order materials, hire more labor, and do on. Forecasts should be on target. Therefore, many business-to-business marketers use rolling forecasts that are updated monthly. A forecast is not an objective or wishful thinking. A forecast is a commitment. It reflects what will be delivered in terms of sales. It is better to underestimate than to overestimate the sales forecast. Firms can choose from an extensive pool of methods and approaches developed to forecast sales. Below we describe some common approaches to forecasting.[13]

Forecasting techniques are often divided into two categories – qualitative and quantitative methods. The key qualitative methods are as follows:

- *In-depth interviews* with customers regarding their buying intentions and purchase requirements. Due to the open-ended nature of this approach, it can contain significant bias. It is an excellent way of getting detailed information from important customers, and it allows for two-way interaction between the interviewer and the interviewee.
- *Jury of executive opinion* combines the average estimates of senior executives and knowledgeable individuals within the organization. The weakness of this method is that it strictly depends on the knowledge of executives. But because this method consolidates the knowledge of several people, it is less biased than the in-depth interview.
- *Sales force composites* are forecasts developed by salespersons for their respective territories. Salespeople may be biased. They may be either too optimistic, or, if they are paid a commission, salespersons may manipulate forecasts to plan their income stream. In spite of this weakness, this is still the most frequent used forecasting method in business marketing. It is easy to implement.
- *The Delphi method* is an extension of the jury of executive opinion approach. It is a group forecasting method that incorporates anonymity, forecasting revisions, feedback to other forecasters, and consensus. It is time consuming to implement but usually unbiased due to the anonymity.

Some quantitative forecasting methods are:

- *Survey of user needs* is similar to the in-depth interview, except that the customer fills out a questionnaire about buying needs and intentions. Because of ongoing negotiations, bias is likely to exist.
- *Time-series analysis* includes several methods – moving averages, trend fitting, exponential smoothening, least squares, and Box-Jenkins time-series analysis. All of these methods require historical data. Moving average techniques use the

average of recent periods to predict the next forecast period. Trend fitting and exponential smoothening tries to fit past data with a particular curve or adjusts the forecasting with some proportional weight to predict sales for the next period. Box-Jenkins forecasting is a sophisticated computer model that allows the computer to pick a statistical time-series model that fits the data.

- *Regression analysis* involves identifying the variables that influence sales and building a model that can then be applied to historical data to determine the effect of each variable on sales. For maximum effectiveness, regression analysis requires a large number of past observations and it is limited in its ability to identify major turning points. It is most useful for products in the mature stage of the product life cycle and for products where a constant set of variables, which can be accurately measured, have been identified.

- *Diffusion analysis* is very difficult to use, but it may work when a firm is trying to forecast sales for an entire product class. This category of forecasting models is also useful for forecasting sales of new products. It is quite problematic because it is a form of market simulation and requires significant market research to estimate parameters used in the analysis.

- *Input-output analysis* is an econometric technique that establishes links between sectors of one industry with sectors of another industry. This technique is complex and time consuming.

- *Product life cycle analysis* can be used when it is possible to estimate the parameters of the life cycle s-curve. Using this approach for forecasting requires knowledge of product acceptance rates.

By themselves, none of these methods may give an accurate forecast. A combination of methods integrated with sound intelligence and experience usually gives the best result. The Swedish telecom company Telia AB does not use any particular method of analysis in their intelligence process, but tries to find a process that is efficient from case to case both for the users and the analysts. The company conducts several different types of analysis on the same questions to see if the answers differ. If they do, more analysis will be conducted.[14] For mature businesses, with relatively stable patterns of competitive market shares, forecasting overall industry demand may be the most critical requirement, but estimates also need to be made of the relative marketing effort of competitors. For firms introducing new products, forecasting becomes more uncertain. Sales patterns during previous introductions of similar products may provide guidance as can intelligence gathered from customers by the sales force. Regardless of the forecasting situation, it needs to be recognized that even the best forecasts deal with the future and so are inherently uncertain. However, the better management is able to estimate the future, the better it is prepared to deal with it. Good forecasts, therefore, require both management attention and resources.

How to Use Marketing Intelligence
Companies able to build intelligence and use systems that are better than their competitors often derive sustainable competitive advantage. It is the use of intelligence that represents an important asset. If the intelligence is not used, it is only a wasteful expense. How can companies incorporate market intelligence? Below are a few suggestions about how intelligence can be used:

- Publish internally the objectives of the marketing intelligence unit and explain who is responsible for what activity. Encourage managers to use the BMI resource.
- Periodically develop a presumed competitor business strategy document. Circulate this document to all managers and productively solicit updates and revisions.
- Provide periodic status reports on competitor and customer activities.
- Provide all managers with periodic technology updates.
- Provide an overview catalog or database of available intelligence material on the Intranet. This might consist of a list of electronic databases available, research reports on file, market statistics, e-mail groups, and secondary resources.

How to Protect Intelligence and Business Secrets
There may be said to be two main kinds of intelligence strategies, one active and one passive. The passive is known as counterintelligence. Some companies may find out that their need for marketing intelligence is limited to marketing research, but all companies should make sure they have an efficient counterintelligence capability. Information that is vital for the company's existence must be protected. Examples of counterintelligence measures can be everything from making copies of the content of a server to full Technical Surveillance Counter Measures (TSCM).

TSCM is concerned with the prevention or detection of sensitive information. It typically involves an inspection by a technician or engineer (TSCM specialist) of a physical item or place. The TSCM specialist will do a sweep of the location, detecting any surveillance devices (bugs) and any technical security weaknesses. It was estimated in 1997 that $2,213 million of illegal eavesdropping equipment was sold per year within the United States.[15] For 2002 sales of security and surveillance equipment has grown to a $5 billion industry, up 30% to 60% since last year at spy-gear stores across the United States.[16] Some of this increase in sales is no doubt caused by the growing fear after the terrorist attack known as 9-11 and is not business-related, but the figures, even though rough estimates, show that companies are more willing to consider alternative ways of gathering information with the development of new surveillance technology. Another reason may be that the economic consequences of being detected are not sufficiently severe to prevent these methods from being used. As a result TSCM services are becoming increasingly necessary, even though general caution in many cases will be enough to prevent any serious damage from the loss of information. Managers should know when they are at risk and for what. Confidential meetings and bids are very popular targets for corporate spies. Other situations may be related to *specific events* like negotiations, litigation, lawsuit and layoffs. If your company is involved in the fashion, automotive, advertising, or marketing industry you are considered to be at *continuous risk*. According to the FBI the following types of businesses are under *continuous and special risk*: Materials, Manufacturing, Information and Communications, Biotechnology and Life Sciences, Transportation, Energy and Environment.

It is essential that business intelligence be kept inside of the organization. Intelligence should be treated as sensitive information and considered a trade secret. Such information is usually lost in three ways:

1. Accidental exposure by an employee entrusted with its possession.
2. Intentional theft by an unauthorized outside agent.
3. Internal theft by an ex-employee or a disgruntled worker who has access to the information.

Since there is no possible way to keep all information secret, management must create an awareness and responsibility program that informs and requires employees who work with BMI that it should not be disclosed to outsiders. Employees should be required to sign a statement related to disclosure of information. For example, throughout IBM, during its period of unparalleled success, a responsible and consistent approach existed among employees. Few employees divulged confidential information to outsiders. Internally, IBM was very *open* while to an outsider it appeared closed and little market intelligence was available to non-employees.

Summary

Marketing intelligence is an important business marketing function. It represents a broad set of activities that supports strategy formulation and implementation. BMI is broader than marketing research and is conducted continuously by employees from a variety of company functions. Globalization of business has increased the importance of BMI made it more complex and more taxing on resources. New technology, like the growing use of Internet for the search of information has contributed in the opposite direction, making it faster and less expensive.

The BMI function is often ignored, poorly resourced and inadequately staffed. This chapter distinguishes between problem-oriented and continuous BMI. Companies that conduct both well are often leaders in their field. Their managers are willing to change strategy as MBI requires.

Further Reading:

Bradford W. Ashton and Richard A. Klavans, *Keeping abreast of Science and Technology.* (Columbus, OH: Battelle Press, 1997).

Helen P. Burwell, *Online Competitive Intelligence: Increase your Profits using Cyber-Intelligence.* (Tempe, AZ: Facts on Demand, 1999).

Michelle Cook and Curtis W. Cook, *Competitive Intelligence: Create an Intelligent Organization and Compete to Win* (London: Kogan Page, 2000).

Rhonda Delmater, *Data Mining Explained: A Manager's Guide to Customer-Centric Business Intelligence* (Boston, MA: Oxford University Press, 2001).

Barry De Ville, *Microsoft Data Mining: Integrated Business Intelligence for e-Commerce & Knowledge* (Cincinnati, OH: Butterworth-Heinemann, 2001).

Alan Dutka, *Competitive Intelligence for the Competitive Edge* (Lincolnwood, IL: NTC Business Books, 1999).

Liam Fahey, *Competitors* (New York: John Wiley & Sons, 1999).

John J. Fialka, *War by Other Means* (New York: W.W. Norton & Co, 1997).

Craig S. Fleisher and Babette Bensoussan, *Strategic and Competitive Analysis: Methods and Techniques for Analyzing Business Competition* (Englewood Cliffs, NJ: Prentice Hall, 2002).

Leonard M. Fuld, *The New Competitor Intelligence: The Complete Resource for Finding, Analyzing, and Using Information about Your Competitors* (New York: John Wiley & Sons, 1994).

Ian H. Gordon, *Competitor Targeting: Winning the Battle for Market and Customer Share* (New York: John Wiley & Sons, 2001).

Charles Halliman, *Business Intelligence using Smart Techniques: Environmental Scanning using Text Mining and Competitor Analysis using Scenarios and Manual Simulation* (Houston, TX: Information Uncover, 2001).

David Hussey and Per Jenster, *Competitor Intelligence.* (Chichester, England: John Wiley & Sons, 1999).

Larry Kahaner, *Competitive Intelligence.* (New York: Simon & Schuster, 1997).

Bernard Liautaud, *E-Business Intelligence: Turning Information into Knowledge into Profit* (New York:McGraw-Hill Education Group, 2000).

Krizan, Lisa, *Intelligence Essentials for Everyone* (Washington, D.C.: Government Printing Office, 1999).

John J. McGonagle and Carolyn M. Vella, *The Internet Age of Competitive Intelligence* (London: Quorum, 1999).

Jerry P. Miller, *Millennium Intelligence: Understanding & Conducting Competitive Intelligence in the Digital Age* (Medford, NJ: Information Today, Inc., 2000).

Washington Platt, *Strategic Intelligence Production* (New York: F. A. Praeger, 1957).

Andrew Pollard, *Competitor Intelligence*. (London, England: Financial Times Professional Ltd., 1999).

John E. Prescott and Stephen H. Miller, *Proven Strategies in Competitive Intelligence* (New York: John Wiley & Sons, 2001).

Nils Rasmussen and others, *Financial Business Intelligence* (New York: Wiley & Sons, 2002).

F. W. Rustmann, *CIA, Inc.: Espionage & the Craft of Business Intelligence* (Herndon: VA: Brassey's, Inc., 2002).

Alan R. Simon and Steven L. Shaffer, *Data Warehousing and Business Intelligence for e-Commerce* (San Francisco, CA: Morgan Kaufmann, 2001).

Jim Underwood, *Competitive Intelligence*. Retrieved August 16, 2004 from Wiley Canada http://www.wiley.ca/WileyCDA/WileyTitle/ productCd-1841122262.html (Capstone Ltd., February 2002).

Carolyn M. Vella, *The Internet Age of Competitive Intelligence*. (Westport, CT: Quorum Books, 1999).

Conor Vibert, *Web-Based Analysis for Competitive Intelligence* (Westport, CT: Quorum Books, 2000).

David Vine, *Internet Business Intelligence* (Medford, NJ: CyberAge Books, 2000).

Alf H. Walle, *Qualitative Research in Intelligence and Marketing: The New Strategic Convergence* (Eastport, CT: Quorum Books, 2001).

---

[1]It should be noted that the term "business intelligence" (BI) has been increasingly related to software over the last several years, and that it is possible that it will be replaced by the term "competitive intelligence" (CI). However, until that happens we shall view CI as a part of BI.

[2]See also Figure 5.6: "The Different Kinds of Intelligence Requested."

[3]These five different intelligence operations are also used to describe the different working procedures for Figure 5.7: "The Types of Competencies Related to the Five Phases in the Intelligence Cycle."

[4]Percentage refers to population asked of firms.

[5]See http://www.scip.org/ci/analysis.asp (August 22, 2002).

Further Reading

6 See *Intelligence Software Report 2002*, Fuld & Company Inc.

[7]For more on OLAP, see http://www.olapreport.com/ (August 22, 2002).

[8]METI was founded in January 2001, incorporating the old MITI (Ministry of Japan's International Trade Industry). See http://www.meti.go.jp

[9]For more information see http://www3.jetro.go.jp/ttppoas/index.html

[10]Examples provided by Hans Hedin, SCIP Scandinavia Chapter Coordinator and Senior Partner at Docere Intelligence AB in Stockholm.

[11]See Figure 5.2: The Business Intelligence Cycle.

12 See http://www.census.gov/epcd/www/naicsind.htm (August 22, 2002).

[13]For a good assessment of forecasting, see D. M. Georgoff and R. G. Murdick, "A Manager's Guide to Forecasting," *Harvard Business Review* (January 1986).

[14]See L. Bertelsen and M. Mathison, "Competitor Intelligence Process – A Case Study of Telia AB." Unpublished paper. Luleå University of Technology, Sweden, 2000.

[15]U.S. State Department/DCI (Bureau of Intelligence and Research), March 1997.

[16]Brooks Barnes, Staff Reporter of *The Wall Street Journal*, February 13, 2002.

Chapter 6

Selecting Business Markets

Few decisions a firm makes are more critical than its selection of the market to be served. Market growth rates indicate the commitment it must make to growth in its production and marketing capacity, and hence its need for capital, physical and human resources. Customers' functional requirements dictate the required product characteristics. Purchasing policies and customer values dictate the nature of buyer seller relations and the communication effort. Levels of competition and customer sensitivity to price significantly influence pricing policies. Size of targeted customers and their preferences influence, and sometimes mandate, choice of distribution channels.

An Overview of Business Market Selection
In broad terms, a *market* can be defined as those potential customers who share a similar want or need and who are able and willing to commit their resources (usually money but sometimes barter or other media of exchange) to satisfy that want or need. Similar wants and needs, however, are still subject to much variation. Having elected to participate in a given market, it is then necessary to decide what portion, or segment, of the market can feasibly be served with a given marketing strategy or mix, and to what extent marketing strategy needs to be varied in order to accommodate variation in the wants and needs of customers.

We define a *market segment* as a group of potential customers who are likely to respond similarly to one or more elements of marketing strategy. Market segmentation is the process of identifying those segments that can feasibly be targeted and that represent profitable opportunities for the firm. In some instances, firms can achieve their aspirations for growth or financial performance by focusing on just one segment. In other instances, achievement of goals may require targeting several segments. In some instances, this may require variation in just one element of marketing strategy; the promotional message, for example. In other instances, this may require variation in all the strategy elements of product, price, promotion and distribution.

Competitive forces and unique customer requirements argue for defining segments narrowly. Economies of scale, with respect to marketing as well as manufacturing, argue for a broader definition of a segment, or aggregation of several segments. The final match of marketing strategy to a segment, or segments, will, therefore, depend on the particular situation of the firm. Hoover Universal, for instance, a diversified U.S. manufacturer, with strong historical ties to the automotive industry, once stated its view as follows:[1]

> *One final future direction concerns key customers. Industrial manufacturers such as Hoover exist to serve others. We design our products to fit the needs of our customers, to accommodate their timing and their geography, and importantly, to adjust to the dollars they have available. In a very real sense, our destiny is tied to our customers. Fortunately, or unfortunately, all customers are not equal. Some are more growth oriented and are prepared to make the serious commitments necessary to achieve that growth. It is imperative that we identify in our present markets the key customers who are making commitments. If we make the right identification, and if we find the way to build partnerships instead of simply a supplier relationship, then we can assure our future success. Or, said another way, if there are markets where we find that the key customer has already been usurped by one or more of our competitors, we must either find a way to displace a competitor or, failing that, cut our losses and move to another market. Happily for Hoover, we have strong relationships with key customers in most of our markets and are moving positively toward partnership relationships which can have such significant dividends in the future.*

For Hoover, the question of market selection was simplified by the existence of relatively few customers. For most firms, however, the issue is more complex. Consider, for example, Loctite Corporation, a U.S. manufacturer of high-performance adhesives and sealants. The company had developed Bond-a-Matic®, a new instant adhesive dispenser. Its studies indicated 1,028,223 U.S. establishments, in 16 categories of SIC Codes,[2] used adhesives. Depending on SIC Code, something between 13% and 48% were either current or potential users of instant adhesives and so were potential customers for the new dispenser. Customers varied in the amount of adhesive use, however; both as a function of the size of the firm and the nature of the manufacturing process. Some customers were sophisticated in their knowledge of adhesive technology, others were not. Some preferred to deal directly with the manufacturer whereas others preferred to deal with distributors, some of whom were very specialized. As the company developed its plan to launch Bond-a-Matic®, it was faced with a number of questions. Should it target all potential customers or some sub-set? Would one marketing plan be suitable for all customers? If not, should a number of plans be developed, each tailored for a particular set of homogeneous customers or should it develop just one plan, focused on just one homogeneous segment. Still further, what characteristics would indicate homogeneity? Would just the size of the firm or the nature of its product be sufficient indicators or would it be necessary to take other variables into account?[3]

The notion of finding a market segment, whose wants and needs are closely met, that responds more favorably to the firm's marketing strategy than to the strategies of its competitors, and is potentially profitable, is intuitively attractive. The search for such segments, however, is highly situation specific. With new to the world products, for instance, precise segmentation may be difficult and market selection may need to be broad, taking into account a wide range of possibilities. When Federal Express introduced Courier Pak, an overnight delivery service of packages of less than two pounds, it placed its introductory media messages in general business publications such as the Wall Street Journal and Business Week, designed to reach organizations of all sizes and in all industries, rather than in more narrowly targeted trade journals. On the other hand, for Mid-Continent Computer Services, having successfully designed and produced a software system for its savings and loan parent, it was clear that its communications should be targeted just to other savings and loan institutions. In the growth stage of the product life cycle, major segments may emerge, requiring completely new strategies. This was the case in the personal computer industry when the corporate segment emerged, some few years after initial introduction of personal computers by Apple Computer, Inc. and Tandy Corporation, focusing principally on the school and consumer markets. By contrast, in mature industries the search for new segments may focus on narrow segments, requiring modification to only some part of marketing strategy. Micro Motion, for instance, initially dominated the worldwide mass flowmeter market with a proprietary, premium priced, full function product. As the market matured, a segment emerged interested in less functionality at a lower price.

Examples abound of firms that successfully serve a particular segment; so successfully, in some cases, as to dominate the segment to the exclusion of competitors. Given the variability in situations, is this the result of careful planning or is it the result of some fortuitous set of circumstances, not particularly amenable to analysis? As we discuss in Chapter 7, failure rates of new products indicate that finding such segments is not an exact science. A number of approaches, however, have been developed which can materially assist the search for characteristics that might identify customers who would respond favorably to a particular marketing strategy.

The Search for Business Market Segments

The process of selecting the market segment, or segments, to be served starts with the identification of potential segments. Once potential segments have been identified, they need to be considered as to their usefulness for further evaluation. Finally, they are evaluated on the basis of their feasibility for the firm and the likelihood that electing to serve them will meet the firm's financial or other objectives.

Some firms segment a market on the basis of just one variable; typically an industry or the size of the customer. With some reservations, we observe that this may be appropriate for certain broad decisions such as the type of product offerings to be made. For the development of comprehensive marketing strategy, however, it is necessary to take into account a wide variety of variables, relevant to the many decisions associated with the strategy. The starting point of market segmentation, therefore, should be the identification of all possible segmentation variables. Generally, these are divided into macro and micro categories. Macro variables are those that focus on the buying organization, and include size, location, industry, market level (e.g., OEM or end user) or the end market served by potential customers. Micro variables are those that focus on the decision making unit, and include individual characteristics of buyers, decision criteria, type of purchase situation, benefits sought and perceived importance of the purchase. A list of possible variables, and possible categories, for segmenting the computer market is shown in Table 6.1.

While many segmentation variables are reasonably obvious, some are not. Rolm Corporation, for instance, when it introduced the first digital switch for use in telephone switching, included the attitudes of state public utility commissions in the United States toward AT&T as one of its segmentation variables. It elected to enter markets only where it was felt that the regulatory bodies would favor increased competition for AT&T.

Possible Variable	Possible Categories
Industry	Banking, retailing, manufacturing, shipping
Application	General purpose, process control, business computation, scientific research
Geography	United States, North America, Japan, Asia, France, Europe, Brazil, Latin America
Firm size/characteristics	Large multinational, large national, medium, small
Buyer behavior	Sealed bid from multiple sources, negotiated from sole source
Buyer culture	Innovator, follower
Intermediate levels	OEMs, VARs (value added resellers)
Benefits sought	Hardware characteristics, software availability, post-sale service

Table 6.1: Segmenting the Computer Market

Segmentation Approaches

Having identified potential segmentation variables, the most widely cited segmentation approach is a two-stage procedure. As shown in Figure 6.1, this starts with macro segmentation, centering on the characteristics of the buying organization.

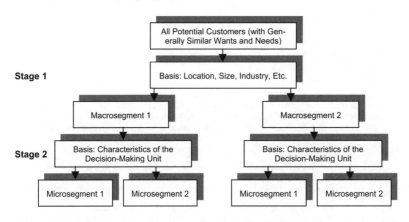

Figure 6.1: A Two-Stage Approach to Segmentation

Within these macro segments, the focus of attention is then on characteristics of the particular decision making unit. This approach needs to be done with care. In particular, it should be noted that many micro segmentation variables are found in more than one macro segment.

A nested, or multi-stage, approach to segmentation has been proposed by Bonoma and Shapiro.[4] Their classification scheme utilizes a number of categories. With some modifications, these are shown in Table 6.2, together with sub-categories and the kinds of questions that need to be asked.

Geographic
- In country: Should we focus on local, regional, or national areas of the country?
- Regional: Should we focus on geographic regions that comprise several countries (e.g., Latin America or Scandinavia), geographic regions that cut across parts of several countries (e.g., the southern portions of European countries bordering the Mediterranean), free trade areas or common markets (e.g., the 15 countries in the European Union or the North American Free Trade Area)?
- Global: Should we select customers without regard to location?

Demographic
- Industry: What industries should we target? In some instances the industry will be defined broadly (e.g., financial services). In other instances, more specificity may be required (e.g., banks or insurance companies).
- Company size: Should we target large, medium, or small companies?
- Level: Should we target OEMs at various intermediate levels or end users?
- End product use: Should we take into account the use of our customer's end product?

Operating Variables
- Technology: Should we target customers who insist on components or capital equipment that utilize leading edge technology or those who prefer more proven technologies?
- User/nonuser status: Should we focus on heavy or light users of the product, on nonusers, or on users who buy from competitors?
- Customer capabilities: Should we target customers based on their need for services, their financial strength, or on the nature of their inventory control processes?

Purchasing Approach
- Purchasing organization: Should we target customers with centralized or decentralized purchasing departments?
- Power structure: Should we target customers where the purchasing or the engineering department dominates the decision-making process?
- Nature of relationships: Should we target customers who prefer a close working relationship with suppliers or those who prefer an arm's-length relationship?
- Purchasing policies:

Situational Factors
- Urgency: Should we target customers for whom fast delivery is critical?
- Specific application: Should we target customers based on application? Should a computer manufacturer, for instance, target a business application or a process control application?
- Size of order: Should we target customers who place large orders with one supplier or those who place many small orders with several suppliers?

Personal Characteristics
- Buyer-seller similarity: Should we target customers who are staffed by individuals whose values or other personal characteristics are similar to our own?
- Attitude toward risk: Should we target customers who are willing to take risks or those who are risk adverse?

Source: From "Segmenting the Industrial Market" by Thomas V. Bonoma and Benson P. Shapiro. Copyright © 1983 by Lexington Books. Adapted with permission from Rowman & Littlefield Publishing Group.

Table 6.2: Market Segmentation Variable for Business Markets

As shown in the nested approach in Figure 6.2, the analysis might start with the outer nests; the general, easily observable segmentation variables, and then move to the inner nests; the more specific, subtle or hard-to-assess variables. Some caveats need to be observed with regard to use this approach. The notion of starting with the outer nests is based on the premise that they are easier to work with, not that there is a rigid sense of hierarchy to the analysis. In some situations, it might be more appropriate to start at a middle point and work inward, or even outward. In particular, it should not be inferred that a pattern of purchasing approaches, situational factors or personal characteristics associated with one geographic, demographic or operating category cannot be found in other categories.

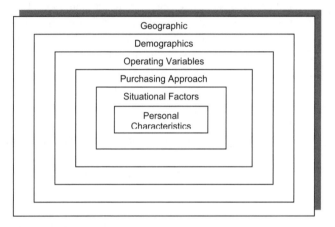

Figure 6.2: A Nested Approach to Segmentation

More recently, a three stage needs-based approach for segmenting business markets has been proposed.[5] The proposed approach is designed to identify potential early adopters of new technologies, using organizational needs revealed by actual purchasing behavior, based on the assumption that past purchase behavior is a good predictor of future behavior. The first stage is macrosegmentation, designed to delineate firms that have broadly similar needs and to reduce the total market to generally manageable segments. The second stage is microsegmentation, to further segment the macrosegments based on benefits and/or needs. The authors argue that while needs are the most logical segmentation base, they provide mangers with only part of the information necessary for target market selection and development of marketing strategy. Hence, the third stage is to further describe microsegments in terms that can be directly linked to specific elements of marketing strategy.

A number of considerations should be kept in mind in conducting a segmentation study:

1. The study should always be guided by its purpose. That is, as potential segments are considered, their usefulness should be tested by their relevance to that aspect of marketing strategy, which is at issue. In some instances, the purpose will be to develop a complete marketing strategy, involving all elements of the marketing mix. We would expect such a study to extensively describe potential segments, in terms of many segmentation variables. In other instances the purpose might simply be to develop an advertising campaign, with messages varied to most effectively communicate with significant groups of customers, or to develop a set of pricing strategies that take into account variations in pricing sensitivity of groups of customers. We would expect such a study might be more limited in its use of segmentation variables.

2. Segmentation requires both rigor and creativity. Secondary data abound on the size of markets based on geographical dimensions, SIC codes or other classifications. Table 6.3 shows a brief discussion of the use of SIC codes for selecting business markets. Additional secondary data usually exist in company files, based on past order histories or other forms of marketing intelligence. In many instances, these data lend themselves to various statistical methodologies such as cluster or factor analysis. There is, however, no set list of variables, which definitively identify a market segment. As indicated in the Rolm example, creative use of variables enhances insights for marketing strategy.

3. The process is, or should be, iterative. Identification of a microsegment in one macrosegment should be followed by consideration of its existence in others. Segmentation on the basis of needs or benefits are particularly likely to cut across several macro segments.

In Chapter 5, we briefly described the North American Industry Classification System (NAICS). NAICS was adopted by the U.S. federal government in 1997 and replaced the 1987 Standard Industrial Classification (SIC). NAICS is a unique, all-new system for classifying business establishments and is the first economic classification system to be constructed based on a single economic concept. Economic units that use like processes to produce goods or services are grouped together. (The SIC, on the other hand, was not based on a consistent economic concept. Some industries were demand based while others were production based.) NAICS is also the first-ever North American industry classification system that will allow business analysts to compare directly industrial production statistics collected and published in the three North American Free Trade Agreement countries. And, it provides for increased comparability with the International Standard Industrial Classification System (ISIC, Revision 3), developed and maintained by the United States.

NAICS recognizes the changing and growing services-based economy of the U.S. and its North American neighbors. It includes 1,170 industries of which 565 are service-based, compared to the SIC which had 1,004 industries of which 416 were service related. Although NAICS is much improved over the SIC, data from the SIC will be used for analysis for several years requiring comparison between NAICS and SIC data and software is now available that provides a crossover from SIC codes to NAICS codes.

As with the SIC, NAICS is an excellent tool to assist in segmenting business activity into fairly homogeneous categories and to provide information on the number of establishments and the revenues in each category. Information from NAICS can assist segmentation in two ways. First, the extensive list of industries coded can serve as an excellent guide or framework for considering target markets. Second, information can be used to estimate the purchases by firms in a particular category and then estimate the size of the segment. A manufacturer of magnet wire, for instance, can total the sales of transformer manufacturers, estimate the percentage of sales spent by these manufacturers on magnet wire, and then estimate the total purchases of magnet wire by firms in this NAICS code.

Some caveats need to be observed. First, statistics for a particular plant are reported in just one category, the activity in which they are primarily engaged, even though the plant may be involved in several activities. Second, the NAICS code does not take into account variation in buying habits of reported firms or variations in product characteristics, either of products produced or of materials entering the product. This information needs to be obtained in other ways.

With these two caveats in mind, the NAICS system, and other similar systems, can be extremely useful as market selection tools. Data are readily and inexpensively available. Where specialization and coverage ratios are high, each NAICS group should be reasonably homogeneous, especially with regard to manufacturing processes and components or raw materials used. NAICS codes should facilitate searches for new customers in unserved categories.

Table 6.3: Use of NAICS Codes in selecting Business Markets

Criteria for Usefulness

The search for market segments is likely to reveal several segments, of varying attractiveness. Some segments may not be real, in the sense that they are not measurable. Others may not be reachable. Before extensive evaluation of potential segments, it is advisable to test their usefulness against the following broad characteristics:[6]

1. Measurability. We can hypothesize a number of variables, which might influence how buyers respond to marketing strategies. However, unless they are measurable it would be impossible to use them to estimate the size of a particular segment. Prime Computer, for example, in its 1977 annual report, stated it estimated the size of its market based on two considerations. First, would a Prime Computer satisfy a customer's requirements and, second, psychologically, would the customers buy from a small company like Prime? While customers who bought from small companies could be identified after the fact, their prior identification on a psychological basis was highly problematic, raising serious questions about the accuracy of Prime's estimates of its market size.

2. Unique Response. For a segment to be meaningful, it must respond differentially from another segment to at least one element of the marketing mix. If, for instance, large and small customers respond similarly to a mail order program for personal computers, then size would not be a useful basis for segmentation.

3. Substantiality. The aggregate demand of the customers making up the segment must be sufficient to cover marketing costs. Anticipated sales, taking into account not just the size of the segment but also expected market share, must generate sufficient contribution margin to cover the added cost of a specialized marketing program.
4. Accessibility. There must be some basis on which we can identify, and hence reach, a particular segment. With new products, we may wish to reach customers who are innovators. Unless there is some characteristic which identifies the customer as an innovator we are not likely to be able to reach this segment.

Dowling, Lilien and Soni propose additional criteria for segments.[7] In particular, they emphasize that segments must ultimately be need based, as needs are the primary determinants of business purchase behavior; and they should be robust, meaning they should not be an artifact of the variability of a particular sample or a specific data analysis technique.

Evaluating Potential Segments
Of the identified segments that are real and reachable, some will represent a better profit opportunity or a better fit for the firm than others. While the ultimate objective in selecting a segment is profitability, there are many other considerations. The following suggest the kinds of questions that need to be answered before concluding to target a particular segment:

- How well do the requirements to successfully compete in the segment fit our distinctive competence? Does, for instance, our sales force have the necessary skills in order to deal with a segment where intense negotiation characterizes the purchasing process?
- How well does the segment capitalize on the firm's current position? Can it be reached, for instance, with our present distributors?
- What are the growth prospects for the segment, either long or short term. Do they match our sales growth objectives?
- Are sales likely to be cyclical? If so, can we adjust our production and marketing efforts to both the ups and downs of demand?
- Does a particular segment exhibit enough difference in response to justify its treatment as a separate segment, with

requirements for a separate marketing program? Would differences in buying behavior, for instance, require separate sales forces, or is the difference something we could reasonably expect the sales force to accommodate as part of its normal work?

- Assuming a successful marketing program for a particular segment, would it be defensible against competitive attack? How likely is it that a competitor could match our offering, and in what period of time? Are buyers likely to be loyal to a pioneer? What would be the switching costs for customers to change to a different supplier?

- Is it within the firm's resources to implement a marketing plan that effectively reaches and serves the segment? Merilab, a small manufacturer of wheel alignment systems for automotive production lines, felt it did not have the resources to reach customers in Europe and so did not target them, despite the fact that these customers represented attractive opportunities.

- Will targeting this segment lead us in the direction we want to go? At IBM, the decision to target personal computer users was seen by many as an undesirable diversion from its traditional mainframe computer markets.

The final test, of course, of the attractiveness of a particular segment is the ability of the firm to develop an implementable marketing strategy. A number of other issues need also be considered.

Additional Issues in Segmentation

Selecting a segment goes beyond simply identifying a potentially attractive segment. How the segment is defined may significantly influence competitor evaluation or future initiatives. Segments emerge, or become clearer, over the product life cycle, raising issues of timing. Finding niches or segments which the firm can dominate to the exclusion of competitors is a special consideration, as is vertical segmentation. Finally, changes in the external environment constantly introduce new possibilities for segmentation variables as is particularly evident in considering opportunities outside of home country markets.

Defining the Market

While the segmentation process is used, primarily, to improve the likelihood of a favorable response to a given marketing strategy from a carefully selected set of customers, it should be recognized that the decision as to which segment, or combination of segments to target, defines the denominator in market share calculations. An excessively narrow definition of the served market, a restrictive geographic definition, for instance, can result in overstating the firm's market share and misestimating the firm's competitive position. In the early stages of CT scanners, GE defined its market as just the hospitals in the United States, leading it to conclude it had a dominant position, based on a 60% share of market. Redefining its market as hospitals worldwide dropped its market share to less than 20%, leading to a significant re-evaluation of its position. Segments, therefore, should be defined to include not just the customers that the firm currently elects to attempt to serve but also should consider those customers with similar wants and needs that are being served by the firm's competitors, in both domestic and foreign markets.

Timing
In the introductory and early growth stages of the product life cycle, customer needs are not necessarily clear or easily definable. Product concepts are new, early acceptance by some buyers may not indicate true market potential and buyers may have little in the way of experience to develop definitive opinions about product features. As product concepts are better understood, new groups of buyers may emerge. Early commitment to one segment, therefore, has the potential to reduce the ability to serve other segments. Apple Computer, for instance, shortly after introducing its personal computer, committed strongly to sell only through distributors. This made it difficult to serve the corporate market which, when it emerged, wanted to buy direct.

As more buyers gain experience, a better basis for specific need definitions is established and the late growth and mature stages of the product life cycle are characterized by the emergence of segments with differentiated needs. Failure to develop specialized offerings for these segments may result in competitive disadvantage. Prime Computer, for instance, with early successes in the mini-computer market was reluctant to commit to any of a number of emerging segments. Subsequently it struggled through a number of reorganizations, each characterized by comments that Prime's biggest problem was its lack of focus. Unfortunately, by the time it did commit to a segment which, it felt, represented a good match between needs and its competence, the segment was crowded with other suppliers and Prime was not able to compete effectively.

Niche Markets
When products are beyond the introductory stage of the product life cycle we expect to find several firms competing for share in the mar-

ket. Within market segments, therefore, we frequently find firms looking for groups of customers, or niches, where a very specialized marketing strategy can establish a position not easily duplicated by competitors. Looking for such niches does not assure they will be found. For ten years, Data Card Corporation had virtually cornered the market for the high-speed machines that emboss plastic credit cards. As growth slowed, the chairman said its strategy was to find narrow markets for specialized office machines that it could overwhelmingly dominate. Their subsequent deliberate search for another lucrative niche proved disappointing.[8]

It would appear the Data Card dominance of the machine market was the fortuitous result of product development at the right time, not the result of a methodological search. Segments can be evaluated, however, on the basis of customer loyalty to pioneers and switching costs. More particularly, good competitor analysis can evaluate the likelihood of competitor response or the timing of such response.

Vertical Segmentation
Unique to business marketing is the opportunity for firms to target markets at various levels. ALCOA, for example, having invented a new alloy with desirable properties for diesel engine bearings, had a number of options.[9] It could sell the alloy to bearing manufacturers, partially fabricate the alloy for sale to bearing or engine manufacturers, or make the complete bearing for sale to engine manufacturers or for sale in replacement markets. In this instance, the value of the new alloy was most salient for purchasers of replacement bearings. ALCOA, however, was not willing to make the commitment necessary to reach the replacement market and attempted to sell the alloy to bearing manufacturers. Despite the alloy's favorable characteristics, it was not a commercial success. Similarly, the Graphics Division of Gould, Inc., when it introduced an electrostatic printer, was not willing to make the commitment necessary to sell the product to end-users, for whom the printer had great advantages. Rather, it attempted to rely on computer manufacturers, for whom the printer had little benefit, to sell the product with disappointing results.

Selling to intermediate market levels, more easily reached than end users is inherently attractive and, in many instances, such as components that completely enter the final product, there may be no alternative. As these examples illustrate, however, the decision to target intermediate market levels requires careful analysis of the potential benefits at each level.

Global Considerations

Despite country differences, the nature of business products and services, with heavy emphasis on functionality, is such that foreign sales have long been important for most firms. Since World War II, this importance has increased significantly. The work of the World Trade Organization (WTO), and its predecessor, the General Agreement on Tariffs and Trade (GATT), has dramatically reduced tariff and other barriers to trade. Improvements in communication and transportation have further facilitated trade across national borders. For business marketers, therefore, failure to consider foreign markets may result in missed opportunities; opportunities which in many cases may be more attractive than opportunities in the domestic market.

The traditional approach to foreign markets has been to segment on the basis of countries. Few segmentation variables would seem more straightforward. An atlas easily provides the basis for delineation of segments. In most instances, language, laws and currencies vary as a function of nationality. As we have previously described, business customs also may vary; sometimes between regions, sometimes between countries. As a result, there has been a tendency to develop marketing strategies for individual countries; the so-called polycentric approach, which assumes that each country is so different as to require a unique marketing strategy.

The obvious differences between countries frequently obscure the many similarities, which argue for global or regional strategies. Many firms, however, are developing strategies that are essentially common across countries except with regard to language and currency denomination. In the chemical industry, for instance, DuPont and Dow in the U.S., Hoechst and BASF in Germany, Rhone-Poulenc in France and Asahi in Japan all compete on a worldwide basis with essentially standardized products, sold at world market prices. In the computer industry, IBM in the United States, Toshiba in Japan, Olivetti in Italy and Bull in France compete on a world-wide basis with increasingly standardized products and prices that are slowly converging to a world level.

To the extent that strategies are less than global, many are being crafted for major economic regions such as the United States, Europe or Asia. Numerous U.S. firms are consolidating their subsidiary operations in the various countries in Europe into centralized European operations. Electro Scientific Industries, Inc., a U.S. manufacturer of sophisticated manufacturing tools for the worldwide electronics industry, for instance, has established such a centralized operation in the Netherlands, where ESI Europe will be the head sales and marketing office

132

that will handle customer support, order processing and distribution of spare parts.

For market segmentation purposes, this mandates consideration of other variables. One possibility is free trade areas or other forms of integrated economies, such as the European Union, the European Free Trade Area (closely associated with the European Union), the Andean Pact and the Mercado Sur in Latin America, the Association of Southeast Asian Nations (ASEAN) and, most recently, the North American Free Trade Agreement (NAFTA). Another is countries, that exhibit similarities along political or historical dimensions such as Scandinavia. Still another is the similarity of business customs, as might be found in the southern parts of European countries that border the Mediterranean or in the German speaking countries of northern Europe. Still another might be to group countries that exhibit similar levels of political risk.

Summary

The fundamental objective of marketing strategy is to meet customer wants and needs more effectively than competitors and at a profit to the firm. The ultimate extension of the objective of meeting customer wants and needs would require a unique strategy for each customer. In some instances, this indeed happens. Defense contractors supplying military needs in just one country frequently have just one customer. In markets with many customers, economies of scale with respect to production and marketing push firms in the other direction, with the extreme found with commodity products where there is essentially no attempt by sellers to determine individual customer's wants and needs. Most business marketers operate somewhere between these two extremes and are constantly faced with pressure either to aggregate segments, in order to achieve economies of scale or critical mass, or to further segment markets to better meet customer needs or respond to competitor threats.

As we have described in this chapter, the process of market segmentation is both analytical and creative. It is also dynamic, as changes in the firm's internal situation and the broader external environment change the context within which the process takes place. Flexible manufacturing, for instance, is increasing the ability of firms to respond to unique customer needs and so is increasing the number of segments a firm can feasibly target. Increasingly sophisticated marketing information systems are dramatically improving the ability of firms to more accurately identify customer's needs and responses to marketing strategies and thereby capitalize on enhanced capabilities of the firm. In particular, segmentation processes need to take into account changing customer needs which, for business customers, develop from their strategies which similarly evolve from their efforts to adapt to their circumstances.

Finally, it should be remembered that the purpose of market segmentation is to improve the process by which firms decide which markets to pursue and which segments to target. These are the critical decisions. They must be accompanied by decisions that commit the firm's resources, its talents and its energies. Without such commitment, even the best marketing strategy targeted at the most appropriate segment is not likely to succeed.

Further Reading

James C. Anderson and James A. Narus, "Business Marketing: Understand What Customers Value," *Harvard Business Review* 76 (November/December 1998): 53–65.

George S. Day, "Continuous Learning about Markets," *California Management Review* 36 (summer 1994): 9–31.

Per Vagn Freytog and Ann Højbjerg Clarke, "Business to Business Market Segmentation," *Industrial Marketing Management* 30 (August 2001): 473–486.

Rashi Glazer, "Winning in Smart Markets," *Sloan Management Review* 40 (summer 1999): 59–69.

V. Kasturi Rangan, Rowland T. Moriarty, and Gordon S. Swartz, "Segmenting Customers in Mature Industrial Markets," *Journal of Marketing*, 56, (October 1992): 72–82.

Thomas S. Robertson and Howard Barich, "A Successful Approach to Segmenting Industrial Markets," *Planning Review*, (November/December 1992): 4–11, 48.

---

[1]*First Quarter and Annual Meeting Report* (Ann Arbor, MI: Hoover Universal, Inc., 26 November 1980): 6–8.

[2]Standard Industrial Classification Codes: A system developed by the U.S. federal government to segment business activity into fairly homogeneous categories, based on products produced. Similar systems exist in most developed countries.

[3]*Loctite Corporation: Industrial Products Group*, Harvard Business School, Case 9-581-066, Revised October 1983.

[4]This section draws heavily on Thomas V. Bonoma and Benson P. Shapiro, *Segmenting the Industrial Market* (Lexington, MA: Lexington Books, 1983).

Further Reading

[5]Grahame R. Dowling, Gary L. Lilien, and Praveen K. Soni, "A Business Market Segmentation Procedure for Product Planning," *Journal of Business-to-Business Marketing* 1, no. 4 (1993): 31–57.

[6]Modified from Philip Kotler, *Marketing Management: Analysis Planning, Implementation and Control*, 11th ed. (Englewood Cliffs, NJ: Prentice Hall, Inc., 2003), 283–86.

[7]Dowling, Lilien, and Soni, "A Business Market Segmentation Procedure for Product Planning."

[8]*Business Week*, (8 March 1982): 88A.

[9]As described in E. Raymond Corey, "Key Options in Market Selection and Product Planning," *Harvard Business Review* (September–October, 1975): 119–28.

Chapter 7

Business Product Management

The product or service produced by the firm lies at the heart of business and marketing strategy. When translated into customer benefits it is the product or service that creates new markets or serves existing ones. Managing the process by which new products are developed to serve emerging needs, and by which existing products are modified to better serve existing needs, is critical to the success of the firm.

In this chapter, we discuss key product management concepts for business customers. We begin with concepts of product, product line, and how product management decisions are influenced by the nature of buyer-seller relations. We then address the role of quality, product market choices, including global considerations, and new product development. We conclude with a discussion of positioning and branding.

The Concept of Product
As we have previously described, business customers use products or services to directly or indirectly derive sales revenue and profit from their operations. Capital goods are major elements in the production process. Raw materials are critical to the production of many products. Components may be integral parts of an assembled product, or may be bundled with another product or system and resold. Maintenance, repair and operating supplies are necessary to keep the production process going. Similarly, a host of services are necessary to the production process and other functions of the firm. It cannot be overemphasized, however, that despite the importance of the physical characteristics of the product or service, the customer is looking for benefits, not just physical characteristics, and that the product or service the customer buys is far more than just its physical attributes. In very real sense, the product is not what it is but what it does. Intimately linked with benefits is the concept of quality, a concept that transcends physical characteristics and takes into account the totality of the firm's offering. Finally, from the firm's standpoint, the product needs to be considered in terms of its role in the overall business strategy. That is, beyond its

contribution to the firm's profits, what other objectives does the firm have for the product, how does the product relate to other products, and what is the impact of the product on the firm's operations?

As shown in the example in Figure 7.1, the "whole product" that the customer buys should be viewed as a bundle of tangible and intangible attributes, from which customers derive benefit and value. The example is meant to be illustrative, not comprehensive, and the attributes of importance to a particular customer will vary. For some customers joint product development might be an important attribute. For others it might be support of the firm's marketing effort. As this suggests, the product is not a fixed element of marketing strategy. Rather, it is a variable whose attributes can be changed, added, or subtracted, depending on the needs of the particular customer or market segment.

Source: Adapted and reprinted with permission from Regis McKenna from a presentation made by Regis McKenna, Summer 1994.

Figure 7.1: The Whole Product Approach to Value

Where intermediate distribution is involved, it is important to recognize that the services provided by a distributor, such as availability, credit, or service, are also part of the whole product. Even in instances of commodity products, normally considered to be undifferentiable, the whole product concept suggests that opportunities exist for differentiation on such attributes as packaging, comprehensiveness of the product line, affording one-stop shopping, or special services. For all products, then, the core or generic attributes should be the starting point of development of a whole product, from which point consideration can be given to other product features that might be appropriate for particular customer needs.

The concept of quality is inextricably intertwined with the concept of product. Initially focused on manufacturing, with Deming's emphasis on statistical approaches or Crosby's emphasis on conformance to specifications, the concept of quality has broadened to take into account all aspects of the firm's offering, as seen through the eyes of the customer. The PIMS studies, described in Chapter 2, introduced the notion of relative quality; that is, quality as perceived by the customer relative to competitors, based on those principal tangible and non-tangible attributes used by the customer in the buying decision.[1] Despite the evidence from the PIMS studies, indicating that relative quality is a key determinant of a firm's profitability, it appeared to require competition from Japanese firms to convince the rest of the world of the importance of quality, the potential of quality programs, and, most importantly, that quality is not static but should be the focus of a constant and ongoing effort. As we will subsequently discuss, there is an increasing imperative for those in marketing to be involved in the firm's quality processes.

In addition to satisfying customer's wants and needs better than competitors, the concept of product also needs to take into account its role for the firm; a role which almost always goes beyond just providing profits. The BCG approach, described in Chapter 2, develops the role of cash cows as providers of cash to fund question marks, support R&D, fund dividends and so forth, and the role of stars to establish dominant positions such that when growth slows they can become productive cash cows. There are, however, many other roles for products. One may be to support the sale of other, more profitable products, as in the case of Bond-A-Matic®, Loc-Tite's adhesive dispenser, introduced to increase sales of adhesives. Others may be to defend against competitor attacks, to lead the way into new markets, to complement and facilitate the sale of existing products, or, perhaps inadvertently as in the case of IBM, to pioneer a new organizational form with the personal computer product line.

The Product Line

As important as the product itself is the concept of product line; a group of products that are closely related by virtue of performing similar functions. Management of the product line is one of the most important product management tasks. While most firms start with a single product, or a very limited product line, almost inevitably the product line is expanded, raising a number of questions. Under what circumstances should we increase the variety of our product offerings? Should we add a product at the high end of the line? Should we add one at the low end? Should we extend our product scope into new arenas?

Increased variety, or depth, may respond to specific customers' needs, enhance the firm's image as a full line provider or thwart competitor attack; but at the expense of increased complexity and added manufacturing cost. A large industrial firm, for instance, introduced a product consisting of five individually packaged components, carefully selected, the firm thought, to meet the needs of the market. The package was offered as one catalog number. Within three years, customer requests for variations in the individual components that made up the package resulted in over 2000 catalog numbers. In total, the packages were produced in high volume. Some catalog numbers, however, were sold in relatively small quantities, raising questions as to their profitability. Manufacturing and engineering departments complained that this kind of product line proliferation was unacceptable. Although extreme, this example indicates the problems that can arise in the name of responding to customers needs. For most firms, periodic pruning of the product line is a must, in order to achieve balance between customer responsiveness and internal operations. Frequently described as the 80-20 rule, Pareto's Law holds that a small percentage of a list of items represents a large percentage of value or impact. Analysis often reveals that the majority of the firm's profits are provided by a relatively small percentage of products. Judicious pruning of the product line can frequently improve profits and release engineering and manufacturing capacity, without seriously impacting customer relations.

The product line may be lengthened. Adding products at the high end of the line may represent opportunities to achieve higher margins and enhance image; but may invite competitor retaliation, encounter customer resistance and take the firm away from its basic competence. Products added to the low end of the line may thwart competitor attack, capitalize on the firm's image and represent opportunities for increased volume; but may cannibalize the existing product line, negatively impact the firm's image or, again, take the firm away from its basic competence. GE's Medical Systems business, for instance, was faced with an attack on its CT scanners by a Japanese competitor that planned a smaller and less expensive machine. Introduction by GE of a similar machine might thwart the attack but with the possibility of cannibalizing sales of its larger, and very profitable scanners. In this case, the firm concluded the new product was close to its competence and that it was better to cannibalize its own sales than to let the Japanese do it. In other instances, however, firms have discovered that manufacturing low-end items is incompatible with a culture that has long focused on features, not cost.

Extending the scope or breadth of the product line may capitalize on existing competence, expand the firm's horizons and establish major new opportunities; but at the risk of diverting managerial attention from the existing business and going beyond the firm's competencies. Exxon, for instance, which had developed a proprietary technology for variable speed motors, acquired Reliance Electric; a major player in variable speed drives, on the supposition that Reliance's experience could be used to commercialize this new technology. In this case, it developed that the promise of the new technology had been overestimated and the challenges of managing a variable speed drive business were very foreign to Exxon's experience as a major producer and marketer of petroleum products. The venture was unsuccessful.

Buyer-Seller Relations: A Key Contextual Element

The close relationship between business customers and their suppliers, and their mutual dependency, described in Chapter 3, strongly influences the product management process. As we will subsequently describe, many new business products are developed at the specific request of customers. The nature of buyer-seller relations can take many forms and decisions with respect to these relations can materially influence the product management process.

Increasingly we see decisions by both buyers and sellers to move toward close relations, sometimes taking on the nature of a partnership, in which product decisions are made by mutual agreement. These relationships are particularly strong in Japan. Shikoku Kakokki, for example, a manufacturer of packaging machinery, has approximately sixty small, long-term vendors that provide the company with parts and components for its products. These suppliers are literally partners in the "Shikoku family." They not only provide Shikoku with machine parts, but also actively try to design new, innovative, and cost-saving solutions for the customer. Part of their motivation to continue these efforts is the knowledge that Shikoku will keep them as suppliers through good times and bad.

Close buyer-seller relationships that are the norm in Japan are also characteristic of business marketing in other countries, particularly in countries in Latin America and Europe, and to a lesser extent in the United States. While they have many desirable aspects they need to be carefully managed. Large customers can significantly influence product development, but sometimes in a direction, which may conflict with the supplier's ability to serve other customers. A large electric utility, for instance, worked closely with one manufacturer to develop a particular piece of equipment for use in underground electrical systems. As the market for these products matured, only this one customer continued to be interested in the design. In some instances, the customer may view a joint development as proprietary and attempt to restrict the supplier from offering the product to others. Manufacturers of paper machines who work closely with paper mills to come up with new and improved designs usually agree to refrain from offering the improved designs for periods up to two years, as a condition of being the mill's sole supplier. As relations become close, the potential exists for the customer to represent the major, or only, source of orders. This has the potential to give the customer excessive bargaining power and ties the supplier to the customer's fortunes.

The Role of Quality

We have previously discussed the increasing importance of quality. From the early interest in quality, with emphasis on manufacturing and conformance to specifications, we have seen the widespread adoption of some form of total quality management (TQM). Unfortunately, according to a recent survey, most marketing managers do not really understand the concept of quality, nor its impact on profitability. As the authors of the study argue, however, the concept of total quality, with its emphasis on quality as perceived by the customer, mandates that marketers become full-fledged members of the quality team, leading or cooperating, as may be appropriate.[2]

In the United States, quality efforts have been widely publicized by means of the Malcolm Baldrige Award. Awards are determined using a 1000-point scoring system to weight the evaluation of a host of quality related factors. Of interest to marketers, the scoring system allocates 300 points to customer satisfaction, indicating the importance of marketing involvement in the quality process. A recent development in the quality arena, of particular importance to business marketers, is ISO9000, an international standard promulgated in 1987 by the International Organization for Standardization. ISO9000, and its various components, provides business customers a well-defined way to specify quality processes to their suppliers, with the provision for compliance certification by outside auditors. Originally adopted in Europe, where conformance to ISO9000 is mandated for many products, interest has spread to the United States and Japan. First viewed by many non-European firms as a deliberately erected trade barrier to doing business in Europe, ISO9000 has since become accepted by many manufacturers as a valuable guide to quality processes. As of December 2002, 561,747 ISO9000 certificates had been granted in 159 countries and economies, up from 27,816 in January 1993. Informed observers have indicated they feel that ISO9000 will become the de facto starting point for the quality processes of most firms, both producers of goods and services. For those who adopt the standard ahead of competitors, this presents an opportunity for significant competitive advantage. To fully capitalize on ISO9000, however, marketers will have to be involved in the quality process in order to ensure that products and services not only meet design specifications but also meet customer requirements better that competitors.[3]

Product/Market Choices

As we discussed in Chapter 6, market selection is fundamental to product decisions, with an attendant number of questions. Can the one product design serve a number of segments? If not, should the firm attempt to serve just one, or a few, segments? Alternatively, should it modify the product in order to serve a number of segments, with the attendant complexity of proliferation of product designs?

For International Paper Company (IP), one the largest paper firms in the world, a question was which of several opportunities should be considered for two recently acquired packaging systems. The Resolvo system, acquired from an Italian manufacturer, made it possible to package milk, juice, and other still drinks in flexible paperboard containers, to provide virtually unlimited shelf life. The Evergreen system, acquired from a U.S. manufacturer, was a system designed for fresh milk and juice products where limited shelf life was satisfactory. IP developed a matrix, as shown in Table 7.1, based on products to be contained and present packaging approaches. The matrix indicated commonly used packaging methods for the various products, and those applications where it was felt the Resolvo or Evergreen systems could successfully compete. Based on their knowledge of these applications, IP was able to develop a better view of those opportunities where one or both of the products had a competitive advantage. Combined with other segment characteristics, the choice could then be narrowed to those, which represented the best opportunities for IP.

Product	Flexible Packs	Metal Cans	Glass Bottles	Plastic Jugs	Folding Cartons	Bag-in-Box
			Market/Application			
Alcoholic Drink						
Spirits			✓	✓		
Beers		✓	✓			
Wines	✓R	✓R	✓R			✓R
Nonalcoholic Drinks						
Carbonate		✓	✓	✓		
Still juice	✓R	✓R	✓R	✓R	✓R	✓R
Fresh juice	✓E		✓E	✓E	✓E	✓E
Noncarbonated mineral water	✓E/R	✓E/R	✓E/R	✓E/R		
Dairy Products						
Fresh milk	✓E		✓E	✓E	✓E	✓E
Long-life milk	✓R	✓R	✓R		✓R	✓R
Other	✓E/R	✓E/R			✓E/R	✓E/R
Culinary Products	✓E/R	✓E/R	✓E/R	✓E/R		✓E/R

Note: ✓ = indicates common method for packaging product; R = indicates a possible market application for the Resolve system; and E = indicates a possible market application for the Evergreen system. *Source:* This matrix was developed by Nils-Erik Aaby, Elopak Americas, Inc.

Table 7.1: Product Market Matrix Analysis of IP's Liquid Packaging

Unique to business marketing is the notion of varying the product on the basis of vertical market segments. Various horizontal segments might desire the same tangible attributes but vary as to desired intangible attributes. Vertical segments present the business marketer with a different set of choices. As we previously indicated, ALCOA could provide its new aluminum alloy in ingot form to bearing manufacturers. Alternatively, it could provide a casting to bearing manufacturers or to diesel engine manufacturers. Finally, it could supply finished bearings to diesel engine manufacturers or to industrial supply houses, for sale as replacements. Similar choices exist for many other products, requiring product adaptation to the needs of the chosen market. Computers, for instance, can be sold without application software to equipment manufacturers such as Rolm, who resell to end users, adding necessary software and other customizing features, but frequently must be sold with software if sales are to be made directly to end users.

Global Considerations

Almost without exception, major suppliers of business products and services do business globally. Boeing and Airbus conduct business with airlines in every country. For many years, GE, Caterpillar, and other producers of industrial goods have been major exporters, making positive contributions to the U.S. balance of payments. Asea Brown Boveri (ABB), Hitachi, Komatsu, Ericsson, Alcatel, Siemens, Olivetti, and a host of other non-U.S. manufacturers similarly do business worldwide. The Big Four accounting firms have offices in every major city in most countries in the world, as do major consulting firms such as McKinsey, A.D. Little, and others. In the heavy construction industry, Bechtel, Ebasco, and CH2M-Hill are all major players on the global scene.

Despite the international participation of such well-known firms, large numbers of business marketers have not pursued global markets, or have done so only on an opportunistic basis, usually when demand is slack in home markets. We first consider the circumstances, which suggest attractive market opportunities and then identify options for product management.

In broad terms, most business products, and many services, travel well across country borders. For many firms, foreign markets should represent profitable opportunities. The normal approach, nevertheless, at least in the United States, seems to be to design new products to sell primarily in the domestic market. Only after the product is successfully introduced in the home market does the firm consider exporting, either to neighboring countries or to world markets, preferably with a minimum of product modifications. In a study by Cooper and Kleinschmidt, this was the approach of 83% of the firms studied compared to 17% who initially designed products with world markets in mind. Of interest, however, was that these 17% had a higher new product success rate and achieved higher profits, both at home and abroad.[4] Apparently, the extra care in naming the product, choosing materials, designing its features, and so on, paid off in domestic markets and ensured that subsequent alterations for non-domestic markets, if necessary, would be less costly. In many instances, taking world markets into account can be as simple a matter as designing dual voltage capability into electrical devices. Even in more complex situations, taking world markets into account pays off. For Microsoft, for instance, taking into account programming requirements for various country markets in the early stages of development would have greatly simplified the introduction of Microsoft Works.

Clearly, world market opportunities are more attractive for some firms than others. Much depends on the managerial philosophy or the firm, as we will discuss, and its comfort with world markets. Global strategy experts provide three important guidelines for designing successful global products:[5]

- In examining customer needs around the world, business marketers should search for similarities as well as differences.
- Global product designers should try to maximize the size of the common global core of the product while also providing for local tailoring around the core.
- Rather than being adapted from national products later, the best global products are designed with the global market in mind from the start.

Assuming world markets offer potentially attractive opportunities, what should be the firm's product strategy? Three general approaches are possible. The first, and simplest, is to export products with no adaptation. This approach may be successful for products that have enormous competitive advantage with respect to functionality or that can offered at extremely low prices. It is usually associated with the so-called ethnocentric view of the world—a view, which assumes the rest of the world, is "like us." For most firms the choice is between a multi-domestic strategy and a global strategy. The multi-domestic strategy is usually associated with a polycentric view of the world—a view that assumes that each country is sufficiently different as to require a unique marketing strategy. In this case, the firm makes extensive adaptations of the product, and other elements of the marketing mix, for each country in which it does business. Global strategies are usually associated with a geocentric view of the world—a view that holds that there are more similarities across world markets than differences. In this case, the firm assumes that products can be designed with a high degree of standardization and only modest adaptation to meet local requirements.

Much discussion has centered on which of these approaches work best. Ted Levitt has argued that technology is driving the world toward a converging commonality, that the globalization of markets is at hand, and that the objective of international marketers should be standardized products that can be offered at low cost.[6] Kenichi Ohmae, on the other hand, argues for an approach, which involves extensive local adaptation of the marketing mix.[7] In point of fact, there is less difference in these points of view than would first appear. Both recognize that some modification of products is necessary to accommodate local preferences and practices. The point to be made is that decisions as to the extent of adaptation need to take a host of circumstances into account. Standardization may be mandatory if economies of scale are important. Standardization may be appropriate where language is not a significant factor or where international standards prevail, as might be the case for microelectronics components, chemical processes and machine tools. Adaptation is a must where standards vary, as in the case of some electrical devices or video equipment, or to meet country specific requirements, as in the case of such products as accounting and tax software.

New Product Development

Product development has long been a key element of product management. In recent years, with rapidly changing technologies and shortened product life cycles, the importance of new products has increased dramatically. At 3M, products less than five years old now account for 25% of sales.[8] A study of 700 industrial and consumer firms in Europe and United States by Booz, Allen and Hamilton supported the importance of new products.[9] Senior executives in these firms indicated they expect to derive significant sources of revenue and profits from new products and new technology. This importance has stimulated research designed to find ways to improve new product development processes. The Marketing Science Institute (MSI) in the United States, a quasi industry-academic research organization, recently announced that enhancement of product development processes is one of the highest priorities among its clients with key issues as shown in Table 7.2. The European Union has initiated a number of initiatives in support of research and development focusing on new technologies and products, including the European Strategic Program for R&D in Information Technology (ESPRIT), R&D in Advanced Communications Technology for Europe (RACE), and Basic Research in Industrial Technology for Europe (BRITE).[10] In Japan the Ministry of Internal Trade and Industry (MITI) organizes industry wide efforts to enhance Japan's capability through new products.

Despite the importance of new products, and the interest in new product development processes, for many firms new product development has been largely fortuitous. In these firms, new products are frequently the result of creative individuals taking a new idea and running with it, or a customer bringing a new requirement to the right individual in the supplier's organization, rather than the result of a well-managed process. In many instances, firms seem to accept the notion that development of new products is not amenable to normal management processes and failures of new products are often justified with statements such as "90% of all new products fail." In fact, nothing like

90% of new products fail. According to one study, only 24% of new industrial products failed.[11] Other studies report similar numbers. More importantly, the success rate of new products can be influenced by good management.

Problem Identification	Product Use	Improvement Opportunities
• Does the product function as planned? • Does the product's performance meet design expectation? • Does the performance meet user expectations? • Are there differences between the firm's management and the user's management as to what adequate/superior performance is? • Is the product's ease-of-use acceptable (i.e., interface, commands, operating instructions, control panel, etc.)? • Do the required interfaces with other hardware, equipment, material, software, and communications media function properly? • How easy was the product to install, initialize, troubleshoot, repair? • Did the product malfunction, shut down, or perform unexpectedly? • Were the causes identified?	• Which applications were expected/unexpected? • How often is the product used? • For how long and by how many people? • What benefits do the users report? What drawbacks? • What changes, if any, has the product made in work procedures? • What changes in work habits or procedures, if any, does the product require of users? • Who benefits the most/least from the product? Is anyone impacted negatively? • What functions/features are used most/least?	• What additional functions and/or features are required to meet minimal customer requirements? • What functions/features now appear unnecessary or optional? • Do the patterns of usage and/or applications suggest any changes in physical design of the product, user interface speed, capacity, or other functions? • How can the product be made easier to install? • How can the product be made easier to diagnose and/or repair? • Should the product be offered in more/fewer models or configurations? • What lessons should be incorporated into the user manual?

Source: Adapted from Voedisch, Lynn. "For Beta or For Worse." *The Industry Standard*, May 8, 2000, pp.239–42.

Table 7.2: Beta Test Questions

In a study of industrial firms in Canada, for instance, Cooper found that market orientation, product uniqueness, and fit with the firm's technical/production processes were key success factors.[12] As shown in Figure 7.2, when market orientation, product uniqueness, and fit were high the success rate was 90%. On the other hand, where all three factors were low, the success rate fell to 7%. The challenge, then, for business marketers is to manage a process that effectively introduces products that are truly unique or have competitive advantage and that have good fit with the firm's manufacturing and other competencies. While research efforts continue, the last 20 years major advances have seen major advances in our understanding of how to do this.

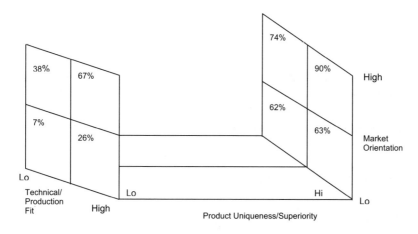

Source: Robert C. Cooper, "The Myth of the Better Mousetrap: What Makes a New Product a Success?", *Ivey Business Journal* (formerly *Ivey Business Quarterly*), Spring 1981, Volume 46/Number 1, p.75, Copyright © 1981, Ivey Management Services. Reprinted with permission from Ivey Management Services.

Figure 7.2: New Product Success Factors

The Product Development Process
Certain basic elements are common to all studies that have been made of the product development process; Crawford describes them in terms of the following five stages:[13]

Strategic Planning. Concerned with goals and guidance of the process, this stage takes inputs from the annual marketing plan, which may call for a particular feature to meet the encroachment of a new competitor; ongoing business planning, which will establish a sense of direction or market focus for product development; and special opportunity analysis, based on audits of relevant markets and internal resources. A key point is the development of a product innovation charter to provide guidance to the overall process and to ensure that developments are consistent with business goals and market choices.

Concept Generation. The creative part of the process requires establishment of a team or nucleus of individuals for ideation and screening, and a process to stimulate the input of ideas from customers, employees, universities or other potential sources.

<u>Pretechnical Evaluation</u>. This stage focuses on concept development, testing and screening, both for customer understanding and technical feasibility. It may involve a preliminary business analysis and development of a budget, based on preliminary marketing, technical, and operations plans.

<u>Technical Development</u>. In this stage the final concept is prepared, resources are gathered and teams are formed, prototype work is done, alpha tests (i.e., tests of the prototype within the firm) and beta tests (i.e., tests of prototypes with customers) are conducted, work starts on the development of a marketing plan, and a comprehensive business analysis is prepared.

<u>Commercialization</u>. In this stage the organizational structure necessary for production and marketing is put in place, initial product runs are made, marketing plans are further developed, market testing is done, primarily to test the elements of the marketing plan, plans are fine tuned and the product is launched.

As Aaby and Dicenza suggest, the product development process can also be thought of as a funnel, as shown in Figure 7.3. In the collaboration stage, the approach is broad and open to new science and creative ideas. In this early stage, efforts are concerned with benchmarking (of science, technology, and competitors), idea generation, product-market choice, positioning, concept development and testing. Cumulative investment of resources is low and management involvement also tends to be low. However, it is at this stage that concepts with little likelihood of success can be terminated with only modest financial consequences. Management's role should be to ensure disciplined choices, as well as collaborative involvement of marketing, R&D or engineering, and manufacturing in the process. In the implementation stage, the approach becomes more narrowly focused and tightly controlled. It is during this stage that costs escalate, suggesting the need at each step to review the decision to continue. Management becomes more involved in the process but, aside from termination, its role is limited to ensuring that all aspects of the process are carried out.

New Product Development

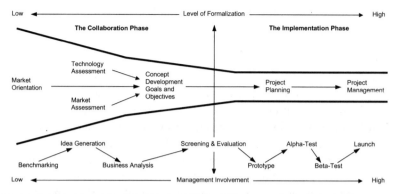

Source: Adapted from Nils-Erik Aaby and Richard Discenza, "Strategic Marketing and New Product Development: An Integrated Approach," Journal of Business and Industrial Marketing, 8(2), 1993, 61–69. Reprinted with permission from Emerald Group Publishing Limited.

Figure 7.3: The Product Development Process Funnel

Lead Users

For business products, and especially for high-tech products, a frequent issue is market pull versus technology push. Ken Olsen, the founder of Digital Equipment Corporation, has been reported as being fond of saying that no amount of market research could have revealed the need for a mini-computer. On the other hand, when electrostatic printing technology indicated a promising approach to high-speed printers for computers, founders of Versatec spent six months talking to prospective customers before developing what turned out to be a highly successful product. In contrast, Gould Graphics developed its offering without customer input and the product was never a success.

In a sense, the argument between market pull and technology push is inappropriate, as technology must always match the needs of the market. However, a unique aspect of development of goods and services for business markets is the extensive involvement of users, who have been found to be the actual developers of most of the successful new products eventually commercialized by manufacturers. One study, for example, found users were the developers of 82 percent of all commercialized scientific instruments.[14] Studies of this kind suggest that analysis of needs and solution data from "lead users" (defined as those who face needs that will be general in a market place, but face these needs months before others, and who are positioned to benefit significantly by obtaining a solution to those needs) can improve the productivity of new product development in fields characterized by rapid change. Lead users are those who face needs that will be general in a marketplace, but they face these needs months before others and are positioned to benefit significantly by obtaining a solution to those needs.

Beta-Tests

Many aspects of the lead user concept apply to beta-testing, a key activity for field-testing of prototypes; a requirement for effective launch of most industrial products. As elaborated in Table 7.3, beta-testing is used to identify problems in product design or function, to understand how the product is used, and to identify opportunities for improvements. As with lead users, a key to success is to find good beta-test sites, desirably potential early adopters, or customers that perceive the new product to have high incremental value. Some characteristics of good beta-sites are as follows:

- Does the firm belong to one of the target segments?
- Does the firm have experience with the technology or product class?
- Is the firm known to have a potential need for the new product solution?
- Does the firms show evidence of using advanced technologies?
- Does the firm face stiff competition and new product time-to-market pressure that force it to be innovative?
- Does the firm make frequent changes in product lines such that all possible options can be tested?
- Is the company recognized as an industry leader?
- Is there an influential "high profile" person within in the company who takes leadership and is willing and able to work with the suppliers?
- Will the individual/firm be willing to be used as a reference?

New Product Introduction

When introducing products to new customers, or significantly different products to existing customers, business marketers need to take into account the fear, uncertainty, and doubt (FUD) that supplier changes or new products can foster, particularly in situations where the customer's ability to perform is highly dependent on the supplier's product. Small suppliers, with limited resources or unknown reputations, may particularly experience FUD. The introduction process, therefore, needs to recognize that FUD may prolong the customer's decision-making process. As shown in Figure 7.4, there are a number of ways to do this, particularly with performance proof and evidence of acceptance by industry leaders. [15]

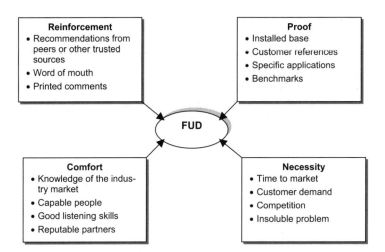

Source: Adapted from "Relationship Marketing" by Regis McKenna, Addison-Wesley, 1991, pp. 86–87, published by Century Business Books. Reprinted by permission of The Random House Group Ltd.

Figure 7.4: What Reduces FUD?

Positioning

Product positioning is concerned with the position the product holds in the customer's mind, based on perceived benefits as compared to those offered by competitors. Although the nature of the business purchasing process suggests comprehensive analysis of the benefits offered by various competitors, it is strongly influenced by customers' a priori perceptions which, in many instances, may be the major determinant of the buying decision. For years, for instance, customers' perceptions of IBM reliability and service were reflected in the comment "you can't go wrong buying IBM." Ultimately, of course, the position the firm occupies in the customer's mind will be the result of the customer's experience with the product. The objective of positioning is to influence product design, development, and customer interfaces to maximize the likelihood that this position corresponds to the firm's intent. As Dovel argues, positioning should be the backbone of product design and development and a key theme in the firm's business plan.[16]

We previously stated that a key element of product development is a positioning statement that clearly spells out the position the firm wants to occupy in the customer's mind. Most products will have a host of attributes, but the firm's position will be established on two or three attributes or benefits, which are most important to the customers in the target segment. Hitachi, for instance, positioned its 256K integrated circuit chip on the core benefits of reliable and fast information storage and retrieval. This simple statement, easy to understand and expressed in terms that reflected the customer's perspective, guided subsequent product development work and became the basis for developing the communications program.

Conceptually straightforward, the development of a good positioning statement is a demanding but important exercise. A variety of processes have been proposed, most of which have steps similar to the following:

- Establish the target market
- Ensure your product strategy is consistent with your business strategy
- Understand the key attributes or benefits from customers' perspectives
- Identify the relevant set of competitors
- Understand their positions
- Pick the position you want to, or can, occupy
- Write your positioning statement
- From the view of competitors, identify its weaknesses
- Test the positioning statement against others, including peers, the sales force, and customers

It should be noted that concepts of product positioning also apply to companies. Consider the situation of Xerox. Firmly established as a copier manufacturer, Xerox purchased Scientific Data Systems to enter the computer business. The subsequent disappointing results were, at least in part, attributed to the market's refusal to recognize Xerox as a serious player in the computer business. Today, Xerox positions itself as "The Document Company," a position that customers understand and that provides a strong sense of direction to the firm's product development efforts.

For international marketers, there are additional issues. In the early years of Microsoft, subsidiary companies had been allowed to tailor positioning strategies to individual countries, based on the needs of target markets within each country. With the advent of other products, it became clear that many products should be targeted at horizontal segments; that is, at segments that crossed country borders. For Microsoft, as for other companies in similar situations, this raised some difficult issues. Who, for instance, should be responsible for worldwide product positioning: Headquarters or individual subsidiary managers? Still further, what problems would be encountered if headquarters insisted on subsidiary companies repositioning their offerings? As we discussed in the section on global considerations, product planning that takes a global perspective initially can help to address such issues.

Once a desired position is determined, the firm has the further issue of how to most effectively communicate the intended position to the marketplace. The nature of business marketing, with professional purchasing, very knowledgeable buyers, and close buyer-seller relations might suggest that this communication can be done exclusively in comprehensive technical or performance terms, and, in fact, much communication is of this nature. Strongly associated with the marketing of consumer goods, brands can also play an important role in communication programs for business products and services, either to identify the company, the product, or both.

Branding

According to the American Marketing Association, a brand is a name, term, sign, symbol, or design, or a combination of them, intended to identify the goods or services of one seller or group of sellers and to differentiate them from those of competitors. Used properly, brands can convey a number of meanings. At the company level, a brand can convey messages about the nature of the company, the kinds of products it makes, its level of reliability or service. In some markets, the firm may desire to establish a reputation for leadership, based on its new technology. At the product level, a brand can convey tangible or non-tangible attributes or proposed customer benefits. In some markets, the firm may desire to establish a reputation for high quality products, in terms of benefits to customers. In these instances, communication efforts are focused on its product brands. All these purposes have the same ultimate goals: to create new sales (market share taken from competitors) or induce repeat sales (keep customers loyal).

As in consumer markets, brand equity affects business-to-business markets by influencing the buyers' choice processes by creating brand awareness, increasing the probability that the brand will be included in the consideration set, and providing a strong positive brand image. However, due to the unique environmental factors inherent in business-to-business exchanges and the complexity and formality of the organizational buying process, the difference in context may have a notable effect on the development and utilization of brand equity. Existing models of brand equity, because of their consumer goods focus, fail to adequately address these differences.

Figure 7.5 represents a model of brand equity form a business marketing perspective.[17] In essence, the model builds upon an expansion of Aaker's model of brand equity to account for the unique characteristics associated with business market exchanges.[18] The basic elements of the model are (a) seller variables/marketing efforts, (b) environmental factors, (c) buying firm factors, (d) seller's brand equity, (e) level of risk, and (f) outcomes/indicators of brand equity. As represented in this model, a seller's brand equity is the result of the seller's marketing efforts. These efforts, however, are moderated by both environmental and buying firm factors. A seller's brand equity, in turn, will impact their market position and strategic capabilities by influencing the choice process of the buying organization. This relationship between brand equity and the outcomes is moderated by the level of the buyer's perceived risk.

Establishing brands, and deciding on how heavily to promote them, raises a number of questions. For some firms, it is the extent to which a strong brand identity could develop product preference, resulting in higher prices or greater market share. For other firms, a brand identity can pave the way for initial calls by the sales force. In some instances a brand can provide a convenient way to both to describe a particular product, as in the case of the Intel, a major producer of microprocessors which are the heart of personal computers. Their successive product generations were called the 8086, 286, 386, and 486 microprocessors. Unfortunately, Intel did not obtain trademark protection on its number system, and thus the 386 and 486 names were available to competitors such as AMD, Chips and Technologies, and Cyrix who made their own chips and applied the X86 name to them.

Intel responded in 1991 by encouraging firms like IBM, Compaq, Gateway, and Dell to put the "Intel Inside" logo in their ads and on their packages. The enticement was a cooperative advertising allowance from Intel amounting to 3 percent of the companies' Intel purchases (5 percent if they used the logo on packaging).

The campaign, which was initially budgeted at $100 million per year, worked on several levels. It generated more than ninety thousand pages of ads in an eighteen-month period, which translated to a potential 10 billion exposures. During that period, the recognition of Intel among business end-users increased from 46 percent to 80 percent, the same level that Nutrasweet enjoyed among consumers after years of exposure of the Nutrasweet logo. The brand equity of Intel, as measured by the price discount needed to get a customer to accept a computer without an Intel processor, appeared to be positively affected. During 1992, the first full year of the Intel Inside campaign, Intel's worldwide sales rose 63 percent.

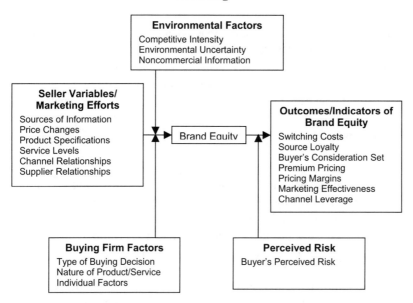

Figure 7.5: Model of Brand Equity in Business Markets

Interestingly, the Intel Inside campaign actually originated in Japan, where Matsushita used it as a way to build high-tech credibility for its computers. Japan is a country in which the prestige and visibility of corporate names is extremely important. By building up the Intel corporate name, Matsushita created credibility for itself.[19]

Frequently there are conflicting objectives with respect to brands. Schuller International, a subsidiary of Manville Corporation, sold most of its roofing and insulating products under the Manville brand which, according to market research reports, was viewed very favorably by distributors and contractors. On the other hand, financial analysts advised Manville that use of the Manville name was adversely affecting its stock price because of the association of Manville with asbestos related health problems, even though Manville no longer made asbestos products. In this case, the company rebranded its products under the Schuller name but with recognition that some customer goodwill or identification might be lost.

In general, it appears that selecting a brand name is more art than science. Firms are advised, for instance, that brand names should convey the use or function of the product and some do, such as Loc-

Tite's Bond-a-Matic® adhesive dispenser, but there are many examples of well recognized brands that do not, such as Apple's Macintosh® computers, Digital's Alpha® microprocessors, and AT&T's Merlin® line of PBX systems. What is more important than the brand name, per se, is the message which accompanies the brand, with respect to the benefits or attributes the firm wants to be associated with the brand, and the clarity and creativity with which the message is communicated.

Summary

Product management and new product development should be high on managers' list of priorities. Traditionally the product is the most important element in the business marketing mix. However, development of individual new products is not sufficient to compete effectively. Firms that can manage the product mix in the context of correctly chosen markets and that can develop new products through effective development processes that increase new product success rates will have a competitive advantage over those that do not. Key success factors will be the development of whole product solutions that satisfy a wide range of customer needs, management of the product line to ensure balance between customer needs and operational requirements, involvement of marketing in the firm's quality processes, and communication strategies that overcome fear, uncertainty, and doubt related to new technology and increase the firm's ability to conduct effective product launches. This will require new and different organizational approaches, commitment of resources, enhanced collaboration with those in other functions, improved product development processes, effective new product testing and comprehensive relationships with early adopter customers.

Further Reading

David A. Aaker, *Managing Brand Equity,* (New York: The Free Press, 1991).

David A. Aaker, "Measuring Brand Equity Across Products and Markets," *California Management Review* 38, no. 3 (1996): 102–20.

David A. Aaker, *Building Strong Brands* (New York: The Free Press, 2002).

David A. Aaker and Robert Jacobson, "The Value Relevance of Brand Attitude in High Technology Markets, "*Journal of Marketing Research* 38 (November 2001): 485–493.

Further Reading

David A. Aaker and E. Joachimsthaler, *Brand Leadership* (New York: The Free Press, 2000).

Clayton M. Christensen and Michael Overdorf, "Meeting the Challenge of Disruptive Change," *Harvard Business Review* 78 (March/April 2000): 66–76.

Robert G. Cooper, Scott J. Edgett, and Elko J. Kleinschmidt, "New Product Portfolio Management: Practices and Performance," *The Journal of Product Innovation Management* 16 (July 1999): 333–351.

Robert G. Cooper and Elko J. Kleinschmidt, "New Product Processes at Leading Industrial Firms," *Industrial Marketing Management* 20 (1991): 137–147.

Robert G. Cooper and Elko J. Kleinschmidt, "Benchmarking Firms' New Product Performance and Practices," *Engineering Management Review* 23 (fall 1995): 112–120.

David W. Cravens, Nigel Piercy and Ashley Prentice, "Developing Market-Driven Product Strategies," *Journal of Product & Brand Management,* 9, no. 6 (2000): 369–88.

Marion Debruyne, Rudy Moenart, Abbie Griffin, Susan Hart, Erik Jan Hultink, and Henry Robben, "The Impact of New Product Launch Strategies on Competitive Reaction in Industrial Markets," *The Journal of Product Innovation Management* 19 (March 2002): 159–170.

George P. Dovel, "Stake it Out: Positioning Success, Step by Step," *Business Marketing* (July 1990).

Abbie Griffin and John R. Hauser, "Integrating R&D and Marketing: A Review and Analysis of the Literature," *Journal of Product Innovation Management* 13 (May 1996): 191–215.

Cornelius Herstatt and Eric von Hippel, "From Experience: Developing New Product Concepts via the Lead User Method: A Case Study in a Low-Tech Field," *Journal of Product Innovation Management,* 9 (1992): 213–221.

Eric von Hippel, "Get New Products from Customers," *Harvard Business Review* 60 (March/April 1982): 117–122.

Ralph W. Jackson, Lester A. Neidell, and Dale A. Lunsford, "An Empirical Investigation of the Differences in Goods and Services as Perceived by Organizational Buyers," *Industrial Marketing Management* 24 (1995): 99–108.

Jon R. Katzenbach and Douglas K. Smith, "The Discipline of Teams," *Harvard Business Review* 71 (March/April 1993): 112.

Kevin. L. Keller, *Strategic Brand Management: Building, Measuring, and Managing Brand Equity* 2nd ed. (NJ: Pearson Higher Education, 2003).

Eric M. Olson, Orville C. Walker, and Robert W. Ruekert, "Organizing for Effective New Product Development: The Moderating Role of Product Innovativeness," *Journal of Marketing* 59 (January 1995): 48–62.

Barry N. Rosen, "The Standard Setter's Dilemma: Standards and Strategies for New Technology in a Dynamic Environment," *Industrial Marketing Management* 23 (1994): 181–190.

Glen L. Urban, Bruce D. Weinberg and John R. Hauser, "Premarket Forecasting of Really-New Products," *Journal of Marketing,* 60, 47–60.

---

[1]Robert D. Buzzell and Bradley T. Gale, *The PIMS Principles: Linking Strategy to Performance* (New York: The Free Press, 1987).

[2]David W. Cravens and others, "Marketing's Role in Product and Service Quality," *Industrial Marketing Management* (May 1988): 285–304.

[3]H. Michael Hayes, "ISO9000: The new Strategic Consideration," *Business Horizons* (May-June 1994): 52–60.

[4]Robert G. Cooper and Elko J. Kleinschmidt, *New Products: The Key Factors in Success* (Chicago: American Marketing Association, 1990), 35–38.

[5]George S. Yip, *Total Strategy* (Englewood Cliffs, NJ: Prentice Hall, 1992), 85–102.

[6]Ted Levitt, "The Globalization of Markets," *Harvard Business Review* (May–June 1983): 92–102.

[7]Kenichi Ohmae, *The Borderless World: Management Lessons in the New Logic of the Global Marketplace* (New York: Harper Collins Publishers, 1991), 58–60.

[8]George S. Day, "Managing the Markeitng Learning Process," *Journal of Business & Industrial Marketing* 17, no. 4 (2002): 246.

[9]Booz, Allen & Hamilton, *New Product Management for the 1980s* (New York: Booz, Allen & Hamilton, 1982).

[10]It is of interest to note that these European programs are open to non-European firms. U.S. participants include Apple Computers Europe, Motorola, IBM Europe, and DuPont de Nemours.

[11]Robert G. Cooper, "New Product Success in Industrial Firms," *Industrial Marketing Management* (1982): 215–23.

Further Reading

[12]Robert G. Cooper, "The Myth of the Better Mousetrap: What Makes a New Product a Success?" *Business Quarterly* (Spring 1981).

[13]C. Merle Crawford, *New Products Management*, 4th ed., (Homewood, IL: Richard D. Irwin, 1994).

[14]Eric von Hippel, "The Dominant Role of Users in the Scientific Instrument Innovation Process," *Research Policy* 5 (1975): 212–39.

[15]Regis McKenna, *Relationship Marketing* (Addison-Wesley, 1991), 86–87.

[16]George P. Dovel, "Stake It Out: Positioning Success, Step by Step," *Business Marketing* (July 1990).

[17]John Kim and others, "Examining the Role of Brand Equity in Business, A Model, Research Propositions and Managerial Implications" *Journal of Business-to-Business Marketing* 5, no. 3 (1998): 65–89.

[18]David A. Aaker, *Managing Brand Equity* (New York: The Free Press, 1991).

[19]David A. Aaker, *Building Strong Brands* (New York: The Free Press, 2002): 12–13.

Chapter 8

Marketing of Services

Should marketing of services be managed differently than marketing of products?[1] The notion of services has been defined in a number of ways. One of the more common descriptions is "any act or performance that one party can offer to another that is essentially intangible and does not result in the ownership of anything. Its production may, or may not, be tied to a physical product."[2] Based on this definition we argue that the answer to the question is both Yes and No. No, because we believe that many of the fundamental principles espoused in this book very much apply equally to marketing of products and of services. Yes, because we also believe that a number of arguments can be made for different perspectives on marketing when it comes to services. The added benefit of including this perspective is that most "product businesses" actually can learn much from marketers of services because these product businesses often focus increasingly on service provision as they reach the mature stage of the product lifecycle.

Specific Characteristics of Business Services
We believe it is useful to provide a framework that differentiates services from goods. Traditionally, four characteristics of services have been identified: *intangibility* (services cannot be seen tasted, felt, heard, or smelled before purchase); *variability* (the quality of the service depends on who is providing it and the interaction between the provider and the customer); *inseparability* (services usually cannot be separated from their provider); and *perishability* (most services cannot be stored for later use or sale). With this perspective, services in business markets can range from after-sales support of a product, in the form of repairs, technical assistance, training, monitoring and surveillance, installation and engineering services, through to highly complex outsourcing projects involving IT operations, production and facility management, and on to management consulting and investment banking services as well as the elusive area of executive education and coaching.

- Intangibility. In many instances, customers have no way to evaluate a service before it is performed. . Management consultants, for instance, are sometimes accused of *selling smoke*, because of their inability to provide verifiable evidence that the service to be purchased can actually be delivered as requested by the client. Clearly, the reputation of the service provider can be critical in overcoming this drawback. The old adage, "No one is fired for buying from IBM," also has parallels when clients have been purchasing management consulting services from the well-known McKinsey & Co. Productization can be another way of addressing this issue. Originally coined to apply to software, rising out of concerns that excellent software is not enough, software suppliers are now focusing on what customers need; namely a total package that includes high quality documentation, training, and services. Usable features, it is held, delivered in a well-balanced package, are the heart of productization. Similarly, intangible services can be made more tangible, and therefore more understandable, if augmented by documentation, evidence of previous success, etc.

- Variability. Whereas products are usually developed and assembled under the scrutinizing eyes of a quality control team in the firm's facilities, services differ in that they are often created away from the firm's offices and sometimes in the client's facility, with the direct or indirect participation of the customer. Thus, some business-to-business services are highly dependent on the customer's involvement in the process, and may require the customer to be heavily engaged in creating the offer. For example, a strategic management workshop for the top executives requires that the clients be heavily involved in the creation and delivery in order to ensure success of the service offered. At other times, the client is only required to participate at the beginning and at the end of an engagement as in the case of a marketing research study or a tax solution. In either case, training of the deliverer of the service becomes highly important to ensure the service is provided as intended.

- Inseparability. Most services are produced and consumed simultaneously. The provider-client interaction is, therefore, critical. Training the provider not only to provide the service as intended but also in the skills to interact appropriately

with the customer is necessary to ensure appropriate outcomes.

- Perishability. Critical to many services is the firm's inability
to store them. As we will discuss in Chapter 10, some services which are being provided on the Internet are, in effect,
stored until delivered to customers. In most instances (e.g.,
maintenance providers, management consultants, etc.), however, the capacity exists to supply, whether it is used or not,
and capacity management becomes critically important. The
service provider is highly dependent on the ability to forecast demands or to work closely with the customers to
achieve optimal utilization. Some strategies can be employed on the demand side to address this issue. Differential
pricing, for instance, can be used to stimulate "off-peak"
some demand for services. On the supply side, use of part
time employees can help to address the issue.

In some instances, the value of the service can also be increased by involving other customers. Consider a top management development
program, such as provided by the Harvard Business School, the International Institute for Management Development (IMD), or the China
Europe International Business School (CEIBS). Such a program has
value, per se, because of the interesting and insightful lectures. However, as important as the lectures from esteemed professors might be,
equally, or more, important is the interaction with other executives
from different companies and industries attending the program who
might share ideas and insights with fellow participants. Similarly, services provided by the A.C. Nielsen survey organization are often
highly dependent on the participation of competitors of the client in
order to have the best comparisons.

Marketing Implications of Services Characteristics

For new managers joining a service company, one of the first insightful observations is the intensity and involvement of contact personnel
as part of the service experience. Service professionals, unlike providers of goods, are not static objects and the variation in expressed behavior is less predictable and controllable. Furthermore, the intensity
of contact between staff and customers is often quite high in services
and the client's experience with staff members and their attitudes,
competence, and personalities have an immediate impact. Thus, the
attention to recruitment, staffing, development, motivation and conflict
handling is highly important in services; these matters are of course
also important in other businesses, but the occurrence in services

should not be underestimated.[5] In Figure 8.1, it is abundantly clear that the people side of the business is central to the strategy of the firm.[6]

The model in Figure 8.1 suggests that the Service Marketing Strategy must take as its starting point the organizational purpose of the service offering. In some firms, services are the core business, whereas in others the service offering is an augmentation which helps differentiate its core product strategy.[7] Therefore, the firm may want to forgo pure profit optimization for the service bundle, and might even be willing to provide services, such as customer support or technical service at no charge, making its profits on the sale of the products.[8] As with all marketing, the service strategy must be driven by client needs. Thus, segmentation is of paramount importance, as is the specifications of client needs or *customer care-abouts* (i.e., what the clients are concerned about).[9]

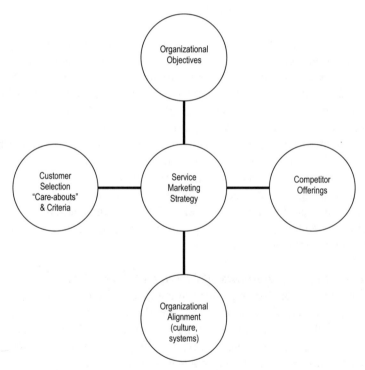

Figure 8.1: Service Marketing Strategy Framework

Figure 8.2 shows other implications as well. In Quadrant A1, the services demanded are standardized in the market place where pure competition exists and margins are low. In Quadrant A2, customers are demanding more than standardized services, and require some degree of customization. Although customers do not perceive the high complexity, the services are seen as critical to the firm. Thus, relationship management and reputation often provide the supplier with higher margins. For services that are not seen as critical, although they may be viewed as complex, (Quadrant A3), there are limits to how much customers are willing to pay, despite the lack of competition. In Quadrant A4, the importance of the services and the perceived complexity will generally cause pricing to be of much less importance for the customer.

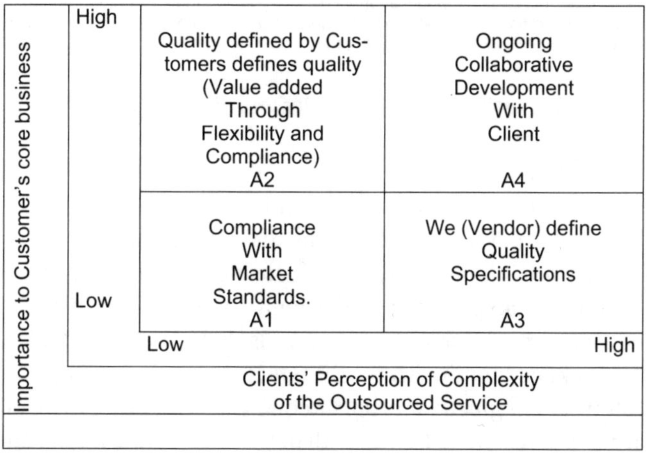

	High	Quality defined by Customers defines quality (Value added Through Flexibility and Compliance) A2	Ongoing Collaborative Development With Client A4
Importance to Customer's core business	Low	Compliance With Market Standards. A1	We (Vendor) define Quality Specifications A3
		Low High	
		Clients' Perception of Complexity of the Outsourced Service	

Figure 8.2: Framework for Segment Identification

The variation in needs among customer segments also suggests differences in the decision-making process, as discussed in Chapter 6. For a European firm specializing in facilities management, this difference led to extensive marketing research for the firm to better understand the arguments used for deciding the appropriateness of outsourcing facilities services. As seen in Figure 8.3, *less dependence on staffing* and *cost reduction* were the two most important motivations for outsourcing.[10]

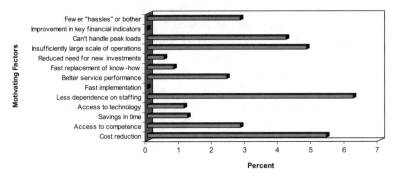

Source: Martin Fog, Mikkel Skov and Per Jenster, "Integration af Internettet i Firmatets For-retningsstrategy; Teoretiske og Praktiske Vurderinger fra en Industriel Virksomhed" *Ledelse og Erhvervsøkonomi* 63. 3 (September 1999):191.

Figure 8.3: Motivating Factors for Outsourcing of Facility Services

Productizing Services

In recent years, the term *productization* has come into use with respect to software. Rising out of concerns that excellent software is not enough, software suppliers are now focusing on what customers need; namely a total package that includes high quality documentation, train-ing, and services. Usable features, it is held, delivered in a well-balanced package, are the heart of productization. In essence, this is an extension of the *augmented product* concept, which recognizes that the customer is interested in far more than just the physical attributes of a product. The term "productizing" is used to apply this augmentation concept to services.

In working with business organizations, we often see the chal-lenges of heterogeneity and of managing the quality of delivery. Be-cause of difficulties of separating products and services, ensuring that the offering provides the customer with a pre-defined experience cre-ates challenges. When the service is delivered by a number of employ-ees, frequently in close interaction with the customer's organization variations it becomes difficult in managing both the *quality of the ser-vice* and the *level of service* provided.[11] What is the meaning of these two concepts? The level of service relates to how much activity is allo-cated to the service engagement. The quality of the service focuses on the perceived experience of the actual service level delivered. As shown in Figure 8.2, the level of service relates to the defined func-tionality of the offering, which differs significantly from quadrant to quadrant. The quality of the service refers to the clients' perceived ex-perience and criteria. These criteria include the following:

1. Customer satisfaction, overall or as sub-categories, such as ordering, ease of access, availability, listening to needs and empathy
2. Quality of the work performed
3. Understanding of customer requirements
4. Efforts to improve service.

The *productization*, or the creation of packages of pre-defined service activities, is also necessary for other reasons. By carefully defining the specifications for a specific bundle of services, the company will also be able to identify the cost of the service. This is not a trivial problem. Many firms have little understanding of the profitability of the services offered. By defining the activities associated with a specific bundle of activities in a service offering, the cost of these services can be established.[12] In the PC marketplace, Hewlett-Packard was one of the first companies to not only bundle its services in pre-specified offerings, but also to sell extended services beyond the warranty period, as a package (very much like a software or package) to small and medium-sized business, through the distributor network.[13]

> An international firm in the specialty chemicals in the food and flavor industry had been struggling with its technical support and *free sample* strategy. The company discovered that some customers were actually ordering *free samples* and that these samples largely satisfied the annual needs of these customers. The firm changed its approach by segmenting the customer base, and decided to charge for samples to "C" and "D" level customers. These customers would then be credited for the charges of samples if orders of a certain size were placed with the company.

Illustration 8.1: Dealing with Free Samples

Not all customers are looking for standard treatment. For some it is very important that their specific needs are met, as is the case for quadrant A2 and A4 in Figure 8.2. Such tailoring can be difficult to manage, if it is not internally managed though the use of modules. Even a firm doing contract research for customers whose needs are highly specified must use *building blocks* internally know the cost structure for a given project. This is also the case for investment bankers, and management consulting firms.

A distributor of stationary compressors had defined three levels of after-sales services, following the product warranty expiration:

(A) **Basic**. Repair and maintenance in the company's workshop; customers would bring the compressor to the workshop and pick the unit up after repair. Turnaround time within 8 days.

(B) **Silver**. On-demand technical support where the tech-service engineer would solve the problem at the customer's facility. Response time within 48 hours.

(C) **Gold**. Techical service response within 6 hours. The package also included a preventive maintenance service contract in which technical support would guarantee operating time of more than 99.6% for the unit.

The pricing for the three levels of services varied significantly.

Illustration 8.2: After-Sales Services

No matter whether the offering is standardized or customized, the marketing team must carefully select the relevant activities for the specific customer or customer segment. The Service Offering Model shown in Figure 8.4 provides a useful tool.

At the core of Figure 8.4 is the fundamental service, which can be thought of as the most basic activities, which must be performed in order to justify the commercial activity. Surrounding the core, are the essential delivery and internal processes. The augmented service activities refer to additional services that are not part of the core activity, but are added to create a differentiated offering. For a legal office, this might include a quarterly updates to customers concerning legal changes. Finally, the extended service characteristics are activities, which enhance the general reputation of the office in order to establish uniqueness through brand equity. This model is also used in defining offerings involving physical products; however, services, such as training, technical support, customer service, and logistical services are frequently used to augment the physical product.

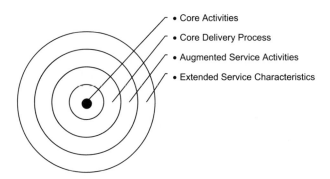

Figure 8.4: The Service Offering Model

Digitizing Services

We earlier touched on the challenges involved in the perishable nature of some services. One of the ways that firms are attempting to address this challenge is through automation or digitization. On-line diagnostics have become standard for many products, not the least of which is IT equipment, but other products ranging for paper machinery to trucks are now aided by remote diagnostics. Consultants such as Ernst & Young have created Ernst & Young Online to allow clients to access service and information, most of which has been digitized for immediate access and delivery.

After the Sale

Many manufacturing firms are increasingly realizing that there is money to be made after the sale of their products, often with higher margins than obtained from the initial product. Producers of cooling systems, elevators and trucks (products with extended durability) are finding that the revenues from design, installation, maintenance, and repair services are a significant part of the revenue. For certain markets, these opportunities constitute as much as four to five times the market for the original product sale.[14] The concept of the service life cycle and the exploration of this potential revenue stream is shown in Figure 8.5. Yet, too often companies squander the potential by not attending to the opportunity. Poor service marketing plans, understaffing, or simply incompetent personnel, systems and organization are often to blame for suboptimal contributions from services.[15]

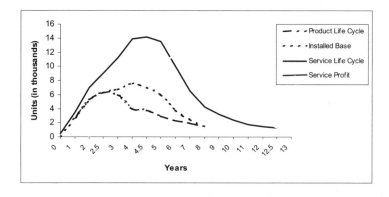

Figure 8.5: The Service Life Cycle

First, management should focus on defining the right service offering, rather than merely responding to customer requests for parts and services on demand. Similar to what firms must do when approaching product markets, their marketing departments must carefully segment the customer base, taking into account different needs and ability to pay for services. Whether some customers are classified as "basic-needs customers" and others as "risk avoiders" or as "hand-holders" is just one indicative illustration of how the offerings may have to vary from one customer group to another.[16] The concept of capturing lost sales revenue is shown in Figure 8.6.

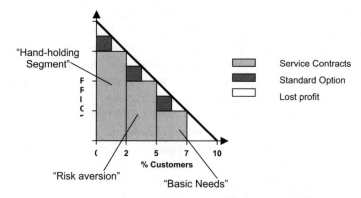

Figure 8.6: Capturing Lost Sales

Summary

All goods and services consist of a core element that is surrounded by a variety of optional elements. If we look first at the core service products, we can assign them to one of three broad categories depending on their tangibility and the extent to which customers need to be physically present during service production. The perceived service quality has two factors: a technical or outcome factor and a functional or process-related factor. The technical quality of a service process is normally a prerequisite for good quality. It has to be at an acceptable level. After-sales service adds to the product's value and is often treated as an integral part of the product.

Further Reading

Donald Cowell, *The Marketing of Services* (London: Heinemann Professional Publishing, 1984).

Christian Gronroos, "Relationship Marketing: Strategic and Tactical Implications," *Management Decision* 34, no. 3 (1996): 5–14.

Philip Kotler and Paul N. Blood, *Marketing Professional Services* (Upper Saddle River, NJ: Prentice Hall, 1984).

John R. Johnson, "Service at a Price," *Industrial Distribution* (May 1998): 91–4.

Saeed Samiee, "The Internationalization of Services: Trends, Obstacles and Issues," *Journal of Services Marketing*, 13, no. 4/5: 319–28.

Arun Sharma, R. Krishnan, and Dhruv Grewal, "Value Creation in Markets: A Critical Area of Focus for Business-to-Business Markets," *Industrial Marketing Management* 30 (June 2001): 391–402.

Stefan Stremersch, S. Wuyts and R. T. Frambach, "The Purchasing of Full-Service Contracts," *Industrial Marketing Management* 30 (2001): 1–12.

Timothy L. Wilson, "International After-Sales Services," *Journal of Global Marketing* 13, no. 1 (1999): 5–27.

Valerie A. Zeithaml and Mary Jo Bitner, *Service Marketing: Integrating Customer Focus Across the Firm*, 3rd ed. (Boston: McGraw-Hill Irwin, 2003).

[1]Donald Cowell, The Marketing of Services (London; Heinemann Professional Publishing, 1984), 73.

[2]Philip Kotler, *Marketing Management: Analysis, Planning, Implementation and Control,* 11th ed. (Englewood Cliffs, NJ: Prentice-Hall, Inc., 2003), 200.

[3]Michael D. Hartline, James G. Maxham III, and Daryl O. McKee, "Corridors of Influence in the dissemination of Customer-Oriented Strategy to Customer Contact Service Employees," *Journal of Marketing* (April 2000): 35–50.

[4]Scott Ward, Larry Light, and Jonathan Goldstine, "What High-Tech Managers Need to Know About Brands," Harvard Business Review 75 (July/August 1999): 85–95.

[5]Cowell, *The Marketing of Services*:110.

[6]Ibid.

[7]Valerie A. Zeitham and Mary Jo Bitner, *Service Marketing: Integrating Customer Focus Across the Firm*, 3d ed. (Boston: McGraw-Hill Irwin, 2003), 2.

[8]Joseph P. Guiltinan, "The Price Bundling of Services: A Normative Framework," *Journal of Marketing* 51 (April 1987): 74.

[9]Ibid.

[10]Martin Fog, Mikkel Skov and Per Jenster, "*Integration af Internettet i Firmatets Forretningsstrategy; Teoretiske og Praktiske Vurderinger fra en Industriel Virksomhed"* Ledelse og Erhvervsøkonomi 63, 3 (September 1999): 191.

[11]William H. Davidow and Bro Uttal, "Service Companies: Focus or Falter," *Harvard Business Review* 67 (July/August 1989): 84.

[12]Valerie A. Zeithaml, A. Farasuramen, and Leonard R. Berry, "Problems and Strategies in Services Marketing," *Journal of Marketing* 49 (spring 1985): 34.

[13]Diane Lynn Kastiel, "Service and Support: High-Tech's New Battleground," *Business Marketing* 73 (June 1987): 66.

[14]George W. Potts, "Exploit your Product's Service Life Cycle," *Harvard Business Review* (September-October, 1998): 32–33.

[15]Ibid, p.36.

[16]Russell G. Bundschuh and Theodore M. Dezvane, "How to make after-sales services pay off," *McKinsey Quarterly* 4 (2003).

Chapter 9

Pricing Strategy for Business Markets

Few marketing decisions have the apparent simplicity of the pricing decision. This simplicity is suggested by the fact that, in sharp contrast with other marketing decisions, the pricing decision can be made quickly, can be implemented almost immediately, and is viewed by many as no more than a matter of marking up an easily determined cost by some "fair" amount. Reality is that the pricing decision is one of the most complex decisions facing the marketer. More than any other marketing decision it has an almost immediate impact on sales volume and revenues, and thus on profits, often in unexpected ways. Because the price a customer will pay reflects the customer's perception of the value of the product or service, all other marketing decisions come together in the pricing decision. That is, the price at which the firm elects to offer its product or service should represent the firm's belief as to the value of its offering to a particular target market and should, therefore, take into account all the benefits the customer may receive, including both tangible and intangible aspects of the product offering, how the product is made available, any value added by the sales force and, importantly, its appraisal of competitive offerings. Finally, to the extent that costs influence the firm's price, they seldom are easily determined and it is not at all clear what might be a fair markup.

In this chapter, we will review the considerations that must be taken into account in making the pricing decision in business markets, and in developing and implementing pricing policies.

The Economists' View of Price

Because most economic textbooks deal extensively with price, we feel it is useful to differentiate the views of economists and marketers on the subject. For the economist, price plays a major role in allocating resources among a host of competing uses. Economic theory, therefore, is concerned with how the price system operates, in order to allocate resources and combine them to produce some optimum level and composition of output. In studying the pricing system, a principal objective is to answer questions such as "what determines the price of various commodities?" Implicit in such studies is the imperative to make simplifying assumptions about demand curves, marginal cost curves and marginal revenue curves.

As a general observation, economic theory has been most successful at considering the question of price determination in markets where so-called perfect competition exists (i.e., markets where there are large numbers of buyers and sellers and products are essentially identical) or where monopoly exists. It is in markets characterized by this perfect competition that we see the determination of price as the intersection of the familiar upward sloping supply curve with the equally familiar downward sloping demand curve. In markets characterized as monopolistic, with only one supplier, we see the determination of a profit maximizing price, associated with the quantity at the intersection of a firm's marginal cost and marginal revenue curves. It should be recognized, however, that in either case there is the notion that the demand curve, the marginal cost curve and the marginal revenue curves are well known and that there is one right or optimum price for the conditions specified. This is seldom the case for marketing decision-making.

Economic theory has been far less successful in considering the question of price determination in oligopolistic markets, characterized by a relatively small number of competitors who are keenly aware of each other and constantly strive to differentiate themselves through such things as product features, superior service, or personal relationships, and a relatively small number of customers who vigorously negotiate with suppliers, or otherwise design their purchasing policies, so as to achieve the best possible price. With few exceptions, theories that have been developed, such as the Chamberlin Model, the Kinked Demand Curve, and Game Theory, have either been discredited or severely limited by their restrictive assumptions.[1] However, it is in these oligopolistic markets that the vast majority of firms strive for customer patronage, competitive advantage, and market share. Business marketers, therefore, have to look beyond economic theories in the pricing decision process.

The Marketer's View of Price

In sharp contrast to the notion of price as a fixed point, as conveyed by the intersection of supply and demand curves or marginal cost and marginal revenue curves, marketers see price as falling in an opportunity range; a range bounded by the three Cs of the firm's costs, customers' perception of value, and competitors' prices for similar products or services, as depicted in Figure 9.1.

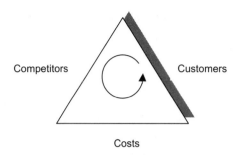

Figure 9.1: The Opportunity Range for Pricing Decisions

In some instances the range may be large, affording the marketer considerable flexibility in price determination, as is the case for new products or those extensively differentiated from competitive offerings. In others, there is little flexibility, as might be the case for mature products or those with little differentiation from competitive offerings. Even in these instances, however, the opportunity may exist to select market segments, which allow a greater degree of pricing freedom.

The extent to which each of the three C's influence the pricing decision also varies. For mature products, competitors' prices may well be the predominant influence on price, and pricing decisions may be made in competitive terms such as premium, meet the competitive levels, or price below them. For new products, in the introductory stage of the PLC, intrinsic customer value and the expected behavior of costs may be the predominant influences on price.

Beyond the three C's, most marketers must also make their pricing decisions in the context of the firm's overall objectives for pricing policy. In the final analysis, of course, the objective of the firm is to produce a profit. Profit objectives, however, may be given to the marketer in a variety of ways. In some firms, they may be stated in terms of return on investment or return on sales. In others, they may be stated in terms of expected gross margin, or profit contribution after marketing expense. Almost always there are other objectives such as attainment or maintenance of market share, avoidance of government antitrust actions, minimizing the cannibalization of other products or services, deterring competitive attacks, or leading the way into new markets.

In the following sections, we first discuss the three C's and then consider a number of other pricing considerations associated with pricing decisions and pricing objectives.

The Firm's Costs

Costs are clearly a major consideration in the pricing decision. While few firms rely solely on a cost-based approach to pricing, their costs are a major determinant of profit and set a finite lower bound for the pricing decision. It is important to distinguish between costs that are fixed, those that are semi-fixed and those that are variable. Fixed costs are those that do not vary as a function of volume produced. These would include such items as physical plant and equipment, long-term leases, or interest on long-term debt. Semi-fixed costs are those that do not vary as a function of volume produced but that can be changed in the short term by management decision. These would include such items as salaries of the sales force or other general administrative expenses, R&D expenses, or advertising commitments. Variable costs are those that vary directly with the number of units produced. These include such items as raw materials, direct manufacturing labor, freight, and salespersons commissions.

For pricing decisions, there are a number of key aspects of cost, which need to be taken into account. First, few firms are likely to make an investment in fixed costs which cannot be recovered in an appropriate time period. Breaking even is a must but few firms are interested in simply breaking even. The price, therefore, must not only cover variable costs but must also result in sufficient volume so that the total contribution (revenue minus variable costs) covers all fixed costs and returns some desired level of contribution to profit, R&D, or investment in other opportunities. Second, even fewer firms are likely to price below variable costs. Hence, a firm's variable cost becomes a floor for the pricing decision. Third, it is important to recognize that the term "total cost" takes on meaning only for a specific volume.[2]

These relationships can be seen in a variation of the familiar break-even chart, as shown in Figure 9.2. A key concept is per unit contribution, or the difference between per unit revenue and per unit variable cost. Breakeven volume, where revenue equals total cost (Q1), is calculated by dividing fixed cost by the per unit contribution. In this illustration, we show the situation where the desired profit contribution is constant, as might be the case with a target ROI. Here the required volume is where revenues equal total cost plus desired contribution (Q2). While most firms will avoid pricing at a level that falls below what are considered total costs, there may be occasions when such a price will make a positive contribution toward fixed costs, even though they are not fully covered.

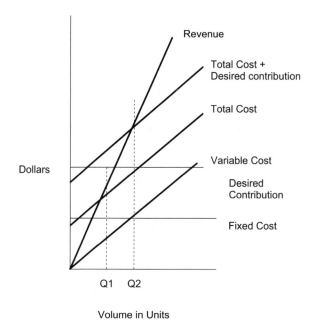

Q1 = Break-Even Volume = Fixed Cost/Contribution Margin

Q2 = Desired Contribution Volume = (Fixed Cost + Desired Contribution)/Contribution Margin

Figure 9.2: Variation on Break-Even Analysis

The relation of fixed to variable costs is a critical aspect of pricing. In high fixed cost industries (e.g., the chemical or paper industries), high contribution margins are necessary to cover fixed costs. In times of economic slowdown, when the level of fixed manufacturing capacity substantially exceeds industry demand, pressures to secure orders that provide at least some contribution margin frequently lead to price wars with large reductions in price that still do not fall below variable cost. On the other hand, in low fixed cost industries (e.g., most service industries, where personnel are the major element of cost), firms feel less pressure to secure orders at any cost and are more likely to respond to an economic slowdown through reductions in personnel or other variable costs.

For most firms, variable costs are not just a function of economies of scale but also can be expected to decline as the firm gains production experience. For some firms this experience curve effect is sufficiently large as to become the key determinant of pricing policy.[3] In the semi-conductor industry, for instance, where experience curve effects as large as 25% (i.e., variable costs decline 25% for every doubling of cumulative volume) have been observed, industry observers

179

have noted that Texas Instruments has introduced products at low prices associated with expected lower future costs which will result from the sales volume stimulated by the low price. This variation of a penetration strategy, which we will discuss in more detail, not only stimulates demand for its products, but also allows the firm to establish a preemptive high share market position. Many Japanese firms employ a further variation of this approach by estimating a target price, which will produce the desired volume, and then working backwards to produce the product at a cost, which will give an acceptable contribution.

Finally, we should note the impact of accounting practices on costs, particularly with respect to depreciation, inventory valuation and fixed asset valuation. Where fixed costs include a depreciation component, accelerated depreciation schedules will show higher costs. Firms that account for inventory using LIFO accounting (last-in, first-out) will show higher variable costs than those using FIFO accounting (first-in, first-out). In some instances, firms will require their businesses to value assets on a replacement cost basis rather than on an historical cost basis, resulting in higher depreciation charges and so higher fixed costs. As a result, the firm which bases its pricing decisions on these more conservative accounting practices may make its pricing decisions very differently from the less conservative firm.

The Firm's Customers

Perhaps the most salient aspect of pricing for business marketers is the fact that its customers are not passive entities in the exchange process but, rather, are professionals who carefully analyze a firm's offerings in terms of their value, both intrinsically and relative to competitive offerings, consider the possibility of make or buy, and develop strategies designed to maximize value received by purchasing at the lowest possible price. This having been said, it still must be noted that buying firms vary enormously with respect to their emphasis on price as a determinant of the purchasing decision.

This variation in emphasis on price comes in two ways. First is the variation in emphasis on price per se. Some firms will indicate their objective is to receive a "fair" price, as viewed by both buyer and seller. In the case of multiple sourcing, such firms will typically solicit quotations or bids from suppliers and will rely on the quotation or bid process to ensure fairness. Where sole sourcing is used, as might be the case where JIT is involved, buyers will frequently require the supplier to provide cost information to justify a particular price and "fair" can become a matter for considerable debate, both with respect to cost calculations and profit margins. Other firms will set aside any notion of fairness and will work aggressively to extract the lowest possible price from a supplier. Typically such firms will engage in extensive negotiation, frequently in connection with the bidding or quotation process, and will not hesitate to use their buying power or superior negotiating skill to their advantage. Still others, albeit in relatively small numbers, may be content to accept a supplier's price, even though it offers the supplier relatively more benefit than the buyer.

Second, firms will vary in their view of required features or functionality. DuPont, for instance, has recognized this variation by offering a certain chemical at both a standard level and a premium level, where the latter includes several added benefits such as fewer impurities, quicker delivery, and high levels of customer support, for which DuPont charges a premium of 5% over the standard level.[4]

The Firm's Competitors

The pricing decision must take into account the presence of existing competitors or, in the case of new products, the existence of potential competitors. For the mature product, with existing competitors, the firm's pricing flexibility will depend on the extent to which customers perceive differences between competitive offerings. Combined with customers' concerns with price this degree of pricing flexibility can be depicted as shown in Figure 9.3.

Customer Concern with Price

		Low	Medium	High
	Great Difference	Great	Substantial	Some
Relationship of Competitive Offers	Modest Difference	Substantial	Some	Little
	Indentical	None	None	None

Figure 9.3: Pricing Flexibility in Competitive Markets

Given significant competitive advantage and large numbers of customers not greatly concerned with price, the firm may elect a premium pricing strategy. Critical to the execution of such a strategy is the ability of the sales force to concentrate on the right customers and to communicate the inherent extra value in the firm's offering to its customers. Inevitably, however, there will be instances where customers become more price-sensitive, where the sales force calls on price sensitive customers, or is unable to convince customers of extra value, or where additional volume may be sufficiently attractive as to require consideration of pricing at or below competitive levels. In such instances, the firm may have to abandon its premium pricing policy or segment the market based on price sensitivity.

The presence of existing competitors, all with at least some knowledge of the actions of others, raises further issues. In an oligopolistic industry, for instance, how are overall price levels established, increased, or decreased? In many industries, we find price leaders; that is, firms that by virtue of size, reputation, or past practice play a major role in determining the overall level of prices in the industry. In some instances, the price leader may take the lead in initiating price changes that are then widely followed by others in the industry. More frequently, and particularly with respect to price reductions, the initiative to change prices is taken by smaller firms but it is the action by the price leader that legitimizes the new price level. The dynamics by which such moves occur are complex. In times of increased demand, the opportunity may exist to increase industry prices but some firms may elect to forego price increases in an attempt to increase share. Similarly, in times of increasing costs the pressure may exist to pass cost increases on to customers but, again, some firms may elect, instead, to forego price increases in order to increase share. The role of the price leader, therefore, is not an easy one. Leading the way in raising prices may expose the leader to significant loss of market share. Leading the way in lowering prices results in loss of revenue and, if competitors quickly follow, will not result in an increase in market share. Despite these difficulties, oligopolistic industries tend to look for price leaders, recognizing the need for some kind of stabilizing force with respect to price levels.

For many firms, a key issue concerns the appropriate response to the move by a competitor to make inroads on the firm's position with a valued customer, usually by offering a lower price. One policy, of course, is to match the competitor's offer. In many instances, however, the special offer may be conditional on not revealing its terms, or the opportunity to match it may not be available. A large European manufacturer of packaging materials, therefore, had a policy of responding to an attack on its positions by quickly making an extremely low price offer to a key customer of the competitor. The competitor could match the price offer, at a significant loss, or lose a significant amount of business; in either case experiencing some loss of profit. The firm's expectation, of course, was that knowledge of past retaliation would dissuade competitors from future attacks on the firm's positions.[5]

Pricing Situations

It is important to recognize the two very different situations firms may face when making pricing decisions. First, is the situation where a new product is being introduced and, second, is the situation with respect to an existing product.

New Product Pricing

As we discussed in Chapter 7, the term *new product* has many meanings. Some use it to describe products that are new to the world, some to describe products that are new to the firm, and some to describe products that are essentially just minor improvements over previous offerings. In this section, we will focus on products that are either new to the world or that are sufficiently different from existing products as to permit substantial flexibility in pricing.

The opportunity range for most new products is large. Its upper bound is the maximum price that at least some customers will pay, based on the product's value to them. The lower bound is normally close to variable cost. Cumberland Metals, for instance, when it introduced its curled metal pad for use in pile driving machines felt the upper bound of its opportunity range might have been in excess of $1,000 and the lower bound as low as $50. Pricing at the high end of the opportunity range has come to be known as skimming, thus maximizing per unit contribution. In many instances, skimming is followed by "sliding down the demand curve" in which the product is introduced at a high price, but gradually reduced after those customers for whom the product has the highest value have bought. The personal computer industry is a classic example using this skimming/sliding approach. Pricing at the low end has come to be known as penetration pricing, to maximize unit volume and establish a preemptive market position.

Factors favoring one approach versus the other are shown in Table 9.1. The skimming approach is particularly appropriate where market demand conditions are uncertain or unknown, where strong patent positions or other factors would inhibit competitor responses, and where requirements for extensive promotion require high contribution margins. The rapidity with which one may slide down the demand curve is influenced by a number of factors, particularly customer demand and competitive response. The penetration approach is particularly appropriate where it is expected that low prices will result in high levels of demand, where the experience curve effect can be expected to result in dramatic cost reduction as volume increases, and where it is felt that a low price may deter competitors from entering the market or at least allow the firm the establish a leadership position with respect to market share and, hence, establish a favorable cost position.[6]

183

Skimming	Penetrating
Ineleastic demand	Elastic demand
Uncertain demand	Experience curve effect
Strong patents	Exonomies of scale
Need for promotional dollars	Large capacity increments
Limited capacity	Ease of copying
Small capacity increments	No "elite" segment
Proprietary manufacturing	
New to the world products	
Few substitute products	
Price/quality inference	

Table 9.1: Factors Influencing New Product Pricing

Pricing Existing Products

Pricing existing products must take into account not only customer demand but also the competitive situation. This involves two considerations. First, how does the firm wish to position itself versus its competitors? It has three fundamental choices. It can elect to price at a premium over competitors, at the competitive level, or below competitors. As shown in Figure 9.3, its freedom to price at a premium is a function of both customers' concerns with price and the firm's degree of competitive advantage. As we will discuss in the Value/Quality/Price section, the firm also needs to take into account the profitability of pricing above, at, or below its competitors, while taking into account the customers' perception of its relative quality. In some instances, it may be more profitable for the firm to pursue a competitive price strategy, even when it has a competitive advantage.

The second consideration relates to how industry price levels and policies are established. As we have previously discussed, in many industries price levels and policies are established or significantly influenced by a price leader. According to Sultan, based on his monumental study of pricing in the electrical products industry, the price leader has the option of choosing a pricing strategy, which can also be imposed on the leader's competitors.[7] Two considerations dictate the choice. First, the pattern of pricing over time, as conditions of supply and demand fluctuate and, second, pricing individual transactions.

Over time, the leader may choose pressure pricing and resist the psychological forces that permit a rapid upward movement in market prices during a period of surging demand or tight supply. In essence, the leader holds the lid on any short-term price increases, thus maintaining a price-cost squeeze on it competitors and discouraging entry by new competitors. Alternatively, the leader may choose opportunistic pricing and, when business conditions are good, increase prices to the limit of customer goodwill and perceived fairness. While opportunistic pricing may increase profits, at least in the short run, there is the obvious risk of entry by new competitors, more aggressive moves by existing competitors funded by their short-term profit increases, and customer ill-will with increased likelihood of future loss of patronage.

Two options exist with respect to pricing individual transactions. Gold standard pricing refers to a policy under which all customers are quoted the same price, regardless of the competitive situation. For many years, this typified IBM's pricing policy for mainframe computers and GE's pricing policy for turbine-generators. The alternative is negotiated pricing, used here to mean that prices for various transactions may be established individually, taking into account the particular competitive and customer circumstances, including the customer's desire and ability to bargain. Gold standard pricing has certain attractions. It eliminates uncertainty among competitors and customers as to what is the market price. It has a certain element of fairness in that it treats all customers alike. Negotiated pricing has its attractions as well. For the firm, it may lead to higher profits and avoids the short-term losses of market position that may be associated with gold standard pricing. Additionally, large customers may feel they should receive preferential pricing treatment, and other customers, very concerned with price, may prefer a situation in which they can exercise their negotiating skills.

Possible combinations of the foregoing are shown in Figure 9.4. Strategy sets are designated by letters. Strategy "A" involves a combination of gold standard and pressure pricing, "B" a combination of negotiated and pressure pricing, and so forth. Leader and follower strategies must be considered separately. Thus, A-B would mean an adoption of gold-standard pressure pricing by the leader and negotiated pressure pricing by follower firms. For both the leader and the follower the question is which, if any, combinations are viable.

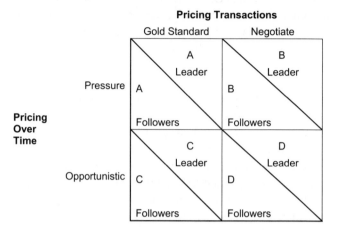

Only AA and DD (and rarely BB) have long-term feasibility.

Figure 9.4: Leader and Follower Pricing Strategies in Concentrated Industries

As a general rule, the leader firm cannot adopt a gold-standard policy unless its major competitors follow it in that policy. This means that in the long run combinations A-B, B-A, C-D or D-C are not feasible. There are exceptions, of course. For many years the A-B combination prevailed in the mainframe computer industry with IBM taking the gold standard approach and RCA, Honeywell, GE and other competitors taking the negotiated approach. In most industries, however, if one major competitor is pricing on a negotiated basis, all others must do so as well, as was the case for manufacturers of electric watt-hour meters, which moved to negotiated pricing when just one player went off the gold standard. A second general rule is that C is not feasible for the leader as a gold standard price policy is incompatible with opportunistic pricing. A third general rule is that if the leader firm imposes pressure pricing, then follower firms must also adopt the same policy. Thus strategies A-C, A-D, B-C, and B-D are typically not feasible. A fourth general rule is that if the leader adopts an opportunistic approach, then the follower firms will do likewise.

As a result, there are only three strategy combinations, which have long-term viability. A-A, B-B, and D-D, and, in fact, it is these forms of price behavior which are most frequently observed in oligopolies. Which, however, to choose? Examples of B-B are rare, probably because negotiating for maximum gain tends to inconsistent with the philosophy of withholding price increases when they are feasible. The choice would seem to be between A-A and D-D. Gold-standard pressure prices are more predictable, thus simplifying long-range planning, and reducing risk, with the prospect of lower marketing and other costs. For A-A to work, however, requires either the willingness of followers to forego the temptation of occasional deviations from the policy or the willingness of the leader to take aggressive downward price action when followers do deviate from the policy, or both. In many instances, the cost to the leader may appear to be excessive. As a result, and because negotiated opportunistic pricing also has its advantages, D-D appears to be the most feasible strategy in oligopolistic industries.

Demand Concepts

The familiar downward sloping demand curve suggests that the quantity demanded will increase if price is reduced. As we have previously described, however, a unique aspect of business markets is derived demand, reflecting the fact that organizations buy only to support their efforts to supply the wants and needs of their customers. Hence, price may influence industry demand very differently than individual customer demand.

Industry Demand

Some products or services are directly related to the quantity of the customer's product or service being produced. In such situations demand is fundamentally determined by the level of the customer's demand and total or industry demand for the product or service may not be influenced by price. In the automotive industry, for instance, the number of mufflers bought by car manufacturers to equip new cars is determined by the number of cars the industry sells. Changes in muffler prices, which represent only a minute portion of a car price, will have no impact on total demand for mufflers. In this case the price elasticity of industry demand for mufflers will be close to zero, with little incentive for muffler producers, collectively, to seek lower price levels for mufflers. On the other hand, in the personal computer industry, memory chips are a significant proportion of the total cost of a personal computer and price reductions, if passed on to customers, are likely to significantly influence industry demand. In this case,price elasticity of demand for memory chips will be something other than zero and producers may well have a collective interest in lower price levels for their products.

In the long run, demand for capital goods is also associated with the quantity of the customers' product or service being produced. Some capital goods have the potential to materially reduce customers' costs. In the early years of the electric utility industry, for instance, lower prices per unit of output and improved efficiency of turbine generators allowed electric utilities to reduce electrical rates, thereby stimulating demand for electricity and, thus, for turbine generators. In this instance, manufacturers of turbine generators had a collective interest in lower prices for their products. Today, however, turbine generators appear to have reached their optimum size and improvements in efficiency are increasingly difficult to achieve. Their demand, therefore, is more likely to parallel that of most capital goods; driven by the business cycle, with most customer's buying for expansion purposes.

The foregoing suggests the difficulty of precisely estimating industry price elasticity of demand. Assumptions, however, can be made as to whether demand is in the elastic zone, in which case an industry price increase will result in a revenue decrease, or the inelastic zone, in which case an industry price increase will lead to a revenue increase. These assumptions play a major role in determining price levels in an industry and can significantly affect responses to competitors' price moves.

Firm Demand

Although business marketers face many situations where industry demand is price inelastic, demand at the firm level is almost always highly cross elastic; either with respect to competitors' prices or with regard to prices of substitute materials. For products or services directly associated with the quantity of the customer's product or service being produced, the price paid is closely related to the firm's profits. While the Ford Motor Company is not likely to buy more mufflers if its suppliers reduce prices, it is certainly likely to buy more from Walker than from Hayes-Albion if Walker offers a lower price. Similarly, automotive manufacturers are not likely to buy more or less steel for bumpers, regardless of price. The price of engineered plastics, however, which have many desirable features as bumper material, can significantly influence steel purchases. For the supplier of products and services, knowledge of prices at the level of individual transactions, both for directly competing products and for substitutes, becomes critically important.

In many instances, purchases of capital goods are not directly associated with the level of output. Rather, they are made to maintain or improve profitability by increased efficiency, or to replace obsolete or functionally inadequate equipment. In these situations, the purchasing decision may be highly discretionary. In some instances price will be important as customers carefully analyze costs and-benefit and the impact of the purchase on their profitability. In others, the emphasis may be on functionality, with less importance on pricing considerations; particularly in such industries as health care where for several years cost increases could easily be passed on the final customer.

Value/Quality/Price Relationships

A major consideration for business marketers is the relationship between features and price. If, for instance, a firm has an advantage over its competitors with respect to functionality or service, should it charge a premium price and thus obtain higher margins, or should it price at competitive or below competitive levels and, presumably, enjoy a larger market share? Using the PIMS database, Buzzell and Gale have framed this question in terms of relative quality, relative price and value.[8] We emphasize here that relative quality in the PIMS conceptualization reflects the customers' perceptions of a firm relative to its competitors on all the product or service attributes, other than price, that affect customer buying decisions. Relative price is simply the firm's price level, relative to its principal competitors (i.e., the largest that compete in the same served market). Value is the relation of relative price to relative quality.

As shown in Figure 9.5, a comparable quality for price curve can be constructed. Most firms fall along this constant value curve, offering the same value in either premium, average or economy positions. Some firms, however, wind up off the curve and fall in the no price premium for superior quality position (more value) or in the premium for less or the same quality position (less value). According to Buzzell and Gale, offerings positioned along the comparable value curve tend to hold share. Businesses in the premium position show, on average, the highest profitability. Somewhat surprising is that the better value position (i.e., superior quality but no price premium) is nearly as profitable. Apparently, what is lost by not charging a premium is made up in lower overall costs, stemming from the tendency to gain market share, and the lower marketing costs incurred selling a superior quality product at less than a premium price.

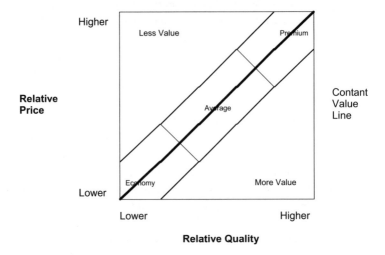

Figure 9.5: Value Map: Five Generic Relative Price/Relative Quality Positions

Pricing the Product Line

So far, we have discussed price determination as if the firm were producing a single product. In fact, most firms offer a group of related products that may differ in size or features or a group of products that are either substitutes or complements. The pricing objective, therefore, is to maximize the profits for this group of products. The basic approaches to pricing the product line are the same as those used in pricing an individual product. Demand or value serves as a ceiling and cost serves as a floor. A number of other factors, however, need to be considered.

Demand Interdependence

If the products complement each other, they may sell in higher volume because they are offered together. In such instances it may be appropriate to offer one product at an attractive price to stimulate sales of the other. Loctite, for instance, needed to take this into account in pricing Bond-A-Matic®, its dispensing system for instant adhesives the firm offered, used to bond metals, plastics, rubber, and other materials in manufacturing operations.

Where products are potential substitutes for one another prices need to be established so that demand for a one product does not erode the sale of a more profitable product. DuPont, in the previously cited example, needed to take this into account in establishing the price difference for its standard and premium products.

Cost Interdependence

In many instances, costs are joint when products are produced together and marketed in a common line. A policy of setting individual product prices so as to reflect differences in full cost (i.e., variable cost plus an assigned allocation of fixed or joint costs) could ignore variations in competition faced or the role assigned to the product in the firm's marketing strategy. Certainly, variable cost should set a floor for prices. If the product cannot support this minimum level, its contribution to the overall line is questionable. The extent to which the product is expected to contribute above variable cost needs to take into account not only competition faced and the product role, but also customer demand and the profit of the overall line.

Products That Differ In Size or Capacity

Frequently the product line will consist of products whose principal difference is size or capacity. An electric motor manufacturer, for instance, may offer a line of motors from one to one hundred horsepower or a manufacturer of disk drives may offer a line with models of several different storage capacities. What, then, should be the relationship of prices for products in the line? Two common approaches are to make them proportional to size or capacity or to make them proportional to cost. These tend to be easy to compute and justify, but they ignore both competitive offerings and customer demand and so are likely to miss significant profit opportunities.

Bundling

In many instances it may be advantageous for the supplier to bundle parts of the product line; either to offer a package combination at a lower price than if the components were offered separately or to tie the sale of components with little competitive advantage to those with significant advantage. The decision to bundle, or unbundle, is influenced by a number of factors. In some instances customers may pressure the supplier to unbundle the package as they may not wish to purchase all the components in the bundle, as might be the case with training or special application assistance. In other instances, tying the sale of a component with great competitive advantage to one with little advantage may by viewed negatively, not only by customers but also by regulatory authorities. The latter was the case when IBM was required by the U.S. Department of Justice to unbundle the sale of mainframe computers and software.

191

Pricing when Distributors are Involved

If the firm sells direct to its customers, it then has complete control over the price at which it offers its products or services. Where distributors, or other intermediaries, are involved, the price at which they offer the product or service must be taken into account in the price determination process. There are two key issues. First, what is the distributor's margin? This should reflect the functions performed by the distributor. In most cases, a normal margin for a particular class of product sold to a particular industry will have evolved over time, reflecting industry experience and competitive practices. In the U.S. machine tool industry, for instance, margins for full service distributors range from 7.5% to 15%, depending on the product.

Second, and importantly, to what extent can the manufacturer control the price at which the distributor offers the product or service? In most industrialized countries, vertical price fixing (i.e., a specific agreement between manufacturer and distributor as to the price to be charged) is illegal. In theory, distributors are free to set prices at whatever level they choose, regardless of the normal margin. In practice, however, manufacturers can exert considerable influence over the distributor's price. In particular,it is usually legal for a manufacturer to indicate, if in fact it so desires, that it expects its distributors to adhere to its suggested user prices. Distributors who do not do so may be terminated.

Price Administration

In this section we address three further considerations: (1) the issue of list versus net pricing, (2) the issue of discounts and, (3) the issue of transaction pricing.

For a number of reasons, manufacturers may elect to publish a schedule of prices in list and discount form rather than as net prices. Where distributors are involved, the list prices may indicate suggested user prices to be charged by distributors. Use of list prices, subject to some level of discount, facilitates price changes, which can be implemented simply by changing the discount rather than by revising prices on an item-by-item basis. Use of list prices also provides a basis for offering quantity discounts, a frequent business marketing practice. Finally, anecdotal evidence indicates that at least some purchasing agents prefer a list and discount approach, as they can report the discount as a saving achieved through aggressive purchasing practice.

Discounts are used in a number of additional ways. As previously indicated, functional discounts to distributors reflect the level of service provided by a distributor, or the manufacturer's cost to serve a particular market. In a particular industry a limited service distributor, providing only stocking and sales, might receive a discount of 20% whereas a full service distributor, providing stocking, sales, and service, might receive a larger discount of 23-25% or, as frequently expressed, 20 and 5. Typically, large original equipment manufacturers receive additional discounts, perhaps another 5%, reflecting both functions performed and volume, frequently expressed as 20%, 5% and 5%. In other instances, discounts may be based strictly on volume, as is the case in the steel industry where specific discounts are offered for carload quantities.

Closely related to list and discount pricing are terms of payment. While many products are offered on a net price basis, with a time stipulated for payment (e.g., terms are net 30 days), many firms offer a cash discount for prompt payment (e.g., terms are 2% 10 days or net 30 days). The decision as to what terms of payment schedule to offer needs to take into account industry practice as well as the firm's own situation. In the highly seasonal table radio business, for instance, speaker manufacturers frequently offer extended terms of payment to the radio manufacturers. In turn, magnet suppliers to speaker manufacturers also offer extended terms of payment. One large magnet supplier, hoping to standardize its terms of payments to all its customers, announced a change to net 30 days to speaker manufacturers. Despite an accompanying price reduction, to reflect the savings associated with prompter payment, speaker manufacturers refused to accept the revised terms as alternative forms of financing were unavailable to them.

The nature of business marketing emphasizes the importance of considering the actual transaction prices at which products and services are actually sold. As Marn and Rosiello point out, most firms are involved in hundreds or even thousands of customer- and order- specific pricing decisions daily, each of which has the potential to enhance or erode the firm's profitability.[9] They use the term *pocket price* to reflect the true price the supplier receives after taking into account trade discounts, prompt payment discounts, quantity discounts, volume bonuses, negotiated discounts, promotional support allowances, and freight. They reported ranges of pocket price bands of 70% for a computer peripherals supplier, 200% for a specialty chemicals company, and 500% for a fastener supplier. In some instances, customers found ways to obtain quantity discounts associated with much higher than actual volumes. In others, sales representatives used pricing authority inappropriately. In still others, customers paid late but still took cash discounts. Frequently, customers perceived by management as profitable ended up at the low end of the band and those perceived as unprofitable at the high end.

As Marn and Rosiello recommend, management needs to understand the price sensitivity of each element of what they call the price waterfall in setting policy, and needs to carefully manage the administration of each element. In particular, the potential of the price waterfall makes the case for carefully thought out, well understood price policies and clearly established pricing authority.[10]

Special Issues

In this section, we briefly describe a number of special pricing issues, including those associated with pricing across country borders.

Sealed Bidding

A unique aspect of business marketing is the frequent use of sealed bidding, in which buyers require formal quotations or bids, with no opportunity for subsequent negotiation. Some buyers will so completely specify the required product or service that the purchase decision can be made on the basis of price alone. More frequently, the decision is made on the basis of the "lowest and best bid," suggesting that some product or service attributes may be evaluated, either adding to or subtracting from the bid price. In the case of public procurement, the norm is for the bids to be publicly opened, affording bidders the opportunity to determine all aspects of competitive offerings. In the case of private procurement, practices vary but the norm is to reveal very little regarding competitive offerings.

In either case, price determination is challenging. A number of models have been proposed to assist in price determination, generally built around an expected value approach based on the following formula:

$$E(X)=P(X)Z(X)$$

where X=the bid price, Z(X) =the profit at the bid price, P(X) = the probability of an award at this price, and E(X) = the expected profit of a bid. The assumption is that the price bid should be the one with the highest expected profit.

Empirical evidence indicates that such models are extremely limited in their application. In a study of the practices of general contractors, for whom sealed bidding is the norm, less than 10% of the respondents reported use of a statistical bidding model, payoff table, or probability model in preparing the bid.[11] This limited use reflects a number of problems in using such a model. Probability estimates are highly subjective, particularly in the absence of a long pattern of similar awards on which to base them. A number of other objectives beyond profit may influence the bid price, such as the prospect of follow-on work, maintaining a stable work force, size of the backlog, and so forth. Still further, the prices bid on one transaction may influence prices on future transactions, and bidders may use a sealed bid, particularly if publicly opened, as a way to communicate future pricing intentions.

Given this complexity, the final determination of the price to be bid or quoted will depend heavily on the experience and intuition of the manager. In appropriate circumstances, however, expected value models can assist this decision making process.

Price Fixing

We have previously discussed the nature of price behavior and the role of the price leader in oligopolistic markets. The kind of stability suggested by firms following a price leader frequently vanishes in the face of profit pressures experienced in times of low demand, and aggressive moves by competitors to obtain orders that provide at least some contribution above variable cost. In many industries, this aggressive pricing has led to price wars, motivating managers to seek agreement with competitors on price levels, or look for other ways to eliminate price competition. In the United States such agreements violate the Sherman Antitrust Act. In the European Union, they violate Article 85 of the Treaty of Rome (the treaty that first established the European Economic Community). Additionally, most industrialized countries similarly prohibit such agreements; particularly those, which prevent, restrict, or distort competition. In Germany, for instance, there is extensive anticartel legislation, administered by the Federal Cartels office; and in the United Kingdom, the Competition Act of 1980 gives powers to the Director General of Fair Trading to investigate anticompetitive practices, including price fixing.

There is a fine line between the kind of stability suggested by the role of a price leader, generally followed by others in the industry, and price fixing. In the United States the Department of Justice has long been concerned with "conscious parallelism," a concept which holds that violation of the Sherman Antitrust Act does not necessarily require a specific agreement to fix prices but can occur where competitors, simply by virtue of long association, have reached some common understandings about pricing that have the same effect on industry prices as overt collusion. As a result, the Department of Justice has frequently sought, and obtained, agreement on the part of firms to discontinue practices that facilitate conscious parallelism, such as price changes that all competitors in the industry make in a short period of time and in the same amounts. Announcements of aluminum price changes in the business press, for instance, were deemed to have been targeted more at competitors than at customers. The Department of Justice successfully obtained an agreement from major producers to discontinue the practice. Other actions have been more stringent. In one industry, the major competitors were required to completely discontinue the use of published prices and to completely revise the basis on which prices had previously been calculated in order to ensure that quoted prices were arrived at independently.

The concern with price fixing, and the degree to which various activities may be illegal, varies around the world. In Switzerland, for instance, some forms of price agreements are still legal. Nevertheless, it behooves business marketers to fully understand and abide by provisions of antitrust legislation or competition policy.

Export Pricing
Pricing in export markets is subject to the same forces as in national markets; namely, customers' perception of value, prices of competitive offerings, and the firm's costs. Because at least first time exporters are less likely to have in-depth knowledge of customers and competitors there is a tendency to rely more heavily on cost based price determination when first entering a foreign market. In this method, the exporter starts with the domestic manufacturing cost, adds for administration, research and development, overhead, freight forwarding, distributor margins, and profit, and denominates the transaction in the home currency or translates the cost of domestic items at the current exchange rate. If the export product has the same relative ex-factory price as a locally produced competitive product, the user price is likely to be considerably higher, particularly if the exporting country's currency is strong, thus resulting in lost sales. On the other hand, if the exporting country's currency is weak, the user price may actually be lower, resulting in lost profit opportunities.

The starting point, then, for export price calculation should be the determination of the customers' perception of value and the local competitive situation. For first time exporters there is a host of resources available to assist in such determination. In the United States, for instance, the U.S. Foreign and Commercial Service provides a wealth of useful services. With a target price established, the firm can work back through the cost chain, taking into account exchange rates, determine the level of contribution associated with foreign sales, and then evaluate the attractiveness of the opportunity.

Once prices are established, fluctuations in the rate of exchange are a matter of concern. Denominating a transaction in ones home country currency has the attractiveness of insulating the firm from the negative consequences of currency fluctuations, but at the expense of competitive position, particularly against local competitors. Caterpillar, with its dominant position in earth moving equipment, and competing principally against U.S. and Japanese producers, is able to denominate its Mexican transactions in U.S. dollars. More common is denomination in local currency with some hedging of transactions or, in the case of multi-product multinationals, a periodic calculation of worldwide transaction exposure with any hedging done at the corporate level. Finally, many firms have simply taken the position that, in the long run, profit fluctuations associated with currency fluctuations will balance out, accept this as a normal business condition and make no provision with respect to currency fluctuation.

Transfer Pricing[12]

A transfer price is the internal price charged by a selling department, division, or subsidiary of a company for a material, component, or finished good or service that is supplied to a buying department, division, or subsidiary of the same company. Transfer pricing may be used both by firms that operate in only one national market and by firms that produce and sell their products in a number of national markets.

The need for establishing a transfer price arises, principally, where the buying and selling departments are SBUs, or components that are established as separate profit centers, and where the selling department also sells in external markets. The presumption, of course, is that the buying department should buy from the selling department rather than its competitors and that the selling department should sell to the buying department for a fair price, usually a market price less some credit to reflect the selling department's lower selling expense. Unfortunately, transactions between departments seldom go smoothly. The selling department frequently tends to assume the buying department is a captive customer and may not provide the same level of service as it does to external customers. At the same time, it may actually charge the buying department something above market prices, particularly when facing profit pressures. Buying departments, faced with what they feel is inappropriate treatment, may elect to do business with external suppliers, leading to strained internal relations and questions from customers. In many firms, these situations have led to the development of complex policies that recognize both the realities of the systems used to measure individual SBU performance and the firm's desire to optimize profits at the firm level. Such policies provide guidance but the wide variety of approaches that have been developed suggests that there is no easy solution to a very complex problem.

The problem becomes more complex when the buying and selling departments are in different countries and transfer prices need to take into account variations in tax rates between countries. From a tax standpoint, the firm would like to establish transfer prices which minimize the firm's world-wide tax liability by reporting high profits in low tax countries and vice versa. Recognizing the potential for tax avoidance of this behavior, many countries have introduced rules constraining aggressive behavior with respect to transfer prices and there is general agreement among countries as to the need for an equitable system for profit and tax calculation. Even so, firms still have considerable leeway with respect to transfer prices, which, if implemented just with respect to minimizing tax burden, has the potential to adversely affect managerial behavior. A large U.S. manufacturer, for instance, raised the transfer prices to its Swedish subsidiary in order to avoid the high Swedish corporate income tax rate. In doing so, it seriously penalized its Swedish country manager whose compensation depended heavily on subsidiary profits. For some firms this has led to two separate profit calculations or to rely on other measures than profit to measure managerial performance.

Dumping
The term dumping generally refers to the practice of selling a product in foreign markets at prices either below cost or below prices charged in the exporter's home market. The practice is attractive in situations of low demand or excess capacity in the home market, as sales at low prices in foreign markets may make a positive contribution to fixed costs without running the risk of affecting prices in the home market. Dumping becomes an issue when a domestic producer claims injury because of lost sales due to the low prices of a foreign competitor.

Few issues have been more contentious with respect to trade policy between exporting nations than laws with respect to dumping. Manufacturers in all countries have vigorously sought protection against dumping. The line, however, between legitimate complaints of injury and efforts to seek protection from legitimate competitors is difficult to draw. Cost determination, as we have seen, is highly problematic. Nevertheless, most countries have antidumping laws, which provide for the imposition of countervailing duties on foreign goods of firms found guilty of dumping.

Provisions with respect to dumping were one of the major issues in the Uruguay Round of the GATT (General Agreement on Tariffs and Trade) and a number of procedural and methodological changes have been included in the agreement. Complaints about country antidumping actions can be brought to the World Trade Organization

(WTO), the successor to GATT. Manufacturers, however, are well advised to be familiar with the provisions of the Uruguay Round and the dumping laws in those countries in which they plan to do business.

Gray Markets[13]

Gray markets refers to circumstances in which goods bypass the normal channel of distribution and are then offered for sale at below the prices offered by authorized resellers. This condition may arise in a variety of ways. Within a country, for instance, an original equipment manufacturer (OEM), to which the manufacturer extends a large quantity discount, may over order and then dispose of the excess goods at a small markup, resulting in a lower price than the normal price through distributors. Control Data experienced a variation of this problem with its disk drives when pseudo-OEMs emerged, purchased under the terms of an OEM agreement and undercut the prices of distributors and other resellers. Across borders, the condition may arise when products are sold, in excess of demand, in one country at a lower price than in other countries, resulting in the surplus goods finding their way into other countries. A large pharmaceutical manufacturer, for instance, contracted through an agent in Hong Kong to sell a large quantity of a particular drug at very attractive price to a customer in China. In this case, the order from China was fictitious and the agent in Hong Kong then offered the entire quantity at below normal prices in other countries, causing serious problems for the pharmaceutical manufacturer and its distributors.

It is unlikely that gray markets can ever be eliminated entirely. A number of steps can be taken to reduce their occurrence. Quantity discount schedules can be restructured to make over ordering less attractive. Discount schedules to various classes of trade (e.g., OEMs, VARs or value added resellers, distributors) can be rationalized to more closely reflect the actual value of services performed. Sales of resellers can be monitored and discontinued to those who participate in gray markets. Warranty policies can require purchase only from authorized distributors. Perhaps most importantly, it needs to be recognized that performance measures that focus on volume, or on profits from particular classes of customers versus optimizing profits across markets, may induce behavior that encourages sales through gray markets.

Escalation Policies

Most transactions involving products and services in business markets are completed in a relatively short period of time; hence, the quoted price is also the invoiced price. In many instances, however, the manufacturing cycle may be lengthy or a blanket order may cover a long period of time. In such instances, there may be some provision for price adjustment, particularly in periods of inflation or where some of the supplier's costs are volatile in nature.

In situations where there is sufficient uncertainty about future costs, some manufacturers will quote prices "subject to adjustment to price in effect at time of shipment." While this protects the manufacturer against profit erosion, it shifts all the risk of cost changes to the buyer and raises questions about the nature of the supplier's price adjustment. As a result, most buyers vigorously seek to require the seller to quote firm prices, even in situations of cost uncertainty. In many industries, compromise positions have developed in which the seller's price may be adjusted to reflect changes in the price of materials or labor, limited to changes in some third party index. In the United States, for instance, it is common to use indexes calculated by the Bureau of Labor Statistics. Although these indexes may not reflect a particular manufacturer's cost changes, their impartiality and the fact that they may go down as well as up have given them some degree of acceptability.

Summary

The complexity of pricing decisions, and the inherent uncertainty of their impact, may lead some firms to avoid the kind of comprehensive analysis suggested in this chapter. However, the inherent potential for profit improvement in well managed pricing practices, where as little as 1% improvement in price can result in as much as 10% improvement in operating profit, suggests the importance of such analysis.

Pricing decisions and price policies must take into account not only the firm's costs but also customer sensitivity to price and the competitive situation. Pricing situations vary enormously but the first distinction to be made must be between new and existing products. For business marketers the concept of derived demand is of critical importance, influencing as it does both industry and firm demand. International pricing involves many of the fundamentals of domestic pricing but must also take into account issues of dumping, transfer prices and fluctuation in exchange rates.

In sharp contrast to the notion of a *right* price that can be calculated as the intersection of a supply and a demand curve, we emphasize the importance of considering the pricing decision in the context of an opportunity range in which all but a few situations present the firm with a wide array of options. Consideration of these options should take into account not just the firm's external situation but also its objectives and the price relationship of products that make up a product line.

Good analysis is not enough, however. It must be accompanied by formulation of policies that are clearly communicated to those responsible for their implementation and managed to ensure that the policies are appropriately executed.

Further Reading

Walter Baker, Mike Marn, and Craig Sawada, "Price Smarter on the Net," *Harvard Business Review* 79 (February 2001): 122–27.

Robin Cooper and W. Bruce Chew, "Control Tomorrow's Costs through Today's Designs," *Harvard Business Review* 74 (January/February 1996): 88–97.

Robin Cooper and Regine Slagnulder, "Develop Profitable New Products with Target Costing," *Sloan Management Review* 40 (summer 1999): 23–33.

George E. Cressman Jr. and Thomas T. Nagle, "How to Manage an Aggressive Competitor," *Business Horizons* 45 (March–April 2002): 23–30.

Robert J. Dolan, "How Do You Know When the Price Is Right?" *Harvard Business Review* 73 (September/October 1995): 174–183.

Robert J. Dolan and Abel P. Jeuland, "Experience Curves and Dynamic Demand Models: Implications for Optimal Pricing Strategies," *Journal of Marketing* 45 (winter 1981): 52–62.

Bradley T. Gale, *Managing Customer Value: Creating Quality and Service that Customers Can See* (New York: The Fee Press, 1994).

Sandy D. Jap, "Online Reverse Auctions: Issues, Themes, ad Prospects for the Future," *Journal of Academy of Marketing Science* 30 (fall 2002): 507.

Michael H. Morris and Roger J. Calantone, "Four Components of Effective Pricing," *Industrial Marketing Management* 19, no. 4 (November 1990): 321–29.

C. M. Sashi and Bay O'Leary, "The Role of Internet Auctions in the Expansion of B2B Markets," *Industrial Marketing Management* 31 (February 2002): 103–10.

Arun Sharma, R. Krishan, and Dhruv Grewal, "Value Creation in Markets: A Critical Area of Focus for Business-to-Business Market," *Industrial Marketing Management* 30 (June 2001): 397–98.

David Shipley and Elizabeth Bourdon, "Distributor Pricing in Very Competitive Markets," *Industrial Marketing Management* 19, no. 3 (August 1990): 215–224.

Hermann Simon, "Pricing Opportunities—And How to Exploit Them," *Sloan Management Review* (winter 1992): 55–65.

Stuart St. P. Slatter, "Strategic Marketing Variables under Conditions of Competitive Bidding," *Strategic Management Journal* 11 (May–June 1990): 309–17.

---

[1]For a comprehensive treatment of the realities of oligopolistic pricing, see Ralph G. M. Sultan, *Pricing in the Electrical Oligopoly: Competition or Collusion*, Vol. 1 and 2 (Boston: Harvard University Press, 1974).

[2]Philip Kotler, *Marketing Management: Analysis, Planning, Implementation and Control,* 11th ed. (Englewood Cliffs, NJ: Prentice Hall, Inc., 2003), 478.

[3]George S. Day and David B. Montgomery, "Diagnosing the Experience Curve," *Journal of Marketing* 47 (spring 1983): 44–58.

[4]Robin Cooper and W. Bruce Chew, " Control Tomorrow's Costs Through Today's Designs," *Harvard Business Review* 74 (January/February 1996): 88–97.

[5]George E. Cressman Jr. and Thomas T. Nagle, "How to Manage an Aggressive Competitor," *Business Horizons* 45 (March–April 2002): 23–30.

[6]Joel Dean, "Pricing Policies for New Products," *Harvard Business Review* 54 (November/December 1976): 151–52.

[7]Kotler, *Marketing Management: Analysis, Planning, Implementation and Control*, 260.

[8]Robert D. Buzzell and Bradley T. Gale, *The PIMS Principles: Linking Strategy to Performance* (New York: The Free Press, 1987).

[9]Michael V. Marn and Robert L. Rosiello, "Managing Price, Gaining Profit," *Harvard Business Review,* (September/October 1992): 84–94.

[10]Ibid.

[11]Paul D. Boughton, "The Competitive Bidding Process: Beyond Probability Models," *Industrial Marketing Management* 16, no. 2 (May 1987): 87–94.

[12]For a short, but comprehensive treatment of this subject, see Clive R. Emmanuel and Messaoud Hehafdi, *Transfer Pricing* (London: Academic Press, 1994).

[13]For an excellent discussion of the gray market dilemma, see Frank V. Cespedes, E. Raymond Corey, and V. Katsuri Rangan, "Gray Markets: Causes and Cures," *Harvard Business Review* (July/August, 1988): 75–82.

Chapter 10

E-Business Marketing

A few years ago, e-businesses were starting up and growing at an astounding pace. We then witnessed the dot.com crash in 2000, and the doomsayers were quick to write off the potential of e-business. In the area of business-to-business marketing, however, the use of electronic forms of communication long pre-dates the dot.coms and even during the dot.com crashes electronic communication developed apace. While the reader can find comprehensive coverage in other places, this book would not be complete without a brief discussion of how e-business, or e-commerce as it is often called, relates to business-to-business marketing.

A precise definition of e-business is difficult as much depends on who is doing the definition. The Word Trade Organization, for instance, defines e-business as "...the production, advertising, sale and distribution of products via telecommunications networks." Merrill Lynch, on the other hand, defines e-business as electronic transactions of information exchange. "These transactions can include business-to-business electronic trading of goods and services; financial payment; credit-card, debit, ATM and electronic funds transfer; card issuing and fund processing; bill payment and presentment; and travel distribution along with other information services."[1]

In some definitions then, e-business is intended to suggest, as in the World Trade Organization definition, that all business activities are conducted via telecommunications networks. In others, e-business is seen as a way to transform business activities through the use of Internet technologies.[2] We prefer to define e-business as the application of electronic communications technology to facilitate the buying and selling of products, services, and information over telecommunications networks, including inter and intra-company sharing of information via various electronic means such as EDI, e-mail, e-forms, file transfer, transmission of CAD/CAM drawings, etc. Within this definition, electronic communications are used in a wide variety of way to increase marketing effectiveness, ranging from application to all marketing functions to supporting some, or all, marketing functions. Throughout this chapter, we will use the term e-business to refer to the use of electronic communications to increase marketing effectiveness.

From small businesses, with niche offerings, to the largest multinational enterprises, use of electronic communications, and, particularly the Internet, must increasingly become an integral part of the firm's marketing strategy. B2B e-business, which encompasses electronic buying and selling transactions between organizations and in which e-procurement is a central function, has become central to doing business effectively. In addition, B2B e-business has replaced B2C e-business as the fastest growing area of e-business in the economy. One of the reasons for this development is that purchasing organizations have been driving down costs of product purchases, resulting in the efficiency of transaction costs. By 2005, some observers have estimated that more than \$4.7 trillion worth of B2B e-business transactions would be completed.[3]

This development is also driven by the phenomenal growth in the global marketplace, where firms of all nationalities can participate in creating both interest and awareness, as easily as organizations that are local. Those firms implementing B2B marketing strategies are also enjoying expanded reach, dramatic cost reductions, increased efficiency, and the opportunities to capture lucrative new markets. Yet, these opportunities are not without risk, and prudent managers require incisive information to create B2B strategies that will work for their companies. E-business will not replace traditional marketing planning, but will be an important addition or supplement to marketing and sales efforts.

Electronic Communications and Applications

Throughout this chapter, we will introduce a number of terms relating to Electronic Communications or e-business applications. We briefly describe a number of key terms here.

With respect to communication networks, three terms have come in to wide use.[4]

- Internet: The Internet is the public global network of networks, which is based on the Internet Protocol (IP) and related standards. This technology was designed to provide a standard means of interconnecting networks so that any system could communicate with any other system. The term often includes the World Wide Web, a powerful, standard facility for network-based publishing, as well as electronic mail and the growing suite of other network application that are based on Internet communications.

- Intranet: An intranet is a private application of the same internetworking technology, software, and applications within a private network, for use within an enterprise. It may be entirely disconnected from the public Internet but is usually linked to it and protected from unauthorized access by security firewall systems.

- Extranet: An extranet uses Internet/intranet technology to serve an extended enterprise, including defined sets of customers or suppliers or other partners. It is usually open to selected partners.

Several broad categories of application software have emerged that are involved either directly or indirectly in e-business.

- Electronic Data Interchange (EDI): Some twenty years before anyone used the term e-business, many firms were using EDI to exchange computer-readable data in a standard format, of some kind, over high-bandwidth telephone connections. Information exchanged was usually transaction related but other uses included securing quotations or other information.[5] Data transfer in EDI is most commonly done using a VAN (a value added network, designed to carry EDI traffic between participants). which provides the necessary infrastructure to bridge incompatible networks and to transmit data securely. A drawback to EDI is the relatively high cost of setting up VAN accounts for the trading partners. EDI can also be conducted over the Internet, but with less assurance of security and reliability.

- Enterprise Resource Planning (ERP): Business software has been developed that integrates all facets of a business, including planning, manufacturing, sales, and marketing. Generally, these are suites that extend the concepts of manufacturing resource planning (MRP) to the whole enterprise.[6] Originally internal to the enterprise, using an Intranet, we increasingly find that that application servers are being used to connect Web-based e-business applications, using an Extranet, with an ERP suite in ways ranging from simply providing access to the firm's website via a browser to integrating ERP functions between business partners.

- Customer Relationship Management (CRM): Generally integrated with an ERP system, CRM systems have been developed to assist firms in targeting, acquiring, and retaining customers. More broadly, CRM can be defined as any system used to enhance relationships with customers.

- Sales Force Automation (SFA): Sometimes part of a CRM system, SFA systems have been developed to allow firms to manage the entire selling process, including order entry, post-sale follow-up, lead tracking, forecasting, and customer historical data.

The Business Marketing Implications of E-Business[7]

This book builds on business marketing management thinking paradigm, in which marketing is seen as the set of organizational activities which effectively connect the firm's, abilities and competence to customer wants and needs. This paradigm remains valid as we discuss the implications of e-business to organizational markets. Analytical thinking and good marketing decision-making are still valid but e-business influences the way the marketing mix is configured and implemented by the use of information and telecommunications technology. In Chapters 11 and 12, we will discuss how the Internet has become a tool to assist in investigating and tracking markets and influencers. In this chapter, we will focus on how the critical marketing decisions are influenced by e-business.

Product (and Service) Implications

Products, and services, that satisfy customers' wants and needs are still at the heart of a firm's marketing strategy. Through the use of the Internet, firms can still further augment the physical product with application information and, in some instances, with product service. Many products such as books and software can be made totally available electronically. An incredible variety of business services are now available via the Internet, ranging from travel services and hotel accommodations to sophisticated databases and consulting reports. In addition, the Internet has facilitated the expansion of customized products and services.

E-technologies have entered all phases of the value-added chain in manufacturing companies. Increasingly, complex products with ever-shorter life cycles call for the automation of design, development and control processes using a variety of new technologies. Co-modeling systems allow multiple engineers in different locations to work on the same computer aided design (CAD) model simultaneously. Visualization software lets people view the design work of others in 3-D. In addition, the changing nature of the supply chain, with outsourcing of design responsibility for parts, assemblies and subsystems is forcing firms to put in place systems to manage the collaborative design efforts of many separate organizations.[8]

Sethi, Pant, and Sethi have observed that many firms are now adopting integrated web-based new product development (NPD) systems. They point out, however, that their mere use is not likely to significantly improve the NPD process.[9] An organization desiring to employ the web in its NPD process can use it at varying levels of functionality and sophistication, ranging from a tool for automating manual tasks and exchanging data to a means of integrating various intra-and inter organization NPD functions and processes. They have developed a conceptual framework to guide firms in effective ways to take advantage of web-based applications.

Pricing Implication

The Internet has created both opportunities and threats to the way firms establish prices and manage the dynamics of pricing in the market. Access to digital data, on the one hand, provides ample opportunity to better understand customer-buying behavior, enhance segmentation and categorization of buyers, and foster more precise pricing strategies. The better access to information allows for faster responses to fluctuating demands and faster implementation of changes. Through the use of customer response data, firms also build a better understanding of the trade-offs that users are making and the value associated with different features. At the same time, through use of the Internet customers become more knowledgeable regarding prices, competitive offerings and price trends and so are better positioned to put pressure on their supplier's prices.

Using Internet technology creates new challenges in managing the firm's pricing strategy. This is particularly true when product strategies vary across regions or national borders, or from one market segment to another. This is also the case when prices on the Internet differ from prices offered through alternative channels. These difficulties do not mean, however, that a firm should abstain from price differences in different regions or channels. However, for customers it must be obvious why such price differences exist (i.e., can the higher price be justified because of easier access, better support, more efficient after-sales service, etc.).

For small players the Internet allows for opportunistic pricing strategies targeting new segments, providing substantial revenue growth. Where economies of scale provide opportunities for cost reductions, use of the Internet can significantly increase the ability of firms to use price reductions to target additional customers. For example, through Internet based pricing strategies, the market share of the top 500 US building-products distributors changed dramatically from 1993 to 2001. In 1993, the top 10 companies shared 40% of the market; this share grew to 70 % over an eight-year period, leaving the remaining 490 firms with only 30% to share.[10]

There are three main routes to profit from flexibility in a firm's pricing policy.[12] First, precision in price levels and price communication is central to enhanced profitability. The key is to understand the "price-indifference" band (i.e., the price band where customers do not change their purchasing behavior). A solid knowledge of where the product is within this price-indifference band can dramatically impact the profit. Finding the boundaries of such a price-indifference band can be difficult, costly and time-consuming. Various techniques, such as conjoint analysis, have been effectively be used for such determinations. The Internet can also be used effectively to determine such boundaries. For example, firms supplying large numbers of customers could increase prices by 2% for, say, every twenty-fifth customer and track the impact on sales.

Second, the Internet can help in responding quickly to market changes. Traditional price changes take time, are costly, and may be difficult to communicate to the distribution channel as new price lists are printed, distributed and put into use. On-line price changes allow companies to make immediate changes, at little cost and inconvenience. For example, on-line pricing can help in clearing slow-movers, or to service larger customer groups at a relatively low cost.

Third, the enhanced ability to understand customer behavior though web-based interactions has substantially improved pricing effectiveness, particularly through the use of *post hoc* segmentation. [12] Apriori segmentation is the traditionally discussed method whereby marketers segment a market based on pre-specified criteria, such as firm size, application market, geographical boundaries or channel preferences, usually relying on managers' intuition, analysis of secondary data sources, analysis of customer databases, etc. Some illustrations of apriori segmentation schemes are as follows but their price sensitivity can only be estimated.

1. Heavy versus moderate and light truck users.
2. North versus south regions,
3. Professional versus non-professional buying organizations.

With *post hoc* segmentation, segments are not defined until after the product or service has been introduced. Primary market research is used to collect classification and descriptor variables for members of the target market. Multivariate analytical techniques are used to define each segment and develop a scoring algorithm for placing all members of the target market into segments. Algorithms can then be developed to utilize the Internet to examine the price sensitivity for the various segments.

In Chapter 3, we discussed the increasing use of the Internet by business buyers as part of the purchasing process. Vertical and horizontal auctions are now common. While these may represent an opportunity for suppliers seeking new customers, they may also represent a threat to existing suppliers with their increased focus on prices as the principal decision factor. Firm must, therefore, decide whether or not to participate in an auction and, if so, must develop an appropriate pricing strategy. Through their use of the Internet, buyers also can develop much larger pools of prospective suppliers, increasing the need for suppliers to understand a larger array of competitors when faced with competitive situations.

Distribution Implications[13]

In the late 1990s, when the dot.com craze was at it highest, one of the predictions was that the Internet would eliminate traditional distribution strategies and all intermediaries between the factory and the final customer. This prediction has certainly not held up. On the contrary, although some *disintermediation* has taken place as firms are optimizing their "go-to-market" strategies, we are also seeing new intermediaries being created.

Regardless of disintermediation or creation of new intermediaries, channel conflict has always been an issue for business marketers and the advent of the Internet has exacerbated the issue. In a recent survey of 50 manufacturers, 66% indicated channel conflict was the biggest issue they face in their online sales strategy, three times as many as the second most frequent response. How suppliers manage this conflict will be an important factor in their success.

Generally, the advent of online commerce has given rise to three types of channel conflicts:

1.   Goal divergence is always a source of conflict when the objectives of the manufacturer and the distributor differ. As manufacturers have introduced Internet options ranging from online product catalogues, training modules, technical specifications and help desks, to online ordering and even monitoring of products in operation, and price lists, these initiatives have not always resonated with distributors who have felt their livelihood threatened.

2.   When the conflicts deriving from goal divergence remain unresolved the disputes pertaining to customer handling, territorial assignments, functions to be served and technology to be used create un-

satisfactory situations. Such unresolved conflicts can do nothing but create lower effectiveness and efficiency in the market strategy.

3.   Finally, there are many instances where there are simply differing perceptions of reality, hence actions may be misconstrued and lead to unresolved conflict in turn leading to a breakdown in the companies channel strategy.

In order to reduce such conflicts, a number of differing efforts are used to avoid disagreement. Some companies have chosen to offer different products online and direct versus the offline and indirect channel. In other cases, distributors have been granted exclusivity or new brands. Alternatively, price differentiation has been used, often supported by value-added activities such as personalization (done by the distributor). In yet other cases, manufacturers have chosen to either take over the roles previously performed by distributors or created their own intermediary sales organizations. Other firms have chosen to strengthen the distributor's role and have even paid financial compensations, to ensure loyalty and ongoing support to products sold online.

Disintermediation takes place when suppliers are offered a direct channel to their customers, eliminating layers of distribution. Re-intermediation is the reverse process and occurs when the shifting or transfer of intermediary functions needs to take place and suppliers or manufacturers add new channels. With the advent of the Internet, the introduction of on-line intermediaries such as electronic malls or market places, directory and search engine services, and comparison aids using agents all have created new needs, as well as new roles of re-intermediation.

The reasons to use online intermediaries are several: In some cases, they know more about the customers, the application areas, the product categories or local markets. They may also be carrying multiple product lines, thus facilitating the purchasing process at the customer level. Some intermediaries also can build profiles of the customer choices based on a much wider array of business than most manufacturers would be able to do by selling directly. As a multi-product vendor, they can learn much more about customers and use this across product categories.[14]

Promotion Implications
Historically, B2B marketers have relied primarily on personal selling, either by a direct sales force or by distributors to promote products and services. These face-to-face contacts by sales persons have been augmented through a wide variety of means, including print advertising, brochures, direct mail, phone contacts by inside sales persons, and trade shows. Now, the Internet and other modern telecommunication

technologies have dramatically altered the way business marketers promote their products and services. E-mail, web sites, and extranets are all now widely used to increase the speed of communication and lower the cost of customer contacts.

As we will discuss in Chapter 11, the cost of an individual sales call has dramatically increased. Routine sales calls, therefore, are being replaced, or supplemented, with various means of electronic communication, including telemarketing, e-mail, and extensive use of web sites. Customer relationship management systems (CRM) have been developed which allow for the integration of data base information based on past history and secondary data concerning customer activities from external sources, on-line monitoring of customer equipment and service operations, supported by video conferencing, and collaborative work spaces on closed intranet links directly with customers.

Few firms today can afford not to have a website providing a way for customers to obtain at least basic information about the firms products or services. In some instances the website may be limited to simply making product or contact information available. In other instances, the website can be used to establish an agreement between the firm and a customer about how to conduct business on-line. GE Medical Systems, for instance, a General Electric Company going to market as GE Healthcare, has a website which provides basic information about the company and its products but which is also linked to a website that has created a "whole new way of doing business electronically", with paper free Internet orders using its eCommerce Master Agreement.[15] Other firms allow customers to have their own web page with tailored access to information on products, in-house experts, or services.

The Internet has allowed firms to build networks of customers, usually called user groups, which intrinsically create value though the membership and interaction possibilities. This notion has been attributed to Robert Metcalfe who founded 3Com Corporation and designed the Ethernet protocol for computer networks. Accordingly, Metcalfe's Law states that, "The usefulness, or utility, of a network is equal to the square of the number of users," as shown in Figure 10.1.[16]

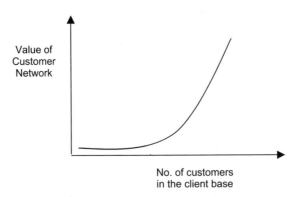

Figure 10.1: Illustration of Metcalfe's Law of Network Utility

Volvo Construction Equipment, for example, is developing strong user groups that enhance customer loyalty and repurchase rates. This is augmented with e-mail newsletters and training courses on demand. Volvo Truck, the sister organization of Volvo Construction Equipment, offers to maintain all fleet information and maintenance records for its fleet customers, thus removing this burden from the customers and providing a differentiation strategy for Volvo Truck.

SAS (a leading supplier of ERP systems) encourages its users to join a SAS Users Group as an excellent way to help get the most value from the SAS System. Users groups, according to SAS, offer a unique opportunity to:[17]

- enhance your understanding of SAS Institute software and services
- exchange ideas about using your software and hardware most productively
- learn of new Institute products and services as soon as they become available
- have more influence over the direction of Institute software and services
- enhance managerial and leadership skills by serving as a user group officer, coordinating involvement in annual and regional SAS user group conferences, or organizing a new user group.

Related to user groups are B2B chat rooms where visitors log on to an on-line chat room and post questions to a moderator and webinars (aka as web seminars/web casts), designed to either provide leads or to lead to requests for proposals.

212

New developments in advertising using the Internet are continuing to but at least the following formats are currently in wide use:

- Banner ads, usually placed on a website featuring complementary projects. In a field research study of 100 business e-marketers, it was discovered that banners are still very effective despite their ease of use. [18]
- Skyscraper ads, running down the right or left side of a website
- Pop-up ads, which burst, open on the computer screen.
- B2B ad networks, which link together B2B websites, either vertically (through an industry) or horizontally (across a mass market).

With the advent of e-mail has come the development of mailing lists, offered by providers such as listserv or listbuilder. According to Network Solutions, successful firms build their own in-house lists and use creative, short write-ups to customer groups, which yield good results. Such lists can be used effectively to distribute a company newsletter or other types of information.

Although many firms have websites and brochures-online, very few ensure that common search engines are optimized; that is, that the firm's name and products are prominently featured when customers are conducting searches. Sometimes the optimization can be supplemented with search engine advertising, which is paid advertising specifically through the Internet search engines promoting the firm's offerings.

Despite the fact that firms use multiple techniques, they often let the click-through links go only to the firm's website instead of connecting potential customers to dedicated offerings or promotion campaigns, and therefore, miss promotional opportunities for reaching new customers. This issue can also be generalized to the design of the firm's web-platform, which should make it easy for the user to navigate. Increasingly, as VOIP (voice over internet protocol) develops, websites (particularly intranet sites) will also allow customers to make audio contact with customer service representatives, by merely clicking on the web page for more personal treatment.

Successful marketing efforts using the web exclusively are non-existent, and the most effective campaigns consist of a multi-prong effort where firms can engage prospective customers through direct mail campaigns, sales calls, email marketing, and websites to capture the attention, interest, desire and choice of potential customers in the marketplace. Successful campaigns must be based on a solid marketing analysis, clearly chosen customer segments, and an integrated marketing mix aimed of satisfying the target market.

Developments of E-Business

Although the failing of the dot.com boom left many early Internet enthusiasts disappointed, when it came to implications for business, great inroads were actually being made, particularly in business-to-business marketing. In a study from October 2003, ISM/Forrester Research Report On Technology In Supply Management it was reported that firms increasingly are using the internet to purchase direct and indirect goods and services with savings as a result. It was reported that the percentage of direct materials purchased using the Internet surpassed that of indirect materials.[19] The study further reported that that it was the better savings opportunities that caused large firms to lead in Internet adoption because the larger buying power helped to contain costs and secure supplier participation.

The study also showed that success in online purchasing is a matter of position, priorities, and persistence, and larger firms are in a better position to afford the available solutions and gain supplier participation. However, only 23% of the 294 participating firms used online auctions whereas 33% used so-called e-marketplaces, with non-manufacturing firms being the most advanced. (An e-marketplace is an Internet-based broker of goods or services within a community of sellers and buyers. It should have an open structure and a level playing field for all participants.) Interestingly, the study also revealed that online collaboration between customers and suppliers were reported by nearly two-thirds of all firm. A similar percentage of participating firms also reported online use of *request for proposals*.

Summary

Business marketers of all types are integrating the Internet and electronic communications into their core strategies. E-business is the broad term applied to communications, business processes, and transactions that are carried out through electronic technology. An intranet is an internal network that is accessible only to company employees and other authorized users. By contrast, an extranet is a private network that uses Internet-based technology to link companies with suppliers, customers, and other partners. Extranets allow the business marketer to customize information for customers and to seamlessly share information with specific customers in a secure environment.

For business marketers, the Internet has been effective as a powerful communication medium, an alternative channel, a new venue for a host of services and a data-gathering tool for integrating the supply chain. The Internet strategy must be carefully woven into the fabric of the firm's overall marketing strategy. The Internet offers important benefits, including reduced transaction costs, reduced cycle time, supply chain integration, information accessibility, and closer customer relationships. Given the failure of many dot.com companies, the lesson for business marketers is that the Internet is an enabling technology that complements, rather than replaces, traditional competitive tools.

The e-business strategy must be carefully crafted, beginning with a focus on objectives. Once the objectives have been established, an Internet strategy can be formulated. Included in the strategy is a consideration of the product-related dimensions of the Internet offering, the most visible of which is the firm's web site. Extranets, electronic catalogs, and customer information must also be integrated in to the "product." Several fundamental channel-of-distribution issues must be evaluated, including the impact of the Internet on present channels and channel partners, channel efficiencies, and the Internet as a separate channel to the market. Pricing issues are also significant, particularly in light of the impact of trading communities and auction sites. Finally, marketing communication strategies consider the extent to which the firm provides transactional capabilities on the Web site and how the Internet strategy is integrated with other promotional vehicles. To an important degree, the Internet provides a powerful medium for developing a one-to-one relationship with customers in the business marketplace

Further Reading

Anitesh Barua, Prabhudeve Konnana, Andres B. Whinston, and Fang Yin, "Driving E-Business Excellence," *MIT Sloan Management Review* 43 (fall 2001): 36-44.

Sandy D. Jap. "Online Reverse Auctions: Issues, Themes, and Prospects for the Future," *Journal of the Academy of Marketing Science* 30 (fall 2002): 507.

Steven Kaplan and Mohanbir Sawhney, "E-Hubs: The New B2B Marketplaces," *Harvard Business Review,* (May-June 2000): 97-103.

Pricewaterhousecoopers, *E-Business Technology Forecast*, (Menlo Park, CA, May 1999).

C. M. Sashi and Bay O'Leary, "The Role of Internet Auctions in the Expansion of B2B Markets," *Industrial Marketing Management* 31 (February 2002): 103-110.

E-Business Marketing

Gary P. Schneider, *Electronic Commerce: Fourth Annual Edition* (Boston, MA: Thomson Course Technology, 2003).

Barry Silverstein, *Business to Business Internet Marketing*, 3d ed., (Gulf Breeze, FL: Maximum Press, 2001).

Stewart McKie, *E-Business Best Practices: Leveraging Technology for Business Advantage*, (New York: John Wiley & Sons, 2001).

---

[1] PricewaterhouseCoopers LLP, *E-Business Technology Forecast*, (Menlo Park, CA: May 1999), 1

[2] For e-business definitions, visit IBM's web-site at http://www.ibm.com/ ebusiness.

[3] Rob Spiegal. "Online Trading Gains Steams," *Electronic News* 48, no.14 (April 2002): 32.

[4] "What's an extranet? and other key terms," Richard R. Reisman, President, Teleshuttle Corporation, http;//www.teleshuttle.com/media/extradef.htm 12/14/04

[5] See Chapter 5, Electronic Commerce, Third Annual Edition, Gary P. Schneider, Thomson Course Technology, Boston, MA, 2002 for a comprehensive discussion of EDI and its transition to e-electronic commerce.

[6] See Chapter 2 in E- Stewart McKie, *Business Best Practices,* (New York: John Wiley & Sons, Inc., 2001), for a comprehensive discussion of ERP and is relation to E-business Management

[7] See Wilson, Susan G. and Ivan Abel, "So you want to get involved in E-commerce", *Industrial Marketing Management,* 31 (2002): 85-94, for further implications.

[8] See http://www.fortune.com/fortune/services/sections/fortune/tech/2003_o4design.html

[9] Rajesh Sethi, Somendra Pant, and Anju Sethis, "Web-based Product Development Systems Integration and New Product Outcomes: A Conceptual Framework," *The Journal of Product Innovation Management*, (January 2003): 37-56.

[10] Walter L. Baker and others, "Getting Prices Right on the Web," *The McKinsey Quarterly*, (2001, Special Edition): 56.

[11] Ibid., 57-59.

[12] For a comprehensive review on the subject, See: http://www.dssresearch.com/toolkit/resource /papers/SR01.asp

[13] See Kevin L. Webb, "Managing channels of distribution in the age of electronic commerce" *Industrial Marketing Management* 31 (2002): 95-102 for a comprehensive discussion of this issue.

[14] Verda Lief, Bruce D. Temkin, Kathryn McCarty, Jerremy Sharrard and Tobias P. Brown. *e-Marketplaces Reshape the B-to-B Landscape.* Accessed on 2 April, 2000. http://www.forrester.com//ER/Research/Report/Analysis/O,1338,8th,FF.html.

[15] http://www.gehealthcare.com/worldwide.html

[16] For a comprehensive review of Metcalfe's Law, see Larry Downes and Chunka Mui. *Unleashing the Killer App: Digital Strategies for Market Dominance.* (Boston, MA: Harvard Business School Press, 1998).

[17] Retrieved December 22, 2004, http://support.sas.com/usergroups/benefits.html

[18] Marketing Sherpa, *SPECIAL REPORT: Top 10 B2B Internet Marketing Tactics that Worked Best in 2000,* (2001, January 1) Know How #13, Retrieved from http://library.marketingsherpa.com/barrier.cfm?CID=1300

[19] Kristin Kioa and Tina Murphy, *ISM/Forrester Research Announce Results of Latest Report on Technology in Supply Management: Online purchasing continues to grow, especially larger companies* (2003, October 27). Retrieved October 11, 2004, from http://www.ism.ws/ismreport/forrester/frob102003pr.cfm

Chapter 11

Business Marketing Communication: Personal Selling

The traditional purpose of communication, as part of the marketing mix, has been to inform, persuade or remind. This may be appropriate for some products but it falls far short of the purpose and nature of communicating with business customers. In this chapter, we develop a more comprehensive framework for considering the purposes of communicating with customers and then address the role of personal selling in the communication process.

An Overview of Communication

Marketing strategies are designed to capitalize on the firm's strengths, in order to exploit opportunities in selected markets or in target market segments. How well these opportunities are exploited is a function of both the appropriateness of the chosen strategies and the extent to which they are understood and accepted by enough customers to achieve the firm's objectives. Emerson's words about the builder of a better mousetrap notwithstanding, few products or services achieve success in the market place without an effective communication program; a communication program which has as its ultimate objective obtaining the customer's order.[1] To achieve this objective, the communication program must also accomplish the following:

1. Ensure that the firm's communication efforts are targeted to those prospective customers whose needs most closely match the firm's product or service attributes.
2. Within the targeted customer organizations, identify decision makers and important decision influences.
3. Create awareness and interest in the product or service.
4. Translate, or assist the customer to translate, product attributes into benefits.
5. Fine tune the product or service to more closely meet customer requirements.

6. Monitor the after sale situation to assure customer satisfaction and to modify the marketing strategy with respect to future customer needs.

The effectiveness with which these elements of the communication program are implemented is critical to the success of the firm's marketing strategy. The nature of the business buying process, with a relatively small number of potential customers, the existence of multiple buying influences, and the frequent need for negotiation, plus the general technical complexity of products or services, is such that the predominant method of communication is personal selling. Non-personal methods of communication, particularly direct mail, telemarketing, and e-mail marketing, also play an important role in communication strategy, either in support of the personal selling effort or as stand alone methods to achieve communication objectives. In this chapter, we first review the principal methods available to firms to communicate with customers and the concept of an integrated approach to communication. We then extensively discuss the nature of personal selling and its management.

The Methods of Business Communication
Traditionally personal selling, advertising, sales promotion, direct marketing, and public relations have been considered the principal methods of communication (or elements of the promotional mix). For business marketing we prefer the following more comprehensive classification scheme of communication methods:

- Personal Selling. Any face-to face interaction with one or more prospective purchasers for the purpose of making a sale. Activities range from prospecting for customers, to providing information on the product or service, to order solicitation, to post-sales service. Personal selling may be done by the firm's own sales force, by others in the firm who have some form of client or customer responsibility, by an agent of the firm (normally a manufacturer's representative), or by a distributor.

- Advertising. Any form of paid non-personal presentation or promotion of ideas, goods, or services by an identified sponsor in print or electronic media. In business marketing this tends to be principally in print media, oriented toward the business community in general, or targeted to selected industry or occupational segments. In addition to providing information, advertising may be used to solicit a specific response such as a request for further information or, in some instances, an order for the product or service.

- Direct Mail. Any communication mailed to a specific individual buying influence. As with advertising, direct mail may be used to provide information on a product or service or to elicit a specific response.

- Telemarketing. Any contact made with a customer or prospective customer by phone. Growth in the use of this form of business communication has been explosive. From its original use as support for the personal selling effort, telemarketing has in some instances replaced personal selling as the principal method of order solicitation and it is now widely used for lead qualifying, for marketing research, and for providing customers with ordering, service, or product information.

- E-mail Marketing. Business communications and transmissions over networks and through computers, specifically the buying and selling of goods and services and the transfer of funds through digital communications.

- Trade Shows. Any participation at an industry or trade show by means of an exhibit, or other form of presence. Trade show participation is usually designed to inform customers about products or services, to identify prospective customers, or to identify prospective agents or distributors.

- Seminars, conferences/technical papers. Any form of technical (i.e., non-commercial) presentation, usually by the firm's technical personnel regarding new products or their application. In some instances the presentation may be made by an industry recognized expert outside the firm.

- Sales Promotion. Any use of samples, contests, catalogs, brochures, or other means to create interest or awareness of products not included above. Some sales promotion efforts, in particular contests, focus on the firm's sales force, or on the sales force of its distributors, and are designed to provide additional stimulus to the sales effort. In many instances, contests are used very effectively to stimulate end user in-

terest in a product or service. (Note: The traditional definition of Sales Promotion usually includes trade shows and
may include direct mail or telemarketing. For business marketing, we believe these deserve separate identification.)

- Public Relations. Any of a variety of programs designed to
  promote or protect a company's image or its individual
  products.

In addition to the foregoing categories, businesses communicate with
customers in a number of other ways. Suppliers' engineers and customers' engineers interact at professional meetings or may jointly participate in standards meetings. Similar interactions take place between
individuals in supplying and buying firms in other functional categories such as finance, production, or human resources and at various
levels of management.

The variety of tools available to communicate with customers,
and the number of non-marketing avenues of communication, suggest
the need for coordination of communication efforts. Much has been
heard recently about integrated marketing communications (IMC), a
concept of particular interest to consumer products companies, but also
of interest to business marketers. According to the American Association of Advertising Agencies, IMC has as its objective the combination
of advertising, direct marketing, sales promotion and public relations
to provide clarity, consistency and maximum communications' impact
through the seamless integration of discrete messages.

The concept of coordinated communication efforts is hardly
new. It has long been recognized that advertising or direct marketing
can support the personal selling effort by introducing the firm and its
products to customers in advance of calls by the sales force, or by
reaching buying influences that the sales force cannot call on. Similarly, it has long been recognized that technical papers describing new
products or their applications can play an effective role in the introduction and acceptance of new products. The changing interest in IMC
may reflect the fact that in many instances communication efforts have
not been well coordinated. Sales promotion material, for instance, designed to support the efforts to the field sales force, frequently goes
unused because the sales force does not feel it is effective. Similarly,
leads developed by advertising messages may not be appropriately
screened, with the potential for wasting the time of the sales force.
Most companies are moving to the concept of a *leveraged sales force*.
A sales force should focus on selling the company's more complex and

customized products to key accounts, and the company should turn over low-end selling through the use of multi-channel integration.[2]

For business marketers, the imperative is a carefully coordinated communication program which effectively and economically utilizes all the tools of communication, that recognizes all the ways in which communications can take place between the firm and its customers, and that is well understood and supported by all those who come in contact with the firm's customers. Given the role of personal selling as the most important element in the communications mix we first discuss the role of the salesperson and management of the field sales force; both because of their importance, per se, and because their understanding is critical to understanding the role of other communication tools which we discuss in Chapter 12 either to support personal selling or as substitutes for it.

Also important to business marketers are the distribution channels. Business partners, in the distribution system, also support the personal selling effort, and are discussed in Chapter 13.

Integrated Multi-Channel Models[3]
Figure 11.1 shows an example of a multi-channel strategy that many firms are using as an innovative sales support function, particularly for small and medium-sized business customers. Note that the channels are arranged in terms of their relative selling expense, in the left column of the model. Sales tasks are arranged across the top of the model as a continuous flow through the sales cycle. The importance in the use of this model is to emphasize that the direct sales channel (personal selling) can be used for maximum effectiveness in serving large customers. Business partners (the distribution channel) can be focused toward middle-market customers, with occasional support by salespersons to help partners close key strategic deals. The smaller customers can be well served through direct marketing, telemarketing, and Internet marketing.

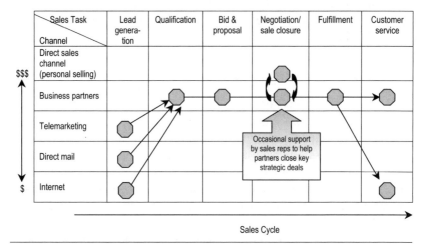

Sales Task / Channel	Lead genera-tion	Qualification	Bid & proposal	Negotiation/ sale closure	Fulfillment	Customer service
Direct sales channel (personal selling)						
Business partners						
Telemarketing						
Direct mail						
Internet						

Occasional support by sales reps to help partners close key strategic deals

Sales Cycle

Source: Adapted from Lawrence G. Friedman, *Go To Market Strategy: Advanced Techniques for Selling More Products, To More Customers, More Profitably*. Boston: Butterworth-Heinemann, 2002, 243. Copyright 2002; Reprinted with permission from Elsevier Science.

Figure 11.1: Multi-Channel Integration Map: Simple Example of High-Coverage Partnering Model

The Role of the Salesperson

What, precisely, should the salesperson do and how should the sales force be managed? These are key questions for marketing strategy. Some years ago, Drucker asserted, "There will always, one can assume, be need for some selling. But the aim of marketing is to make selling superfluous. The aim of marketing is to know and understand customers so well that the product or service fits them and sells itself."[4] To the extent that this statement is rooted in the view that the task of salesperson is to sell things to people that they do not want or need, the assertion may be appropriate. It appears to assume, however, that products or services can be so precisely designed as to require no modification and so comprehensively explained in non-personal ways as to require no assistance in understanding or application; conditions which are seldom the case for business marketers. More recently, it has been asserted, "Selling is Dying."[5] As explained by the author, however, what he really meant was that selling in the future will be different, with emphasis on long-term affiliations and relationships that help people buy; a view that generally coincides with ours. More specifically, however, it is our view that personal selling should reflect the firm's marketing strategy and that each firm should develop its own model of personal selling, which fits its marketing strategy. In some instances, this may be a variation of one of the many generic personal selling models that have been proposed. Hence, we start by examining three such models:

- Stimulus Response. This model is based on the assumption that a standardized message, delivered by a salesperson to a predetermined number of customers, will result in a predictable number of orders. Its key requirement is the salesperson's ability to get the opportunity to deliver the message. The model tends to have limited application in business selling as it is appropriate principally for one-time sales, where there is one easily identifiable decision maker, or for very routine sales situations. It does, however, have the merit of simplicity and is easily implemented.

- AIDA (Attention, Interest, Desire, Action).[6] This model is based on the assumption that there are a number of standardized steps through which the salesperson should lead the customer: first, get the customer's attention; then create interest in the product; then create desire for the product; and finally, get the order. The key requirement of this model is the salesperson's ability to determine when to move from one step to the next. The model has somewhat broader application than the Stimulus Response model. It does suggest some of the dynamics that may be involved in a sales call. Nevertheless, it also has limited applicability in business selling. It presumes that there is a single decision maker and that every sales call has the potential to result in an order. Still further, evidence suggests it is difficult to determine when to move from one step to the next. In generally it is most useful as a starting point for consideration of additional task requirements.

- Consultative Selling. This model is based on the assumption that high margin sales will result from focusing on improvement of customers' profits, resulting in customers willing to share these improved profits with the supplier.[7] While it takes the customer's most fundamental objective of profit improvement into account, it has been criticized for failing to recognize that many customers are not willing to enter into a relationship of the nature proposed by the model; that for many suppliers the opportunity is limited to significantly impact a customer's profit; and that it does not adequately take into account the personal interactions between the salesperson and individuals in a customer's organization.

To the extent that these models are appropriate to a particular strategy they may be useful in suggesting the role of the salesperson, how he or she should be selected and trained, and how the sales force should be organized. As indicated, they have serious limitations. For instance, both the Stimulus Response and AIDA models fail to take the customer into account, either with respect to the individual, and his or her characteristics, or with respect to the customer's organization, its objectives and its way of doing business. In essence, the customer is seen as someone to be manipulated by the salesperson. More broadly, all three models are generic. They fail to take into account the firm's marketing strategy and do not adequately connect marketing strategy to the work of the salesperson. Still further, they do not suggest the extent to which the customer's view of the supplier is influenced by the salesperson's behavior. As the purchasing manager of a large electric utility explained:

> *Our view of a supplier changes substantially every time the supplier assigns a new salesperson. There is enormous variation in how they represent their principals. Some sell on personality, some sell on service. Some try to be the expert on every question. Others act more as conduits to connect us to those with specialized knowledge. In one situation, the salesperson was the only contact we ever had with the supplier. When he was transferred, the new salesperson introduced us to so many people in his firm we thought we were dealing with a different company.*[8]

The key point of the foregoing is that marketing strategy should specify an appropriate model of personal selling. In a limited number of instances, a generic model may be appropriate. In most instances, the model needs to be uniquely crafted to fit the firm's strategy and needs to be changed when the strategy changes. It is used to guide all aspects of personal selling and sales force management, including training, selection and compensation.

To provide the understanding necessary to the development of an appropriate model we first introduce the concept of role as it applies to the work of a salesperson. We next consider how the salesperson's role may be influenced by a number of situational factors. We then address issues in sales force management as well as the special issues associated with national or international accounts and the use of agents versus ones own sales force.

Role Concepts

In this chapter we use the term *role* to categorize a set of activities associated with a particular aspect of a sales position or assignment.[9] In some selling situations, the salesperson may enact a single or limited number of roles, as might be the case in the routine sale of Maintenance, Operating and Repair (MRO) items. In more complex selling situations, the salesperson may have a number of roles, as might be the case where the salesperson is expected to maintain relations with existing accounts, prospect for new accounts, introduce new products, secure orders from existing accounts and, in some instances, provide after sales service. To enhance our understanding of the salesperson's role we introduce a number of role concepts.

Role Set and Role Expectations

As salespersons enact the role specified by the marketing strategy, they relate, directly or indirectly, to individuals in other positions, both within their firm and in the customer's organization. These individuals make up the person's role set. At a minimum, the role set would include the sales manager and key buying influences in customers' organizations. All those in the role set depend on the salesperson's performance to some extent and so develop beliefs as to what the salesperson should or should not do as part of his or her role. These prescriptions and proscriptions are designated as role expectations.

Role Conflict and Boundary Roles

Role conflict occurs when the expectations of one person in an individual's role set are at variance with the expectations of another. Such conflict is a fact of life, in all social situations. Family expectations, for example, frequently conflict with those of employers. For the salesperson, role conflict is particularly acute. Salespersons occupy what are called boundary positions; that is, positions that interface between two organizations. Such positions are particularly susceptible to role conflict, as a result of lack of power over persons in the other firm, from failure of others to understand the demands made on them, and from the great variation in objectives between organizations. The conflict between the firm's desire for a high price and the customer's desire for a low price, and the lack of the salesperson's authority to require the customer to buy, might exemplify this kind of conflict. Even within the firm, opportunities for role conflict tend to be greater for salespersons than for others, particularly in complex selling situations where the salesperson enacts a number of roles or represents products with significantly different marketing strategies. In such situations, it is not unusual for product managers to have very different expectations as to appropriate sales approaches or to attempt to impose conflicting requirements as to time devoted to their products.

Role Ambiguity and Role Inaccuracy
Role ambiguity and role inaccuracy are related but arise very differently. Role ambiguity occurs when the nature of expectations of various members of the role set are unclear. Role ambiguity tends to be high for salespersons. The nature of personal selling, with many unanswered questions as to what makes for success, makes it difficult to clearly spell out all aspects of a salespersons role. Boundary role positions exacerbate the problem, as information about customer expectations may be difficult to obtain. Role inaccuracy occurs when the salesperson has an incorrect understanding of behavioral expectations with respect to some aspect of the job that is, in fact, specified by the job description or is clearly articulated by sales management or others who can legitimately prescribe the salesperson's behavior.

Role Repertory and Role Adjustment
Except for the simplest selling situations, salespersons are expected to have a role repertory; that is, they are expected to be able to enact a number of roles. As in more general social situations, large role repertories are generally associated with increased sales success. Adjustment from one role to another, however, is frequently difficult. The greater the required role repertory, the more likely the possibility for role conflict, ambiguity, and inaccuracy. As a result, many salespersons do not appropriately enact all required roles.

In summary, the salesperson must be able to enact a variety of roles in such a way as to be perceived by various constituencies in the firm as representing their interests and in such a way as to be perceived by the customer as representing the customer's interests. In enacting these roles, he or she will inevitably experience role conflict and is likely to experience role ambiguity, role inaccuracy and problems in role adjustment. These problems cannot be eliminated. Managing them appropriately, however, is the key to sales success. The imperative for marketing strategy is to provide the framework within which the sales force is managed. This can be done only with a good understanding of the selling task, based on comprehensive understanding of the specific selling situation.

Understanding the Selling Situation

Most business selling situations share certain characteristics.[10]

1. Relations between buying and selling organizations tend to be long term, as a result of either repetitive transactions or the length of the buying cycle.
2. Multiple buying influences are the norm.
3. Salespersons are generally assigned to call on specific accounts, or specific geographical territories.
4. Demand is derived. Hence, available business from individual accounts may be subject to substantial fluctuations.
5. Customer contact is primarily, and sometimes only, through the salesperson.
6. The salesperson's responsibilities usually include more than just selling.

A number of classification schemes have been developed to elaborate on these characteristics. In Chapter 3, we described the BUYGRID model, which suggests how the selling task may vary as a function of the buyer's situation, in terms of the newness of the product to the buyer. The classification schemes described below provide further insights into the nature of the selling task in a particular situation:

The Sales Cycle

The old idea was that the sales force should *sell*. More recently, the concept of *solutions selling* has proven to be the most effective use of the sales force, and is based on relationship selling in business markets.[11] Sales people may show a customer prospect how their company can help the customer improve its profitability. They seek to join their relationship with the customer's company as *partners for profit*.

Companies need to define the specific objective they want their sales force to achieve. The specific allocation scheme depends on the products, service, or industry. But regardless of the selling context, there is a typical sales cycle of tasks performed throughout the sales process, as shown in Figure 11.2.

Classification According to the Nature of the Product, Service, or Industry

The nature of the product, service, or served industry has a major influence in shaping the nature of the selling task. The tasks associated with selling a main frame computer or a turbine generator, for example, which involve large expenditures and long buying cycles, vary significantly from those associated with the sale of highly standardized supply items. Similarly, the sales approach to contractor markets, with short-term relationships and emphasis on negotiation, is significantly different from the approach to the electric utility market, with its emphasis on long-term relationships and sealed bidding.

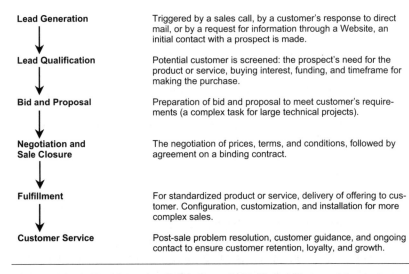

Lead Generation	Triggered by a sales call, by a customer's response to direct mail, or by a request for information through a Website, an initial contact with a prospect is made.
Lead Qualification	Potential customer is screened: the prospect's need for the product or service, buying interest, funding, and timeframe for making the purchase.
Bid and Proposal	Preparation of bid and proposal to meet customer's requirements (a complex task for large technical projects).
Negotiation and Sale Closure	The negotiation of prices, terms, and conditions, followed by agreement on a binding contract.
Fulfillment	For standardized product or service, delivery of offering to customer. Configuration, customization, and installation for more complex sales.
Customer Service	Post-sale problem resolution, customer guidance, and ongoing contact to ensure customer retention, loyalty, and growth.

Source: Adapted from Lawrence G. Friedman, Go To Market Strategy: Advanced Techniques and Tools for Selling More Products, To More Customers, More Profitably. Boston: Butterworth-Heinemann, 2002, 234–36. Reprinted with permission from Elsevier.

Figure 11.2: Typical Sales Cycle: Tasks Performed Throughout the Sales Process

Product or service categories useful for consideration of the nature of the selling task include raw materials, components, capital goods, supplies, professional services, and maintenance services, each of which may suggest variations in the nature of the selling task. A complete list of categories where sales approaches vary would be quite lengthy but the key is to recognize or identify the key aspects of the product, service, or industry that significantly influence the role of the salesperson.

Classification According to Selling Activities

A number of schemes have been proposed that consider the selling task in terms of the required activities. A now classic study by Newton found sales forces organized around the following activities:[12]

- Trade Selling. The principal activity focused on increasing business from customers by providing promotional assistance, either to some element of the distribution channel or to a manufacturer purchasing for resale.

- Missionary Selling. The principal activity focused on increasing business by providing a direct customer, such as a wholesaler, with personal selling assistance to indirect customers, such as small businesses, architects or doctors.
- Technical Selling. The principal activity focused on increasing business from existing customers by providing technical service and assistance.
- New Business Selling. The principal activity focused on increasing business by obtaining new accounts for the firm.

Classification According to Strategic Fit

The salesperson's job is to exploit the opportunity made possible by the supplier's strategy and marketing program. We define strategic fit as the match between the supplier's strategy and the wants and needs of individual customers. Achieving strategic fit is the purpose of market segmentation. Realistically, a high level of strategic fit with every customer in a targeted segment is difficult to obtain. Economy of scale considerations restrict opportunities to segment markets. Within narrowly defined market segments business buyers are highly idiosyncratic in their business strategies as they strive for competitive advantage. Joint development efforts with one customer, for instance, may be seen as a competitive threat by another. Successful implementation of a pull strategy may interfere with at least some customers' efforts to achieve product differentiation with respect to their competitors. Even where competition between customers is not a factor, as may be the case with electric utilities or telecommunication companies, variation in their business strategies may make a one marketing strategy fits all difficult.

Finally, strategic fit is dynamic, not static. Economies of scale change as new technology influences manufacturing processes. Individual customer's strategies change as they pursue their changing market opportunities or respond to competitive threats. Environmental forces can influence the strategies of all or some of the firms within an industry. Some shifts may enhance strategic fit between supplier and customer. Others may detract from it.

In the long run, suppliers have the option to change their strategies to more nearly meet customer objectives or to attempt to influence favorable changes in customer strategies as ways to achieve strategic fit. The salesperson, however, solicits orders from assigned accounts in the short run and in the context of current strategies and programs. *The role of the salesperson is, therefore, materially influenced by current levels of strategic fit.*

High Level of Strategic Fit

Where strategic fit is high, the salesperson's opportunity is generally favorable. He or she enjoys significant competitive advantage, or at least has competitive parity. Securing a large share of the customer's business is important but success is assumed. The salesperson needs to understand the customer's decision-making process but the nature of communications to individuals in the customer's organization is explanatory rather than persuasive. Equal emphasis is placed on management of the systems that support pre- and post-order activities. The salesperson develops an extensive network of contacts in the customer's organization and close personal relations may develop. The importance of continued strategic fit is recognized and the salesperson is expected to monitor changes in customer strategy and needs and to use this knowledge to guide the supplier's continued fine-tuning of strategy and marketing programs. Competitive activity is monitored as a defensive tactic to guard against encroachment of the salesperson's favored position.

Low Level of Strategic Fit

Where strategic fit is low, the salesperson's role is very different. Opportunity is not as favorable. The competitive position is one of disadvantage. The salesperson is expected to get orders, but these expectations are not high. Understanding the buying decision process is important, but communications are persuasive rather than explanatory, as the salesperson attempts to influence change in the customer's evaluation system, objectives, or, in some instances, even the customer's strategy. The flow of orders is small or erratic and systems to support pre- and post-order activity are modest or nonexistent. The salesperson's network of personal contacts is small and the opportunity to develop close personal relations is limited. Customer strategy is monitored primarily in hope of a change in a favorable direction. Competitive activity is monitored, but the emphasis is on identifying weakness in competitors' approaches or failure of competitors to respond to changes in the customer's strategy.

Although we have described the salesperson's role for two levels of strategic fit, in actuality strategic fit is a continuum, not a dichotomy. As a result, many variations are possible in the salesperson's role. Still further, in the case of a pooled sales force or a manufacturer's agent selling many products, strategic fit can vary not only by account but also by product within accounts. In some instances, the

230

salesperson will manage an ongoing relationship for one product and emphasize opportunistic positioning for another.

Personal Interaction Between Salesperson and Buyer

We have described a number of classification schemes, or frameworks to assist in better understanding the tasks and role of the salesperson. The essence of personal selling, however, is the one on one interaction with an individual in the customer's organization. In the final analysis, sensing how the prospect expects the salesperson to behave and how effectively the salesperson reacts to these expectations is a matter of the individual skill and personality of the salesperson. A number of classification schemes have been developed to assist the salesperson in thinking about the dynamics of this personal interaction. It is beyond the scope of this text to extensively explore the nature of this interaction. However, we briefly describe one classification scheme, which suggests the complexity of possible interactions between salesperson and buyer.

The scheme developed by Buzzotta and his colleagues classifies the salesperson and the buyer on two dimensions: dominant-submissive and a hostile-warm.[13] Using these dimensions, they then describe four sales approaches and four buying approaches, as shown in Figures 11.3 and 11.4.

Dominance

Q1. Dominant-Hostile	**Q4. Dominant-Warm**
Customers don't buy willingly. Salesperson must impose his or her will on the customer through strength. Selling is a struggle; the salesperson must win.	Customers will buy if they can satisfy a need. Salesperson must show customer his or her product will best satisfy customer's needs. Selling is a win-win process for customer, salesperson, and company.

Hostility   **Warmth**

Q2. Submissive-Hostile	**Q3. Submissive-Warm**
Customers buy when ready. Little the salesperson can do to get them to buy. Survive by taking the order when the customer is ready.	Customers buy from friends. The salesperson's job is to make friends.

Submission

Source: Adapted from V. R. Buzzotta and R. E. Lefton, and Manuel Sherberg, *Dimensional Selling*, McGraw Hill, New York 2005. St. Louis: Psychological Associates, Inc., 1972, 22. Reprinted by permission of Psychological Associates, Inc., St. Louis, MO 63105. All rights reserved.

Figure 11.3: Dimensional Model of Sales Behavior

Dominance

Q1. Dominant-Hostile	Q4. Dominant-Warm
Salespersons can't be trusted. They want to sell me something I don't want or need. I control them by being tough and resistant. The best defense is a good offense.	I buy because I expect to benefit. I buy from salespersons who prove they can help me get more benefit than their competitors.

Hostility

Q2. Submissive-Hostile	Q3. Submissive-Warm	**Warmth**
Salespersons can't be trusted. They want to sell me something I don't want or need. To defend myself, I try to avoid them. If I can't, I try to stay uninvolved.	Competitive products are all alike. Since it really doesn't matter which one I buy, I might as well buy from a salesperson I like.	

Submission

Source: Adapted from V. R. Buzzotta and R. E. Lefton, and Manuel Sherberg, *Dimensional Selling*, McGraw Hill, New York 2005. St. Louis: Psychological Associates, Inc., 1972, 22. Reprinted by permission of Psychological Associates, Inc., St. Louis, MO 63105. All rights reserved.

Figure 11.4: Dimensional Model of Customer Behavior

The value systems underlying the four sales approaches can be paraphrased as "make em buy" (dominant-hostile), "whatever will be, will be" (submissive-hostile), "you can't say no to a friend" (submissive-warm), and "get 'em committed" (dominant-warm). Similar value systems can be inferred for buyers. These can then be used to examine the nature of the interaction between the various categories of salespersons and buyers, and to suggest how salespersons can more effectively adapt to individual buyers.

Managing the Sales Force[14]

While marketing strategy should specify the major aspects of the selling task, directing the selling effort is the responsibility of the sales manager. A number of management tools can assist the sales manager in accomplishing this goal.

Job Description: The Starting Point

The job description should be the starting point of sales force management. All else flows from a good understanding of selling objectives and how they are to be accomplished. It is not enough to say the objective is to get orders. The job description must spell out the firm's sales approach, the desired balance between new and existing accounts, the desired balance of product line sales, desired activities beyond sales calls (e.g., participation in trade shows), the nature of the sales support and how the salesperson is to use the resources of the firm. To guide the selection process the job description should also include the salesperson's qualifications.

Personnel Selection: The Critical Decision
Few aspects of sales force management are more critical than the selection process. Poor hiring decisions, quickly made, may take months to undo and in the process may excessively burden management resources. Unfortunately, there is no magic formula to guide the selection process. Despite countless studies, there is no evidence of a universal sales personality.[15] Good selection processes seem to rely on a number of techniques, developed in the context of the firm's particular selling situation and taking into account the characteristics of successful sales persons in the firm. Multiple interviews, carefully structured, done by individuals trained in interviewing and formal tests (validated against the records of successful salespersons in the firm), improve the selection process.

Training: The Ongoing Requirement
Training is a key aspect of sales force management. It has two principal dimensions:

1. Knowledge, with respect to the company, its strategy, its processes, its products, and its procedures.
2. Skill, with respect to analyzing the customer situation, planning an account or call strategy, and handling the specific call.

Knowledge training is generally straightforward. Marketing managers can explain marketing strategy, product specialists can describe product or service features. Training in selling skills is more complex. Generic sales training programs can be used to introduce basic sales concepts. Sales training that is relevant to the marketing strategy, however, must be specially developed. Sales training for experienced salespersons must also be specially developed, taking into account both the experience of the salesperson and changes in the marketing strategy. As firms move to team selling, training in its unique requirements becomes particularly important.

Coaching: The Changing Element
Traditionally, coaching the salesperson has been an important element of the sales manager's job. This presumes that the sales manager makes calls with the salesperson, observes the sales approach and, subsequently, gives the salesperson feedback. As organizations flatten, in-

creasing the number of the sales manager's direct reports, and as sales forces organize on other than geographic dimensions, the opportunity for the sales manager to make calls with the salesperson decreases. As a result, the nature of coaching is changing. Increasingly, there is emphasis on working with the salesperson to develop account or territory strategies, or to manage teams, with emphasis on how the team functions rather than on an individual's personal selling skill.

Sales Support

Few salespersons today can operate effectively without extensive support. Business partners and inside sales personnel, backing up the salesperson, are common. Computer technology is used to facilitate making the sales presentation, to enhance the ability of the salesperson to check order status, and/or to reduce the time required for administrative tasks. Increasingly, direct mail, telemarketing, and the Internet are used to reach small customers and/or to make customer contact between personal calls. [16]

Compensation[17]

Compensation is one of the most complex aspects of sales force management. Options include:

- Straight salary
- Straight commission, paid as a percentage of gross sales
- Commission paid as a percentage of gross margin
- Bonuses or a percentage of salary paid on performance relative to quota
- A combination of straight salary and some form of incentive payment

In the United States, straight salary is common but the predominant form of compensation is a combination of salary and incentive, usually based on performance with respect to quota. Typical combinations range from 50-50 (i.e., 50 percent salary and 50 percent incentive for meeting quota) to 80-20.[18] The variation in compensation plans, however, is enormous. Cultural norms significantly influence plan selection. Firms in Northern Europe, for instance, tend to favor straight salary plans. Even within industries in the same country, there is great variation. For many years, Digital Equipment paid its sales force on straight salary, whereas the rest of the computer industry relied heavily on some form of incentive compensation.

While there are no rules for the *right* compensation plan, there are some guidelines:

- The plan should reflect the reality of the selling task. Incentive compensation tends to be less appropriate in long selling cycle situations or in situations where the salesperson is just one of many factors that may determine the order placement.
- The plan must be understandable. Incentive plans that attempt to pay for performance based on a large number of variables are generally too complex to be understood by the sales force and lose their ability to motivate.
- The plan should not attempt to be a substitute for good management. It is simply impossible to devise an incentive plan to guide or evaluate all dimensions of the salesperson's work.
- As firms move to more team selling, compensation planning must account for the impact of an incentive plan on all members of the team; both those in sales and those in support roles.
- The plan should be perceived as fair. Plans that are perceived to establish arbitrary quotas or that penalize the salesperson for events beyond his or her control will fail to motivate the sales force.
- The plan should take into account the values of those in the sales force. That is, to what extent are individuals in the sales force motivated by monetary incentives and how might this vary as a function of age or stage of career?

Career Pathing: Frequently Forgotten

Managing the sales force must take into account growth in sales competence, marketing personnel needs, and the future managerial needs of the sales force. It is important, therefore, to recognize the various career paths that salespersons may take within the firm. A typical career path to accomplish this might include the following assignments:

- A starting assignment at marketing headquarters, designed to acquaint the individual with the marketing strategy and the products and procedures of the firm.
- A low-level sales assignment, followed by a mid-level sales assignment, to demonstrate selling skills and leadership potential.
- A marketing headquarters assignment in a key activity such as pricing or field sales support.

- A high-level field sales assignment, possibly directing a sales team.
- A management position, either in field sales or in headquarters.

Where the opportunity does not exist for an extensive array of assignments, changes in sales assignments with increasing levels of responsibility, combined with special assignments to new product development teams or to product introduction task forces, should be considered.

Special Issues

It is beyond the scope of this text to extensively treat all aspects of sales force management. Five issues, however, merit particular attention.

Use of Agents vs. Direct Sales Force

Traditionally manufacturers' agents have been considered as part of a channel of distribution; much in the same context as wholesalers. It has also been traditional to frame the decision to use agents principally in economic terms. That is, because they are not under the direct control of the manufacturer, they are thought appropriate just for small firms that cannot afford their own sales force, or for large firms who cannot justify a full-time salesperson in new territories or other special situations.

We treat the topic here because it is more appropriate to think of a manufacturer's agent as a substitute for the manufacturer's own sales force. Consider the typical agent, either an individual or a small firm that exclusively represents one manufacturer, or several manufacturers of complementary lines, in a specified geographic area. The agent does not take title to the product, does not handle invoicing, and sells at the manufacturer's price and in accordance with the manufacturer's policies. To earn the right to represent the manufacturer, the agent fields skilled salespersons, who are both competent with respect to the product and knowledgeable with regard to their customers. In short, the agent performs almost the same functions as does a manufacturer's sales force.

The issue, then, of using agents is not simply a matter of economics, but should take into account the specialized knowledge or relationships of the agent, and the ability of the firm to manage the agent. The economics of the decision are fairly straightforward. Commission expense paid to an agent can easily be weighed against the cost of a salesperson or the establishment of a sales office. In some instances, however, agents may have specialized knowledge or have relationships with customers that would be difficult to duplicate, whose value would transcend pure expense considerations. Finally, while agents are not directly under the control of their principals, it would be inappropriate to conclude that they are not responsive to their needs or desires. As with a manufacturer's sales force, agents' selling efforts can be influenced by a number of factors beyond just the commission rate. In particular, high levels of sales support can significantly increase an agent's effectiveness.

Organizing the Field Sales Force

How should we organize the field sales force? The difficulty in finding the correct answer to this question is indicated by the frequency with which sales forces are reorganized. Frequent reorganizations have characterized both IBM and AT&T, for example, with changes from one general sales force, selling all products and services to all industries, to various combinations of multiple sales forces, selling limited lines of products to targeted industries. Customer focus remained a key issue for Louis Gerstner, the CEO at IBM, who promised, "We're going to organize the sales force to give customers what they want. We're going to start with the customer."[19]

While giving the customers what they want is critical, this does not necessarily provide a clear path to the right organization. Some customers want to be called on by product specialists. Some want industry specialists. Others want "one-stop shopping" or an account executive who represents the total company. For small companies, selling a limited product line to a restricted number of industries, the issue is relatively simple. One sales force, organized on geographic lines can meet most if not all these requirements and, importantly, can assure the company that all product lines are well represented. As the firm expands its product line or elects to pursue new markets, it faces the choice of establishing several sales forces or, as is common, establishing a "pooled sales force" which represents a number of SBUs or product businesses. The choice is influenced by the ability of the sales force to sell to diverse markets, by its ability to have sufficient product knowledge to represent a variety of products, by the view of the SBU manager as to the adequacy of representation, and by customer desires. Inevitably the chosen form of organization represents a compromise between conflicting objectives. In particular, while pooled sales forces are widely used, SBU managers are frustrated by lack of direct control over the sales force. As with manufacturers' agents, one solution is to look for ways to increase the level of support provided to the sales force; in short, to make it easy for the sales force to sell the SBU's products.

Involvement in Marketing Research and Strategy Development

With few exceptions, business salespersons are knowledgeable about their customers' strategies, product needs, and buying practices. They are also likely to be knowledgeable about many aspects of competitive products and strategies. For the development of new products, or changes in marketing strategy, the sales force represents a rich source of information but one which may be underutilized unless formal processes are in place to ensure an appropriate flow of information.

Systems need to be in place to encourage and reward salespersons who contribute customer and competitive information. At the least this requires (1) that the sales force knows what kind of information is desired and (2) that individuals who provide such information be recognized and rewarded for their contributions. When new products or changes in marketing strategy are being considered, members of the field sales force can make valuable contributions as members of task forces or planning teams.

National or International Accounts[20]

We define a national account as one in which multiple buying influences are located in a number of locations within one country. International accounts are an extension of national accounts, with buying influences located in two or more countries.

Almost without exception, national accounts require some form of sales team to handle all the buying influences. Accounts are frequently large enough to require specialized sales support, provided by individuals who are also often members of the sales team. We describe three key issues in management of national accounts.

Sales Coverage

Options include coverage of all buying influences from a central office location, a dedicated national account team with salespersons strategically located throughout the country, or individuals in the regular sales force who may be assigned exclusively to national accounts or who may be assigned to a mixture of local and national accounts.

Team Work

Historically, selling has been a highly individual activity. Customer relations tend to be very personal. Information gained from key buying influences is closely guarded. The norm for most salespersons is "I got the order" not "we got the order." Teamwork, therefore, cannot be taken for granted. Extreme perhaps, but illustrative, is the experience of Kraft in the United States, which no longer hires experienced salespersons because of their difficulty in making the transition from operating as an individual to operating as a team member. Careful selection of team members, special training and appropriate management practices are required if, in fact, they are to operate as a team.[21]

Sales Credit and Compensation

Where incentive forms of payment are involved, the importance of allocating sales credit is obvious. Even where members of the team are paid on straight salary, the issue of sales credit is still salient. Salespersons have budgets, and annual raises or promotions are influenced by performance relative to budget.

A variety of approaches to credit allocation have been used. The formula approach gives the office or individual receiving the order a specified percentage of the orders received credit, with the balance of the credit evenly split between other salespersons assigned to the account, without consideration of the actual influence exerted. There may be instances where the office receiving the order exerted no influence and, indeed, was unaware the order was coming.

The drawbacks of the formula approach have led some firms to simply give each salesperson full credit for the order. In a sense, this avoids the issue and, in any event, is generally not practicable if significant amounts of incentive compensation are involved.

Some firms have attempted to assign management the responsibility to subjectively assess the share of influence exerted by members of the sales team. Management, however, may not be close enough to the situation to make an informed judgment. In situations where members of the sales team report to different managers, there is also the potential for bias and a manager's negotiating skill may outweigh the merits of a particular case.

Finally, there is the issue of non-selling personnel who are important members of the team but tend to be left out of incentive compensation schemes based on solely on orders received.

One approach that holds promise is to establish a bonus pool for all members of the team based on the total volume of business or the profit contribution of the team. Shares in the bonus pool are then determined by the team members, by allocating influence shares to other members of the team.

International Accounts

International Accounts. International accounts are an extension of national accounts, with many of the same management issues. Added considerations include language and cultural differences, which add to the imperative for special training and management and the cost of meetings and communication. GE Plastics, for instance, has for several years recognized the need for special attention to communication between far flung team members by establishing a computerized customer database, accessible by team members in any location in the world.

A special consideration in managing sales to international accounts is the firm's organizational structure. For firms with extensive operations outside of their home country, the most common form of organization is country based, with a country manager responsible for all activities of the firm within a particular country. In some instances, the country manager is essentially a sales manager, responsible only for sales and, perhaps, distribution activities. In other instances, the country manager is responsible for a number of additional activities including manufacturing and finance. In these instances, the interests and measurement system of the country manager must be taken into account.

Selling to Distributors
The role of the salesperson assigned to a distributor is significantly different than that of other sales jobs. The object, of course, is to secure orders. Orders from distributors, however, result only if the distributor's customers place orders. Subject to the nature of the relationship the distributor elects to have with its suppliers, the role of the salesperson more nearly parallels that of a sales manager, albeit without any authority over the distributor. Keys to success include training or otherwise assisting the distributor's salespersons, sometimes making joint calls on distributor's customers; assistance to the distributor with respect to overall business planning; and general sales support to various parts of the distributor's organization. The effectiveness with which the assigned salesperson manages the relationship with the distributor can significantly increase the distributor's sales of the supplier's products.

Summary
Frequent reorganizations of field sales forces indicate a continuing quest for that right combination of marketing strategy and field sales efforts. Examples abound of product introductions that were not supported by the field sales force. Tensions between those in marketing and field sales are widely reported. Marketing strategy, therefore, must take into account not only how customers buy but also how the sales force sells. Except in the most standardized situations, the success of

the salesperson is determined by how well he or she orchestrates the firm's resources to connect the business and marketing strategy to the situation of an individual account. While personal selling is the predominant method of communicating with business customers, the efforts of the sales force can be supported and reinforced by a variety of non-personal selling methods which need to be coordinated with the personal effort.

Marketing strategy should establish the context within which the sales force operates, should identify the target customers, or specify their characteristics, and should define the sales approach. Field sales management is the key to ensuring the connection of marketing strategy to the efforts of the sales force. Finally, marketing strategy should take into account the dynamic nature of personal selling and the extent to which the selling task changes as a result of changes in the external environment as well as marketing strategy. As we will discuss in Chapter 12, personal selling should be supported by, and coordinated with, a number of other methods of communication, which also can be used for direct marketing.

Further Reading

Joseph P Cannon and Narakesari Narauandas, *Relationship Marketing and Key Account Management*, ed. Jagdish N. Sheth and Atul Parvatiyar (Thousand Oaks, CA: Sage Publications, Inc. 2000), 407–29.

Gilbert A. Churchill Jr., and others, *Sales Force Management*, 6th ed. (Boston: McGraw-Hill Companies, 2000).

John S. Hill and Arthur W. Allaway, "How U.S.-based Companies Manage Sales in Foreign Countries," *Industrial Marketing Management* 22 (1993), 7-16.

William Keenan Jr., ed., *The Sales & Marketing Management Guide to Sales Compensation Planning: Commissions, Bonuses & Beyond* (Chicago: Probus Publishing, 1994).

George H. Lucas Jr. and others, "An Empirical Study of Sales Force Turnover," *Journal of Marketing* (July 1987): 34–59.

Robert N. McMurray, "The Mystique of SuperSalesmanship," *Harvard Business Review* (March–April 1961): 114.

William C. Moncrief, "Selling Activity and Sales Position Taxonomies for Industrial Salesforces," *Journal of Marketing Research* (August 1986): 261–70.

William C. Moncrief, "Five Types of Industrial Sales Jobs," *Industrial Marketing Management*, 17 (1988): 161-67.

Sharon Drew Morgan, *Selling with Integrity: Reinventing Sales Through Collaboration, Respect, and Serving* (New York: Berkeley Books, 1996).

James A. Narus and James C. Anderson, "Industrial Distributor Selling: The Roles of Outside and Inside Sales," *Industrial Marketing Management* 15 (1986): 55–62.

Charles J. Quigley, Jr., Frank G. Bingham, Jr., and Michael B. Patterson, "The Information Flow for a Business-to-Business Buying Decision Process: A Modeling Approach," *The Journal of Marketing Theory and Practice* 2 (fall 1993): 103–21.

Neil Rackham and Jon De Vincentis, *Rethinking the Sales Force* (New York: McGraw-Hill, 1996).

Bert Rosenbloom, "The World Class Sales Manager: Adapting to Global Megatrends," *Journal of Global Marketing* 5, no. 4 (1992): 11–22.

Madhubalan Viswanathan and Eric M. Olson, "The Implementation of Business Strategies: Implications for the Sales Function," *Journal of Personal Selling & Sales Management* XII, no. 1 (winter 1992): 45-57

John J. Withy and Eric Panitz, "Face-to-Face Selling: Making It More Effective," *Industrial Marketing Management* 24 (August 1995): 239–46.

Thomas Wotruba, "The Evolution of Personal Selling," *Journal of Personal Selling & Sales Management*, XI, no. 3 (Summer 1991).

Eilene Zimmerman, "Quota Busters," *Sales & Marketing Management* (January 2001): 59–63.

Further Reading

[1]"If a man can write a better book, preach a better sermon, or make a better mousetrap than his neighbor, though he built his house in the woods, the world will make a beaten path to his door." Attributed to Ralph Waldo Emerson in Sarah B. Yule, *Borrowings* (Oakland, CA: First Unitarian Church of Oakland, 1889), 138.

[2]Lawrence G. Friedman, *Go To Market Strategy: Advanced Techniques and Tools for Selling More Products, To More Customers, More Profitably* (Boston: Butterworth-Heinemann, 2002), 233.

[3]Ibid., 243.

[4]Peter Drucker, *People and Performance: The Best of Peter Drucker on Management* (New York: Harper & Row Publishers, Inc., 1977), 91.

[5]Don Schultz, "Selling is Dying," *Sales and Marketing Management* (August 1994): 82–84.

[6]Edward. K. Strong, *The Psychology of Selling* (New York: McGraw-Hill, 1925), 9.

[7]For a comprehensive treatment on the subject, see John F. Tanner Jr., "Buyer Perspectives of the Purchase Process and Its Effect on Customer Satisfaction," *Industrial Marketing Management* 25 (March 1996): 125–33.

[8]From a personal communication with H. Michael Hayes (July 1974).

[9]This section draws heavily from Robert L. Kahn and others, *Organizational Stress: Studies in Role Conflict and Ambiguity* (New York: John F. Wiley and Sons, Inc., 1964) and Orville S. Walker, Jr. and others, "Organization Determinants of the Industrial Salesman's Role Conflict and Role Ambiguity," *Journal of Marketing* (January 1975): 32–39.

[10]James Cross, Steven W. Hartley, and William Rudelius, "Sales Force Activities and Marketing Strategies in Industry Firms: Relationships and Implications," *Journal of Personal Selling & Sales Management* 21 (summer 2001): 199–206.

[11]Robert J. Schultz, Kenneth R. Evans, and David J. Good, "Intercultural Interaction Strategies and Relationship Selling in Industrial Markets," *Industrial Marketing Management* 28 (1999): 589–599.

[12]Derek A. Newton, "Get the Most Out of Your Salesforce," *Harvard Business Review*, (September–October 1969): 130–43.

[13]V. Ralph Buzzota, Robert E. Lefton, and Manual Sherberg, *Effective Selling Through Psychology: Dimensional Sales and Sales Management Strategies* (St. Louis: Psychological Associates, Inc. 1991), 23–26.

[14]A comprehensive treatment of all aspects of sales management is beyond the scope of this volume. For more extensive discussion, see Gilbert A. Churchill Jr. and others, *Sales Force Management*, 6th ed. (Boston: McGraw-Hill Companies, 2000).

[15]Wesley J. Johnston and Martha C. Cooper, "Industrial Sales Force Selection: current Knowledge and Needed Research," *Journal of Personal Selling & Sales Management* 1 (spring/summer 1981): 49–53.

[16]Philip B. Clark and Sean Callahan, "Sales Staffs: Adapt or Die," *B to B,* (10 April 2000).

[17]For estimates of sales representative salaries, see *Sales & Marketing Management* (October 1998): 98.

[18]Luis R. Gomez-Mejia, David B. Balkin, and Robert L. Cardy, *Managing Human Resources* (Upper Saddle River, NJ: Prentice Hall, 1995), 416–18.

[19]Geoffrey Brewer, "Rebooting IBM," *Sales & Marketing Management* (October, 1993): 82.

[20]Frank V. Cespedes, *Concurrent Marketing: Integrating Products, Sales and Service* (Boston: Harvard Business School Press, 1995), 186–202.

[21]Victoria D. Bush and Thomas Ingram, "Adapting to Diverse Customers: A Training Matrix for International Marketers," *Industrial Marketing Management* 25 (September 1996): 373–83.

Chapter 12

Business Marketing Communications: Beyond Personal Selling

In Chapter 11, we identified the principal methods of communication with business customers and then extensively considered the role of personal selling and its management. In this chapter, we discuss the communication methods that either supplement personal selling or that, for some firms, carry the full burden of communication, including securing the customer's order. We conclude with a brief discussion of the cost of communication with business customers.

Supplementing Personal Selling

Personal selling efforts, no matter how extensive, can seldom accomplish all the communication objectives of marketing strategy. Personal selling, focused on all buying influences may not be practicable. In what may be an extreme example, Xerox found that its salespersons selling photocopiers could see decision makers in only 1 out of 25 calls.[1] Buyers report that they rely extensively on a wide variety of sources for information about products, services and their characteristics. According to one study, buyers in the machine tool industry actually rely more heavily on advertising than on salespersons as a source of information.[2] In many industries, trade shows are important sources of product information. In some instances, high level management in the customer's organization, not actively involved in the purchasing decision, may influence supplier selection on the basis of overall perceptions of the supplier, based on advertising or other non-personal communications.

Direct marketing, advertising, sales promotion, and public relations support and supplement the personal selling effort. The share of the marketing budget devoted to these functions is smaller in business than it is in consumer-goods marketing. A well-integrated marketing communications program can, however, contribute to the increased efficiency and effectiveness of the overall marketing strategy as shown in Figure 12.1.

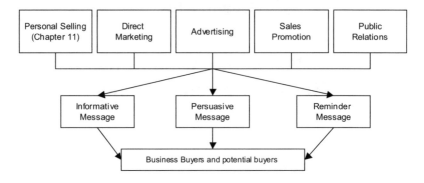

Figure 12.1: Business Promotional Tools and the Flows of Information, Persuasion, and Reminder Messages

Direct Marketing

The predominant role of personal selling in the communications program should not obscure the fact that for many firms, the expense of personal selling, either by the firm's direct sales force or an indirect channel is either prohibitive or unnecessary. Therefore, any discussion or communication with the customer, by means other than the salesperson, needs to take into account the concept of direct marketing, defined as an organized and planned system of contacts, using a variety of media, seeking to acquire or maintain a customer. It requires the development and maintenance of an information base to control targeting, manage the offer and maintain continuous contact.[3]

Direct mail, e-mail marketing, and telemarketing are among the direct marketing tools available to the business marketer. Direct mail delivers the firm's message firsthand to selected individuals. Possible mail pieces range from sales letters introducing new products to lengthy brochures or even product samples. Direct mail can accomplish many functions of advertising, but its real contribution is in delivering the message to a precisely defined prospect. E-mail marketing can have a substantial impact on creating and qualifying customer leads, if some important rules are strictly followed: "always seek permission to send e-mail and always provide the recipient with the ability to 'opt out.'"[4]

Direct Mail

The nature of business marketing, with its relatively small number of fairly identifiable customers, emphasizes the potential usefulness of direct mail in the promotional mix. Key to its effective use is a good database.

Direct mail is commonly used for corporate image promotion, product and service promotion, sales support, distribution channel communications, and special marketing problems. In promoting corporate image, direct mail may help to establish a firm's reputation of technological leadership. Product messages by direct mail can also be used to put specific product information in the hands of the purchasing decision-makers. Timing of direct mail is also flexible; a new price schedule or new service innovation can be communicated to the buyer as needed. Direct mail also makes it easy for the buyer to respond— usually a reply postcard is included or the name, address, and phone number of the local salesperson or distributor are provided.

Mailing lists for existing customers can be developed from company records and kept up-to-date by the field sales force. Price changes can be transmitted simultaneously to all customers. New product or service announcements or extensive technical information can be transmitted to interested customers, for subsequent follow-up by a salesperson. Catalogs or other promotional information can be mailed to key buying influences on a regular basis. Direct mail can also be used to reach key decision makers who cannot normally be contacted by the sales force. Beyond the need for mailing list accuracy and frequent updating, a key to success is creating messages that the sales force believes will assist their selling efforts.

For new customers, commercially available mailing lists can be used to introduce the company, to develop leads for subsequent follow up by the sales force, or to solicit some other direct response. In the United States, there are a number of list providers. Companies such as Dun and Bradstreet offer lists of upward of 10 million U.S. businesses, available for four, six, and eight digit SIC codes. In addition to lists for U.S. businesses, Dun and Bradstreet offers international lists that include another 28 million names. Lists can be obtained just for mailing labels or with more comprehensive information such as years in business, company size, and credit history. Lists can be purchased for one time use, suitable for a single mailing, or for multiple use, suitable for building a permanent data base. Keys to success are correct selection of mailing lists and careful screening of responses to ensure that leads are viable.

For most firms an extensive and accurate database for direct mail, and for telemarketing as well, is a vital component of a marketing communication program. What needs to be recognized in building a database of business customers is the existence of multiple influences. Not only does this require extensive knowledge of the names and positions of all the buying influences in the customer's organization but also may suggest ways in which the message needs to be varied, reflecting the functional interests of the individual. The impact of even the best message can be reduced if the customer's name is spelled incorrectly or the wrong title is used, further emphasizing the importance of accuracy in the database. In his comprehensive handbook on building databases in Europe, Rhind makes the point that it is not enough to translate messages into the customer's language but that titles and form of address also need to take local custom into account.[5]

E-Mail Marketing
E-mail marketing is less costly than direct mail, and sending printed materials by mail. E-mail campaigns often yield higher responses than direct mail campaigns, and the results are generated more quickly.

Firms that plan to fully integrate e-mail into their marketing communications strategy (IMC) should make a special effort to build their own e-mail lists. Often, such information is already available from the firms customer database, including records from all departments, including sales, marketing, and customer service. As a result, if a customer responds to an e-mail (or direct mail) campaign, the system captures that information in a centralized customer information database for all contact employees (salespersons, call center employees, marketing managers) to retrieve.

The Internet changes marketing communications from a one-way to a two-way process that permits the marketer and the consumer to more readily exchange information. Consumers receive and provide information by navigating Web sites, specifying their preferences, and communicating with business marketers.[6] Moreover, marketers can use such communications to provide consumers with better service, such as personalized e-mails and information, customized service solutions, or inks to providers of complementary products and services.

Telemarketing
Contacting business customers by telephone has long been a staple of business communication. Salespersons phone customers for appointments and to communicate information in a timely manner. Inside sales personnel rely on the telephone and the Internet, in their work to support the sales force. Customers contact sales offices to request information and to place orders. What, then, is causing telemarketing to be recognized as a separate and distinct method of communicating with customers? Much of the growth reflects the number of ways that the telephone can effectively be used to communicate with customers including:

- Use as the principal method of communicating with customers (i.e., replacing the sales force)

- Use as a supplement to the sales force, to proactively stay in touch with customers, particularly small or remote customers called on infrequently, in periods between sales calls
- Providing customers a convenient way to place orders in response to direct mail
- Generating and qualifying sales leads
- Conducting market research
- Conducting customer satisfaction surveys
- Providing product service information

Facilitated by the use of direct call or other toll free numbers, and the increase in the number of ways of use, overall growth in telemarketing has been explosive. It has been estimated that business marketers will spend $588 billion by 2006 on telemarketing, and it has been one of the fastest growing methods of business communication. [7] This growth mandates that telemarketing be well organized and managed if it is to be effective. In many instances, this means specialized personnel and procedures, carefully integrated with the rest of the marketing effort. One telemarketing operation, for instance, designed to support the field sales force located all its personnel in a centralized location in the United States. In order to convey a *local feel,* telemarketing personnel assigned to customers on the West Coast subscribed to West Coast newspapers in order to be able to discuss local news with customers. As telemarketing operations continue to grow, problems of coordination must be addressed in order to avoid situations such as that of a company running an advertisement with a toll free number, without notifying the telemarketing center, or generation of leads without the knowledge or involvement of the sales force.

Advertising

We have defined advertising as any paid form of non-personal presentation of ideas, goods, or services by an identified sponsor. It includes the use of media such as magazines, newspapers, radio, TV, and billboards but does not include direct marketing activities. Good use of advertising is rooted in a clear specification of its objectives, which can include the following:

- Introducing the firm to prospective customers to pave the way for the first sales call.
- Providing information about products to buying influences who cannot be reached by the salesperson or who cannot be reached in a timely manner.

- Generally enhancing the image of the firm, particularly with high level buying influences.
- Generating sales leads by announcing new products.
- Directly soliciting the customer's order.

The starting point for developing an advertising campaign or strategy is the determination of objectives. In a typical case, for instance, a brief to the advertising agency might specify that the firm wished to reach a number of audiences, to enhance the overall image of the company as a reliable, modern supplier and to position its brands as high-end products. A comparison of methods used by industrial marketers, to set advertising budgets, is shown in Table 12.1

Method	Percent of Respondents Using Each Method $(n = 64)^a$
Quantitative	3
Percent anticipated sales	16
Match competitors	21
Per unit of sales	2
Percent past years sales	23
Arbitrary	13
Objective and task	74
Affordable	33
^{a} Figures exceed 100% due to multiple responses	

Source: Reprinted with permission from *Marketing News*, published by the American Marketing Association, "B-to-B," July 2, 2001, 16.

Table 12.1: Comparison of Methods Used by Industrial Marketers to Set Advertising Budgets

In the ideal situation, business marketers will use the objective and task method to guide advertising expenditures.[8] That is, objectives of this nature will be quantified, an economic analysis will be made of the costs and expected benefits, and the results of the advertising campaign will be measured and evaluated on a before and after basis. A study in the United Kingdom suggests that this approach is common in Europe.[9] It is not without problems, however. Where the objective of advertising is to enhance the image of the firm, increase brand preference or introduce the firm to prospective customers, establishment of an advertising budget will inevitably involve subjective judgments as to benefits and measuring advertising effectiveness may be difficult. Faced with this subjectivity and difficulty, many firms simply determine advertising expenditures based on rules of thumb such as a historical percent of sales measure or industry norms. A more appropriate approach is to establish objectives and estimate benefits, even if rough, using past expenditures and industry norms as guides for advertising budgets, not as determinants.[10]

Where the objective of advertising is to generate sales leads or solicit direct sales, establishment of objectives and measurement of effectiveness are far simpler. The value of a good lead can be reasonably estimated and the number of responses to an advertisement can be tracked, facilitating reasonably accurate cost-benefit estimates.[11]

A salient characteristic of business advertising is the existence of specialized publications. In the United States alone, there are some 2,700 publications carrying business advertising. Some are vertical publications, focused on a particular industry such as *Electrical World.* Others are horizontal publications, focused on a particular function such as *Purchasing.* The business marketer faces choices between these specialized vertical or horizontal publications or more general business publications such as *The Wall Street Journal* or the *Financial Times.* Selection of the appropriate media must be consistent with the objective of the advertising.

Business marketers should not overlook radio advertising as a communication medium. In Detroit, for instance, radio messages by industrial firms reach large numbers of automotive engineers and purchasing agents in their cars during the morning rush hour.

Finally, for the multinational firm, the choice must be made between a standardized message, worldwide, or one that is tailored to specific markets. In some instances, the answer is clear. Advertising messages directed to engineers in Germany must reflect their desire for extensive technical information. In other countries, conceptual advertising may be more appropriate. Except for language, however, the nature of business markets suggests that standardized messages are appropriate in most situations.

Sales Promotion

Sales promotion was formerly considered by marketers as short-term inducements to create interest among personal selling, channel intermediaries, and business customers. In many firms today, sales promotion ventures beyond creating short-term value for various prospects. It has become the driving force that links personal selling, advertising, and public relations into a meaningful, integrated promotional program. Although there are many forms of sales promotion activities available, business marketers very commonly use trade shows and exhibits; incentives, contests, sweepstakes and games; and advertising specialties.

Trade Shows and Exhibits

One of the most important elements of the communication mix, and yet frequently overlooked in the formulation of communication strategy, is the trade show, which provides a unique opportunity for buyers and sellers to come together in an environment where buyers are actively looking for product information, new products, or new sources of supply.[12]

Most industries stage a business show or exhibition annually to display new advances and technological developments in the industry. Exhibiting firms spend over $10 billion annually on floor space at expositions in North America.[13] Generally, sellers present their products and services in booths visited by interested industry members. The typical exhibitor will contact four to five potential purchasers per hour on the show floor.

Outside of North America, trade shows attract even larger numbers of prospective buyers. The largest industrial trade show in the world is held annually in Hanover, Germany, attended by over 400,000 prospective buyers. The cities of Cologne, Dusseldorf, Essen, and Dortmund in the German state of Northrhine Westphalia are the homes of some 90 trade shows, of which 58 are international in scope and 40 are the largest worldwide in their specific sectors. The importance of trade shows in foreign trade is emphasized by the extensive help offered U.S. exporters by the U.S. Foreign and Commercial Service to participate in international trade shows, and by the help offered all exporters by the Japan External Trade Organization (JETRO) to participate in trade shows in Japan.

When exhibiting outside the United States there is always the question of approach and in Europe the approach of European manufacturers to their exhibits has tended to more conservative than that of U.S. manufacturers. Hence, when General Electric first exhibited its engineered plastics at a European trade show, with much emphasis on showmanship, many of the firm's competitors felt it had made a serious blunder. As it turned out, the showmanship was very effective and the company has since become one of the major players in the European market.[14]

Driving this growth is the evaluation of trade shows as a top-rated source of purchasing information by buyers, attendance by individuals with significant levels of purchasing influence, and studies suggesting that closing a sale to a qualified trade show lead takes significantly fewer sales calls than if all calls are made in the field.

Despite the extensive use of trade shows, the high level of expenditures, the favorable reviews by purchasers, and the general evidence regarding their effectiveness, many executives still question participation in trade shows.[15] Some view participation as a necessary evil, done only because competitors are there. Others view them as little more than vacations for participating personnel, particularly when they are held in attractive locations. More particularly, participation is questioned because of lack of specific evidence of their effectiveness and the high, and rising, cost of participation. For business marketers this suggests the need to have well established objectives for trade show participation, to select trade shows carefully, to staff them appropriately, and to measure their effectiveness.[16]

According to the Trade Show Bureau, and others, companies exhibit at trade shows for a wide variety of reasons, including:

- Generate sales
- Generate qualified sales leads
- Intensify awareness of the company and its products
- Introduce a new product or service
- Create a preference for products and the company
- Find new distributors for their products or services
- Provide distributor support
- Test prototypes and judge reaction to new products
- Find new applications for existing products
- Recruit sales representatives
- Secure information about competitors
- Provide technical staff the opportunity to interface with customers

Selection of trade shows is facilitated by the segmentation that takes place by prospective customers, based either of their product or industry interest. Other factors to take into consideration include the orientation of the show with respect to selling and the level of participants. Some trade shows tend to be more selling oriented (i.e., orders are placed at the show) whereas others tend to be more oriented to future or broader objectives. Some may attract high-level managers with broad interests. Others may attract technical personnel, interested in technical detail.

In many instances, trade shows are staffed with relatively low level, untrained personnel, reflecting the view of trade shows as a necessary evil. Effective use of trade shows, however, is enhanced by careful selection and preparation of personnel for their participation. In many instances, such participation is held out as a privilege that has the added benefit of improving morale.

A wide variety of measures can be used to measure effectiveness, depending on the objectives of the particular show.[17] If the show is oriented toward selling then sales generated is an easy and straight-forward measure. Buying influence of attendees, or buying plans, can be measured through short questionnaires. Leads generated, and sales generated from leads, can be measured with relatively simple tracking systems. On a more subjective basis, customer attitudes can be measured, as can the views of those staffing the trade show.

Finally, it should be recognized that the use of trade shows is not limited to products. A Denver architect, for instance, specializing in designing sports centers, exhibited a model of one of its designs at a trade show, was contacted by a Japanese firm interested in building sports centers in Japan, and now is doing a thriving business designing sports centers for the Japanese market.

Incentives, Contests, and Samples
Incentives, contests, sweepstakes and games are used by many business marketers to stimulate buyer frequency and interest. Incentives include rewards or discounts given to customers who buy often and/or buy large amounts of a firm's product. Some suggestions for getting the most from incentive programs include: (1) being sure that rewards or discounts go only to those customers who buy enough to make the incentive profitable, (2) track buying habits and customer information to help create effective and attractive incentive programs, and (3) recognize your best customers with special rewards.[18]

The use of contests merits particular attention. For the sales force, either that of the manufacturer, an agent, or a distributor, well designed contests can materially enhance the sales effort. There are two basic approaches. The sell harder approach establishes incentives that reward sales personnel for additional sales, either in a certain period of time or of a particular product. Key to such an approach is to ensure that all participants have an equal opportunity to be rewarded and that many personnel will receive rewards. The sell smarter approach establishes certain goals that are steps along the path to a sale and rewards sales personnel for their achievement. More complex to administer than the sell harder approach, many firms have found this to be effective in enhancing communication between marketing and sales personnel.

Contests can also be used effectively with customers, either to stimulate product interest or generate sales leads. A compressor manufacturer, for instance, capitalized on interest in golf to mail a golf quiz to mailing list of contractors. All respondents received a sleeve of golf balls and product information and the winners were publicized in a subsequent mailing. It was the manufacturer's view that the product interest thus stimulated far exceeded what would have been the result of a more traditional mailing.

Public Relations

Public relations has been defined as "the management function which evaluates public attitudes, identifies the policies and procedures of an individual or organization with the public interest, and executes a program of action to earn public understanding and acceptance."[19] Public relations generally has a broader objective than publicity, as its purpose is to establish and maintain a positive image of the company among its various publics.

Public relations uses publicity and a variety of other tools such as publications, participation in community activities, fund-raising, and sponsorship of special events to enhance an organization's image.

Publicity

Publicity, perhaps the least expensive form of communication, can be an effective element of the communications mix. Relations with editors of trade journals enhance the likelihood of feature stories on the firm or its products. In many instances, trade journals will report on, or even publish, technical papers referred to above. Many trade journals include new product and personnel sections. News releases focusing on these new product sections, including how to get further information, can be very effective in generating leads for further selling effort. News releases about personnel changes can be effective in keeping the firm's name before its customers.[20]

Seminars, Conferences/Technical Papers

Often overlooked in the communication mix, seminars, conferences, and technical papers can play an important role in business marketing. Attendance at seminars and conferences by both marketing and engineering/R&D personnel provides the opportunity to interact with buying influences in an environment conducive to open and informative discussion. In many instances, presentation of technical papers by suppliers comprise much of the program, affording suppliers the opportunity to communicate about their product developments or applications in way that is perceived to have less bias then normal marketing communications. In some industries, such as health equipment, papers on favorable test results of a firm's product by a university researcher add further credibility to the supplier's performance claims and are frequently published in trade journals or used as a part of direct marketing.

The Cost of Communication

Cost is clearly a major consideration in developing and implementing an appropriate communication program; increasingly so as organizations reengineer, downsize, or take other steps to improve productivity and meet competitive pressures. What, then, is the "right" amount for the firm to budget for its communication programs. Collectively, business marketers spend more than $5 billion on media advertising. The leading advertisers are shown in Table 12.2, and it is interesting to note the preponderance of high tech firms.

Company	Total Advertising Expenditures (millions)
AT&T	$385.7
IBM	303.4
Microsoft	218.9
Sprint	209.7
Verizon Communications	180.2
American Express	175.6
Hewlett-Packard	168.4
First Union	161.4
Alltel	127.9

Source: Reprinted with permission from *Journal of Marketing*, published by the American Marketing Association, Blasko & Patti, vol. 56 (Fall 1984), 106.

Table 12.2: Top Business-to-Business Advertisers

In the final analysis, the budget for communications must take into account the unique situation of the individual firm. Products in the early stage of the product life cycle, for instance, will require greater expenditures on communication than those in the mature or decline stage. With regard to pricing, which we discussed in Chapter 9, firms that adopt a differentiation strategy may be able to achieve revenue goals with relatively lower expenditure on communication.[21] Uncomplicated products usually require less communication effort than complex ones. Compensation levels of personnel vary widely from one industry to another, reflecting necessary skill levels and availability of personnel. Pressures on communication costs will reflect the firm's profit situation. The variation in these situational aspects suggests there is no *right* amount to be spent on communication programs. It is useful, however, to consider how the budget process should be approached and the experience of other firms or firms in other industries.

We previously referred to the recommended objective and task approach for determining advertising expenditures. Conceptually, the same approach is appropriate for the entire communication program. In essence, the budget can be built based on estimates of the expense of each element of the program, as determined by its objectives and what are required to achieve them. Estimates, for instance, can be made as to the number of sales calls necessary to achieve certain revenue objectives and these estimates can be used to size and cost out the required sales force. In most instances, however, budgets are not built from the bottom up. Rather, programs are ongoing and last year's budget is usually the starting point for the next, modified to reflect changes in objectives and strategies. In either case, some sense of industry norms is a useful way to check on the reasonableness of the firm's budget. A study by Blasko and Patti shows the shift in industrial marketing away from the subjective, arbitrary approach to a goal-oriented objective and task method for budgeting.[22]

Considerable aggregated data are available, such as a study by *Sales and Marketing Management* which reported industrial goods companies spent 11% of sales on selling expenses and 3% on advertising and other promotional expenses, compared to service companies which spent 15.3% on sales and selling and 3.4% on advertising and other promotional expenses.[23] There have been fewer comprehensive studies, however, that provide information by industry on all elements of communication. One such study, consistent with broader studies, indicates that direct selling costs were by the far the largest component of communication programs in all industries surveyed.[24] A key point, however, is the substantial difference in total marketing costs by industry.

These data need to be used with caution. The nature of industry studies, with all the difficulties of sampling and different ways in which firms report data, is such that reported percentages should be taken as no more than general indicators. Still further, it is highly likely that reported percentages have changed over time, and across industries. They do, nevertheless, along with other reports of marketing costs, and data gleaned from annual reports of competitors, provide background useful for development or analysis of the communications budget.[25]

Summary

For business marketers, a number of communication methods are available to support the direct sales and/or indirect distribution channels. Direct marketing is the principal method, through the use of direct mail, e-mail marketing, and telemarketing, as tools. Participation in conferences and seminars, use of contests, brochures, and catalogs, as well as advertising and public relations should all be considered in developing a communications program. Whatever methods are used, coordination is imperative. Sales aids that are not used by the sales force, advertising that solicits calls to an unprepared direct call number, sales leads that are not properly qualified before being given to the sales force, or a website that is outdated, are all examples of uncoordinated efforts that are economically wasteful and, in some instances, counterproductive.

The cost of the communications program is the major portion of total marketing expense. For most business marketers the cost of personal selling is the major portion of the communication program. Careful control of these costs, taking into account the objectives of each element of the communication program, is increasingly important. Although each firm will develop a budget appropriate to its own unique marketing strategy, industry figures can be very useful as checks on the reasonableness of the firm's expenditure on communication.

Further Reading

Susanne Craig, "E*TRADE to Cut Marketing Even as Its Losses Narrow," *Wall Street Journal*, 12 (April 2001), B13.

Susanne Craig, "Bank on It," *Brandweek* (11 December 2000).

Joel R. Evans and Vanessa E. King, "Business-to-Business Marketing and the World Wide Web: Planning, Managing, and Assessing Web Sites," *Industrial Marketing Management* 28 (1999): 343–58.

Yoav Ganzach and Nili Karashi, "Message Framing and Buying Behavior: A Field Experiment," *Journal of Business Research* (January 1995): 11–17.

Paul Herbig, Brad O'Hara, and Fred Palumbo, "Measuring Trade Show Effectiveness," *Industrial Marketing Management* 23 (1994): 165–70.

Earl D. Honeycutt, Jr., Theresa B. Flaherty, and Ken Benassi, "Marketing Industrial Products on the Internet," *Industrial Marketing Management* 27 (1998): 63–72.

Theodore Levitt, *Industrial Purchasing Behavior: A Study in Communication Effects* (Boston: Division Research, Harvard Business School, 1965).

Byron G. Quann, "How IBM Assesses Its Business-to-Business Advertising," *Business Marketing*, (January 1955).

Adrian Sargeant and Douglas C. West, *Direct and Interactive Marketing* (MA: Oxford University Press, 2001).

Don E. Schultz, "The Next Step in IMC?" *Marketing News* (15 August 1994): 8–9.

David Shipley and Paul Howard, "Brand-Naming Industrial Products," *Industrial Marketing Management* 22 (1993): 59–66.

---

[1] Peter Finch, "Xerox Bets All on New Sales Groups," *Business Marketing* (July 1986): 21.

[2] Charles H. Patti, "Buyer Information Sources in the Capital Equipment " *Industrial Marketing Management* 6 (1977): 259–64.

[3] Stan Rapp and Tom Collins, *The Great Marketing Turnaround* (Upper Saddle River, NJ: Prentice Hall, 1990), 220–234.

[4] Barry Silverstein, *Business-toBusiness Internet Marketing*, 3rd ed. (Gulf Breeze, FL: Maximum Press, 2001), 171.

[5] See Graham R. Rhind, *Building and Maintaining a European Direct Marketing Database* (Hampshire, England: Gower Publishing, 1994).

[6] David W. Stewart, "From consumer Response to Active Consumer: Measuring the Effectiveness of Interactive Media," *Journal of the Academy of Marketing Science* 30 (fall 2002): 376–96.

[7] George E. Belch and Michael A. Belch, *Advertising and Promotion: An Integrative Marketing Communications Perspective* 6th ed. (New York: McGraw-Hill/Irwin, 2004), 224–26.

[8] Ibid., 647.

[9] James E. Lynch and Graham J. Holley, "Industrial Advertising Budget Approaches in the U.K.," *Industrial Marketing Management*, 18 (November 1989): 266

[10] See Theodore Levitt, *Industrial Purchasing Behavior: A Study in Communication Effects* (Boston: Division of Research, Harvard Graduate School of Business, 1965).

[11] "New Proof of Industrial Ad Values," *Marketing and Media Decisions* (February 1981): 64.

[12] Thomas V. Bonoma, "Get More Out of your Trade Shows," *Harvard Business Review* 6

[13] Barbara Axelson, "How to Choose the Right Trade Show," *Business Marketing* 84 (April 1999): 14.

[14] Brad O'Hara, Fred Palumbo, and Paul Herbig, "Industrial Trade Shows Abroad," *Industrial Marketing Management* 22 (August 1993): 235.

[15] Srinath Gopalakrishna and others, "Do Trade Shows Pay Off?" *Journal of Marketing* 59 (July 1995): 75–83.

[16] Srinath Gopalakrishna and Jerome D. Williams, "Planning and Performance Assessment of Industrial Trade Shows: An Exploratory Study," *International Journal of Research in Marketing* 9 (September 1992): 207–24.

[17] Thomas V. Bonoma, "Get More Out of Trade Shows," 79.

[18] George E. Belch and Michael Belch, *Advertising and Promotion*, 546.

[19] H. Frazier Moore and Bertrand R. Canfield, *Public Relations: Principles, Cases, and Problems*, 7th ed. (Burr Ridge, IL: Irwin, 1997), 5.

[20] Jack Neff, "Ries' Thesis: Ads Don't Build Brands, PR Does," *Advertising Age*, (15 July 2002): 14–15.

[21] Philip Kotler, "Design: A Powerful but Neglected Strategic Tool," *Journal of Business Strategy* (fall 1984): 16–21.

[22]Vincent J. Blasko and Charles H. Patti, "The Advertising Budgeting Practices of Industrial Marketers," *Journal of Marketing* (fall 1984): 104–9.

[23]*Sales & Marketing Management*, (28 June 1993): 65.

[24]Harold C. Cash and W. J. E. Crissy, "Comparison of Advertising and Selling: The Salesman's Role in Marketing," *Psychology of Selling* 12 (1965): 56–75.

[25]Wesley J. Johnson, "The Importance of Advertising and the Relative Lack of Research," *Journal of Business & Industrial Marketing* 9, no. 2 (1994): 3–4.

Chapter 13

Managing Business Marketing Channels

In Chapters 11 and 12, we discussed communication with customers, primarily from the perspective of a firm doing business directly with its customers. In practice, however, most firms rely at least to some extent on intermediaries to communicate with customers and to perform many of the other functions necessary to satisfy customer wants and needs. In this chapter we first outline the major issues related to channel selection and management. We then describe some of the most common intermediaries and the functions they perform, and discuss some of the major changes taking place in distributions channels. We next discuss channel design and issues related to managing intermediaries. We conclude with a discussion of the role of logistics and physical distribution.

Issues in Distribution Management
Decisions with respect to the use of intermediaries are among the most important that business marketing managers make. In some circumstances, firms elect direct distribution. These firms communicate with customers through their own sales forces, or via some form of direct marketing, accept orders directly from customers, ship products directly to customers from factories or company owned warehouses, bill customers directly, and provide their own after sales service. Most firms, however, use some form of indirect distribution, either exclusively or to supplement direct distribution.

For those firms using some form of indirect distribution, the importance of decisions with respect to the desired pattern of distribution, and the relations firms have with intermediaries, cannot be overemphasized. As Corey has observed:

> *A distribution system, which consists of some combination of agents, jobbers, and distributors, is a key external resource. Normally it takes years to build, and it is not easily changed. It ranks in importance with key internal resources such as manufacturing, research, engineering, and field sales personnel and facilities. It represents a*

> *significant corporate commitment to large numbers of independent companies whose business is distribution—and to the particular markets they serve. It represents, as well, a commitment to a set of policies and practices that constitute the basic fabric on which is woven an extensive set of long-term relationships.*[1]

As the foregoing suggests, decisions with respect to the use of intermediaries are of two very different kinds. At one level, decisions are strategic, concerned with the overall pattern of distribution. These decisions focus on the structure of the channel, the number of levels between the producer and the customer, and the use of mixed patterns of distribution. In particular, should the firm use its direct sales force or manufacturers' agents and should it distribute directly or indirectly? These decisions tend to have long time horizons and are changed only infrequently. At another level, decisions are more tactical and are concerned with how the channel should be managed. These decisions address how channel members communicate and relate to each other, and consider cooperative efforts, trade discounts, inventory levels, responsibility for promotion, information sharing, and so forth. Although the basic pattern of these decisions may have a long time horizon, the associated activities are usually important elements in implementation of the annual marketing plan.

Types of Business Distribution Channel Members

The term channel of distribution has a sense of orderliness about it, suggesting that goods flow from producer to customer in a precise and easily described manner. In fact, channels of distribution are made up of an incredibly diverse and constantly changing set of intermediaries. The structure of channels of distribution varies depending on the industry. Within a particular industry, functions of intermediaries will vary, as will the terminology used to describe them. As we will subsequently discuss, forces in the external environment are reshaping many distribution channels and the roles of intermediaries. There are, however, four broad categories of channel intermediaries and some general patterns of the channel flows, which provide a framework for considering the issues of concern to management.

Channel intermediaries basically fall into four categories.

1. Volume oriented partners. These include corporate resellers, high volume distributors and others who sell products in

large quantities to corporate accounts, or to other distributors and resellers.

2. Value-oriented partners. These include value-added distributors and resellers, consultants and integrators as well as smaller partners such as manufacturers' representatives.
3. Service and support partners. These specialized partners do not sell, but rather come in after the sales transaction to provide customer support and service.
4. Solution partners. These companies combine the offerings of multiple vendors into total integrated solutions.

Figure 13.1 shows the principal elements of business distribution channels, together with a general pattern of channel flows. While some definitions of channels include sales branches (i.e., a manufacturers' sales office and warehouse) as a channel element, it is our view that it is more useful to limit the definition of a channel intermediary to just those which are independent of the producer; thus requiring management or influence without direct control. These intermediaries perform some, or all, of the following functions:

- Promotion.
- Stocking
- Pre- or post-sales service.
- Market research,
- Sales financing,
- A variety of value adding activities.

In a further classification, channel members can be thought of in two categories; based on whether or not they take title to the goods; agent middlemen, whose principal function is to promote the manufacturer's products or services, but who do not take title to goods, and merchant middlemen, who perform a wider variety of functions and do take title to goods. Within these categories, we find a wide range of firms, specialized to serve various markets.

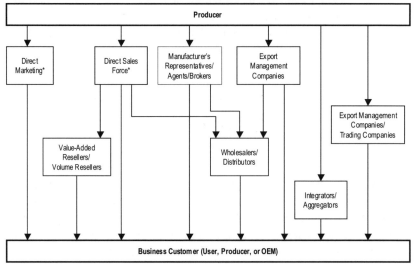

*Not normally considered an intermediary.

Figure 13.1: Principal Elements of Business Distribution Channels

Agent Middlemen
The key characteristic of agent middlemen is that they do not take title to goods. They vary significantly, however, on a number of other dimensions, both with respect to the functions they perform and the nature of the relationship they have with their principals. For business marketers, the two principal types of agent middlemen are manufacturers' agents (or representatives) and export management companies.

Manufacturers' Representatives (or Agents)
In business marketing, the most frequent form of agent is an individual or firm with a formal agreement to represent the producer of a good or service. As we discussed in Chapter 11, such an agent in many ways is analogous to a manufacturer's direct sales force, whose principal function is promotion but who also may be extensively involved in product planning, marketing research, or development of marketing strategy. The rep or agent may be an individual, operating in a limited area, representing a limited number of products to a limited number of customers. Alternatively, the rep or agent may be a firm with large numbers of salespersons, representing a larger number of products, operating in a large geographic area, with sales responsibility for large numbers of customers.

Reps are usually paid a commission on sales; the commission varies by industry and by the nature of the selling job. Commissions

typically range from a low of 2 percent to a high of 18 percent for selected products. Percentage commission compensation is attractive to
manufacturers because they have a few fixed sales costs. Reps are paid
only when orders are generated, and commissions can be adjusted
based on industry conditions. When the electronics industry experienced a severe downturn in 2002, many companies reduced rep commissions to a point where the average commission was only 2.5 to 3.0
percent of sales.[2]

As a general rule, agents specialize by product or market classifications. In the United States, the 1995 Directory of Manufacturers'
Sales Agencies lists agents in 108 separate market classifications, of
which the vast majority are oriented to business markets.[3] Typically,
the agent will be paid on commission for all orders received from a
specified geographical area or a specified set of customers. In some
instances the agent will represent only one principal but more frequently will represent a number of non-competing products, usually
complementary in nature.

In the United States, the terms of the relationship between
manufacturer and agent are usually governed by a formal agreement,
which stipulates the responsibilities of each party. A major bone of
contention between manufacturers and their agents is the basis on
which agreements may be terminated by the manufacturer, frequently
with little notice, and with little or no recognition of the work of the
agent to develop a given set of accounts or a territory. Outside the
United States, termination of agreements between manufacturers and
agents tends to be more difficult. In many countries in Europe, there
are legal stipulations that mandate payment to the agent in case of termination. In Japan, where long-term relations are highly prized, termination of an agreement may be viewed very negatively by customers
or other prospective agents.

Export Management Companies
An export management company (EMC) is a specialized form of
agent, which normally functions as the exclusive export department for
several allied but non-competing manufacturers. As such, it conducts
business in the name of each manufacturer it represents. It negotiates
in the name of the manufacturer and all quotations and orders are subject to confirmation by the manufacturer. An EMC will frequently do
market research for its principals and may play a significant role in
formulation of marketing strategy.[4]

There are many variations of this basic model. EMCs may represent agricultural producers, as is the case in Norway where salmon
farmers have joined forces to promote and distribute products interna-

tionally, or may represent an industry, as is the case in Denmark where the office furniture industry has extensive cooperative distribution organizations. Normally paid on a retainer and commission basis, some EMCs buy the goods and take title to them, in which case they act more as merchant middlemen.

Other Agent Middlemen

Beyond the agents described above are a host of other agents, usually of a very specialized nature. We briefly describe a few of the more common ones. Brokers are agents with a wide network of contacts who can bring buyers and sellers together, usually on an individual transaction basis with more emphasis on knowledge of particular markets and less on the specific product. We particularly find brokers operating in the used equipment market. Selling agents are similar to manufacturers' agents but generally perform a broader range of functions for their clients, sometimes actually serving as the clients' entire marketing department. Commission merchants receive products on consignment and negotiate sales in their own names. Purchasing agents are firms that specialize in representing buyers, generally for a limited number of clients and for a limited set of products.

Merchant Middlemen

The salient characteristic of merchant middlemen, which distinguishes them from agents, is that they buy from the producer, take title to and then resell the goods. As with agents, merchant middlemen vary greatly on a number of other dimensions. Some act principally to buy commodities in bulk, to be resold in small quantities; a role, which requires little promotion or service. Others act to provide an extensive array of services, including promotion, warranty and other after-sales service, and, increasingly, engage in a variety of value adding activities. We describe four major categories of merchant middlemen for business products.

Distributors (or Wholesalers)

The most common type of merchant middleman is the full-function or full-service firm, most frequently referred to as a distributor. At a minimum, the distributor stocks and resells goods, principally to users or OEMs, but may also sell to other resellers. Given the nature of business marketing, with its reliance on personal selling, most distributors will field their own sales forces and may provide extensive product information or application assistance. In some industries, such as the machine tool industry, distributors may also provide equipment installation and warranty and other forms of after-sales service.

In order to create more value for their customers, many large distributors have expanded the range of services provided. Value is delivered through various supply chain and inventory management services, including automatic replenishment, product assembly, in-plant stores, and design services.[5] The most popular services involve assisting customers with the design, construction, and, in some cases, the operation of a supply network. Other value-adding activities include partnerships in which the distributor provides field application engineers who work at a customer's site to help with component selection for new product designs. In order to reap the profits associated with these important services, many distributors are now charging separate fees for each unique service.

As with agents, distributors specialize by product, market, or both, with an almost limitless variety of classifications: abrasives, construction equipment, electrical equipment, janitorial equipment and supplies, MRO items, uninterruptible power systems, and well drilling equipment, to name just a few. In the United States, distributors may be local, regional, or national and may be independent or captive. In the electrical industry for instance, Graybar Electric is a national independent distributor, serving utility, contractor, and manufacturing markets with a broad array of products. General Electric Supply, on the other hand, which serves the same markets, is owned by GE and sells both GE and non-GE products. In the United States the trend appears to be away from captive distributors. Westinghouse, for instance, recently divested itself of Westinghouse Electric Supply. In Europe, on the other hand, paper producers have been aggressively acquiring independent paper merchants (the industry term for distributors).

Increasingly, industry specialization has led distributors to serve international markets. The U.S. firm Medtronics, for instance, a large manufacturer of medical equipment, distributes its products and the products of other manufacturers to hospitals internationally. Unitor, a Norwegian firm that provides specialized services to the shipping industry, has a global network through which manufacturers of maritime products can distribute equipment.

Value Added Resellers

Value adding has long been a characteristic of merchant middlemen. Steel distributors, for instance, buy coils of steel strip from steel mills and then slit and cut the steel to meet the requirements of small customers. The term value added reseller (VAR), however, has emerged from the computer industry, to describe intermediaries who buy and resell computer hardware or software, adding specialized software or other customizing features. Lotus Development Corporation, for example, had its own sales force of some 400 but had 4,000 *business partners*, many of whom are value-added resellers (others are distributors, consultants, and system integrators) who buy and customize Lotus Notes and other company products for specific clients or market segments.

Closely related to the notion of value added resellers is the concept of value added logistics, which goes beyond the value added by virtue of making goods available at the right time and place and actually involves modifications to the product while it is in the distribution channel. In its bid to become a distribution center in Europe, the Netherlands has advocated establishing value-added logistic facilities there that can modify products before being reshipped to other countries in Europe. Computer manufacturers, for instance, can stock computers without electrical plugs and then add plugs in the warehouse as may be required as a function of the country of destination.

Trading Companies
Trading companies are a specialized form of merchant middleman, generally involved in import/export activities. Although we find trading companies in most industrialized countries, it is in Japan where the current form of a trading company has developed as a unique and admired model.

Large Japanese general trading companies, also known as *Sogo Shosha*, such as C. Itoh, Mitsui, and Mitsubishi, engage in a far wider range of commercial activities than simply trade and distribution. They play a central role in such diverse areas as shipping, warehousing, finance, technology transfer, planning resource development, construction and regional development (for example turnkey projects), insurance, consulting, real estate, and deal-making in general (including facility investment and joint venture of others).[6] They have established global sales networks consisting of branch offices overseas, or wholly-owned subsidiaries, but also are heavily involved in domestic distribution. A key to the success of the many of the large Japanese trading companies is that they belong to a keiretsu, a uniquely Japanese institution with large numbers of closely linked firms with significant manufacturing and financial resources who operate with some degree of common interest and coordination. Mitsui, for instance, is part of the Mitsui Group, which recently included some 2300 member firms.

Stimulated by the success of Japanese trading companies, the United States passed the Export Trading Company Act of 1982, designed to encourage U.S. manufacturers to export by offering exporters greater protection from U.S. antitrust laws and permitting banks to own and control export trading companies. A number of export trading

companies were formed. Several failed, or provided disappointing results, raising serious questions as to suitability of this type of intermediary to the needs of the average U.S. exporter. Nevertheless, the successful use of trading companies around the world, including many examples in the United States, suggests that trading companies should
receive serious consideration in developing a distribution strategy.

Office Product Retailers
Few aspects of the dynamic nature of distribution are more evident
than changes in the distribution of office products. Once typified by
small stores, selling mostly stationary products, recent years have seen
the development of chains of large office stores, selling not just stationary products but also business machines and accessories, computers, printers and their accessories, office furniture, and a host of
other products, for large and small businesses alike.

Office Depot in the United States, and OfficeMax, are typical of
such chains. Operating coast to coast, these stores stock some 500
product categories of supplies, software, computers, business electronics, and furniture. In addition to extensive in-store sales, both chains
feature catalog sales and direct delivery to offices. Recently acquired
by Burhmann NV in the Netherlands, Corporate Express, a relatively
new player in office product retailing, is moving away from retail
stores, as the firm has decided to focus on large corporations. It now
has 35 warehouses and offices in 110 cities in the United States and
Canada, and envisions a national network of regional warehouses from
which companies could order office products from a single national
vendor, with reliable next-day service. Already doing business in Aus-
tralia, Jirka Rysavy, the firm's founder, believes the concept will be
viable in Europe and Latin America. According to Rysavy, "We are
competitive, but we really don't sell products. We sell service. We sell
relationships."[7]

The Changing Environment of Business Distribution
The long-term relations, which characterize many channels of distribution, may suggest that the structure of channels, and functions of intermediaries, are stable and unchanging. In fact, forces in the external
environment are exerting a profound influence on patterns of distribution throughout the world. There is concern, however, that many
manufacturers and distributors are resisting adapting to this changing
environment. At least this was the conclusion of "Facing the Forces of
Change 2000: The New Realities of Distribution," a study in the
United States sponsored by the Distribution Research & Education

Foundation of the National Association of Wholesaler-Distributors (NAW).[8] Reasons for this resistance include:

- Strong commitment to original and traditional distribution channels
- Lack of understanding about new roles and requirements of customer relationships
- Inability and/or unwillingness to evaluate new operating alternatives
- Desire to avoid conflict that might threaten testing of market position
- A strong concern that if distribution channel changes are made competitors, might take over the existing channels.

While the study found resistance to change, it is also clear that many firms have recognized the forces of change and are successfully adapting their distribution strategies to them.

Few industries have seen as much change as the information technology industry, where new technology, shifts in customers needs, increased competitiveness, and the changing orientation of key players have forced every information technology supplier to rethink and, in many instances, radically change distribution strategy. Virtually all the players have come to embrace multi-channel approaches to the market. IBM, for example, uses multiple and non-traditional channels to distribute its hardware and software. Its *business partner* program has existed for more than 30 years, on a global scale.[9] The use of intermediaries for software sales for personal computers has grown enormously. Currently software sales go through intermediaries, in sharp contrast to the 1980s, when the bulk of software sales went directly to end users.[10]

Technology is also changing the nature of distribution. The rampant pace of communication technology is facilitating more direct communication with customers. Distributors are able to communicate with distant customers, at the same time that changes in logistics, warehouse automation, and better inventory control procedures are increasing the ability of distributors to offer greater value to larger geographical areas.[11]

During the Internet boom in the late 1990s, many technology experts suggested that channel members would be bypassed by manufacturers who could directly serve customers online. Disintermediation is used to describe the destruction of the intermediary function as manufacturers elect to deal directly with the ultimate customer. However, channel members continue to thrive in many industries, because many customers prefer to work with local channel partners who provide services and solutions that add value to products. Indirect channels assume an important role in information technology (products and services) sales where dealers and distributors will account for roughly one-half of the $1.1 trillion in industry sales for 2003.[12]

A major trend in the United States is the growth in size of some distributors, through mergers or acquisitions. For smaller distributors this has posed a competitive threat, met in many instances by the formation of consortiums, such as Integrated Suppliers Alliance, a group of eight distributors supplying the automotive industry, or by alliances such as the Industrial Supply Division of Affiliated Distributors, a group of 50 industrial and electrical distributors doing $4.5 billion in annual sales. In many instances large distributors or consortiums have elected to represent several competing manufacturers, acting more as purchasing agents for their customers than as representatives for a manufacturer. For manufacturers, these changes, combined with changes in distributor-customer relationships resulting from technology, are having profound effects on their relations with distributors.

Various combinations of intermediaries and direct selling may be employed in the business-marketing channel. In fact, one manufacturer could use several channels. The options reflect the many marketing tasks to be performed and the fact that many business marketers are creating unique channel systems to appeal to a wide variety of customer niches. As business markets evolve, new channel arrangements are formed to reach every one of the identifiable segments. Xerox employs a complex channel strategy that includes retail stores, distributors or dealers, and a large direct sales force.[13] Each channel is designed to serve a particular market segment. For example, some office or small business customers are served through the retail store channel while the company sales force serves large corporate and government customers. Distributors cover the vast middle market composed of a diverse array of medium-sized organizations. Moreover, small and medium-sized customers can purchase some Xerox systems and supplies online through the Xerox Web site. The firm has also developed private extranets (sites) for its largest customers. These customers can use the site to change orders, check delivery status, and make electronic payments. Salespeople continue to work closely with these corporate accounts and receive commissions for sales that come through the Internet.

The increase in world trade and emergence of regional trading blocs is also having a major influence on distribution channels. We have already mentioned the Export Trading Company Act of 1982, passed in the hope that it would stimulate the formation of export trading companies in the United States. Where it was once necessary to have significant distribution facilities in each of the now twenty-five countries in the European Union, the move to a single market within the European Union has made it possible to consolidate many distribution operations. It is likely that the North American Free Trade Agreement will have a similar impact in the United States, Canada, and Mexico.

The emergence of new markets in China, Eastern Europe, and Latin America have required substantial attention to distribution issues. In contrast with more developed markets, distribution channels in these markets are not well defined. In China, for instance, the approach to many markets is not clear. For one thing, China is not one market, but several large markets with regional barriers that serve to discriminate and block distribution of certain goods. Many types of middlemen simply do yet not exist. In addition, the physical distribution channel infrastructure is poorly developed and bottlenecks stifle the flow of goods. The experiences of Shanghai Ingersoll-Rand Compressor Ltd. (SIRC) and Xerox of Shanghai suggest how this can be overcome. Instead of trying the almost impossible task of finding existing agents, SIRC and Xerox elected to build their own direct sales teams, utilizing Chinese nationals.

A very different situation is encountered in Japan, with a long established, unique, and complicated distribution system, controlled in many instances by well-established domestic manufacturers. For many non-Japanese companies the nature of the distribution system, and the differences in ways of conducting business, have made it difficult to penetrate the Japanese market. Joint ventures and strategic alliances with Japanese companies, particularly members of a keiretsu, are often essential to build successful distribution in Japan.

As we have previously mentioned, many business marketers are being asked to follow their customers as they pursue global strategies. Leprino Foods, a major supplier of mozzarella cheese to chains of pizza restaurants in the United States, is now considering the challenge of distributing its products to U.S. pizza chains that are operating in Europe. Patterns of distribution that have worked in the United States will have to be modified to take into account distribution structures in Europe.

In this section, we have identified and discussed just a few of the many forces influencing distribution channels, and some of the changes that are taking place. The key point to be made is the importance of for business marketers to understand the forces influencing channels in their industries, and the changes that are taking place.

Developing a Channel Structure

While there are many types of channels, they do fall into a few major categories. These categories are important, because channels within a particular category tend to offer similar benefits, and also similar disadvantages. The three categories are direct sales channels, indirect channels, and direct marketing channels, as shown in Table 13.1.[14]

	Direct sales channel (Sales force)	Indirect channel (partners)	Direct marketing channels
Purpose	• Complex sales • Control over sales • Process in key accounts • "High-touch" service	• Lower-cost sales • Complete "solutions" • Local customer support and care • Expanded geographic and vertical market "reach"	• Lowest-cost sales • Maximum market "reach" and penetration • Efficient transactions for simpler items and automatic repurchases by existing customers

Major types	• Field sales reps
	  o Global account managers (GAMs)
	  o Key account managers (KAMs)
	  o Corporate account managers (CAMs)
	  o Senior account executives
	  o Account executives
	  o Technical reps
	  o Etc.
		• Distributors
		• Resellers
		  o Volume resellers
		  o Value-added resellers (VARs)
		• Service and support partners
		• Retail stores (partner-owned)
		• Mass merchants
		• Manufacturer's agents, reps and brokers
		• Integrators and aggregators
			• Telechannels
			  o Telemarketing
			  o Telesales
			  o Telecoverage
			• Internet and e-commerce
			  o Public Website
			  o Proprietary Websites (extranets, Web EDI, etc.)
			  o E-marketplace
			• Direct mail (e.g., catalogs)
			• Retail (company-owned) stores

Source: Adapted from Lawrence G. Friedman, *Go To Market Strategy: Advanced Techniques and Tools for Selling More Products, To More Customers, More Profitably.* Boston: Butterworth-Heinemann, 2002, 158. Copyright 2002; Reprinted with permission from Elsevier Science.

Table 13.1: The Three Categories of Go-To-Market Channels

Direct Distribution

Direct distribution, or use of a field sales force (covered in Chapter 11) is a channel strategy that does not use intermediaries. The company-owned, company-paid organization sells products and services directly to end-customers. Direct distribution is frequently required in business marketing because of the selling situation. The direct sales channel is viable in four situations: 1) customers are large and well defined, 2) customers require direct sales, 3) sales involve extensive negotiations with management, 4) control is necessary as part of the total *solutions selling* package.[15]

A direct sales force is best used for the most complex sales situations, but it is becoming a more limited specialized role than in the past. Using a highly focused sales force to serve the top end of the market, and using a mix of other channels to serve the rest of the market is the emerging *best practice* in business-to-business marketing.[16]

Indirect Distribution

Indirect channels of distribution employ at least one type of intermediary, if not more. Business marketing channels typically include fewer types of intermediaries than consumer marketing channels.

Indirect distribution is best used in three situations: (1) markets are fragmented and widely dispersed, (2) low transaction amounts prevail, and (3) buyers purchase a number of items, often different brands, in a single transaction.[17]

Indirect channels (business partners) also offer the ability to reach and penetrate broad, dispersed markets, offering much broader coverage characteristics than direct distribution. Indirect channels also have an understanding of local market conditions, as well as local account penetration.

Agents Versus Direct Sales Force

For small firms, the question is frequently purely an economic one: To use a direct sales or manufacturers' reps or agents? In the early stages of the firm's existence agents may be the only viable way to establish personal selling capacity. The traditional view holds that, as the firm grows, it should transition to a direct sales force at such time as the cost of sales through agents exceeds the cost of sales direct force. There are, however, other considerations that might favor continued use of agents:

- Use of agents, paid on a commission, ensures that selling costs are variable. For many firms this is an attractive alternative to the fixed costs associated with the firm's direct sales force. Still further, in many instances where pure economics might indicate transitioning to a direct sales force, there is the possibility of renegotiating the agent's commission rate.
- Use of agents avoids much of the management complexity associated with a firm's direct sales force, and may be attractive for firms that find it difficult to effectively manage a sales force.
- Many agents have unique skills, market knowledge, or strong customer relations, which cannot be easily replicated.
- In some instances, agents may supplement the firm's sales force, either by selling to small customers, or by taking over account maintenance after the firm's sales force has introduced a new product.
- Although not subject to direct control, agents can be effectively influenced through appropriate processes, similar to

those used by large firms with pooled sales forces, where SBU managers do not have direct control of the direct sales force.

Direct Marketing Channels

A direct marketing channel, which we discussed in Chapter 12, is any channel other than the direct distribution (direct sales force) or indirect distribution channel (channel partners). The three benefits of the direct marketing channel are: (1) low cost, (2) reach, and (3) preferences of business customers.

The three main types of direct marketing channels are: (1) telemarketing, (2) Internet, and (3) direct mail. These channels have been growing rapidly in recent years, and now outpace the revenue growth coming from all other types of channels.

Direct Marketing Versus Indirect Distribution

Another question is the use of other indirect channel intermediaries (i.e., merchant middlemen) versus direct marketing. It is important to understand that no matter which alternative is chosen, major operating activities must be performed for either scenario. The starting point for analysis, therefore, is to identify the necessary activities. Some of the activities that always need to be accomplished are:

- Initiate and maintain contact with customers in local market
- Promote the product, usually by personal selling
- Forecast sales and order products for stock
- Stock the product in local inventories
- Receive and process customers' orders
- Arrange for transportation, insurance and delivery
- Collect, analyze and transmit market information
- Handle warranty claims

If the firm chooses a strategy of direct distribution, it basically elects to perform all the necessary activities to move the product from the point of production to the customer. If the firm decides to use an indirect channel, it elects to delegate some of the activities to an intermediary. The key is to delegate those activities that a distributor can accomplish more effectively than the firm itself. When doing this, it is important to ask at least four questions:

- Of the required activities, which are we willing to (or qualified to) handle internally?

- How do these activities vary depending on the market segments we intend to reach?
- How extensive a distribution effort is required?
- How important is it that we have complete control over the necessary activities?

Another consideration that merits special attention and that is the matter of customer preference based on non-task variables. A large computer manufacturer, for instance, identified what it called "strategically important" customers for direct handling, with all others to be handled by distributors or VARS. A number of customers, however, were highly offended when told they were not strategically important, even though they were to receive the same level of service. Smaller customers, on the other hand, may prefer intermediaries over large suppliers simply because they are uncomfortable in situations where there is an obvious imbalance in relative power.

In Table 13.2, we list a number of specific factors that bear on the decision.

Factor	Direct	Indirect
Sales cycle	Long	Short
Required product knowledge	Extensive	Modest
Nature of the selling task	Complex	Simple
Personal relations	Close, long-term	Impersonal
Product line	Broad or extensive	Narrow or limited
Target market(s)	Homogeneous	Segmented
Customer location	Concentrated	Dispersed
Product development	Extensive end-user involvement	Limited end-user involvement
Order size	Large	Small
Order placement	Infrequent	Frequent
After-sales service	Specialized or limited	Extensive
Management resources	Extensive	Limited
Financial resources	Extensive	Limited

Table 13.2: Factors Influencing Distribution Decisions

Mixed Patterns of Distribution
Some firms elect one mode of distribution and adhere to it over long periods of time. For over forty years, Thomas and Betts, a manufacturer of electrical and electronic connectors in the United States, sold its products only through electrical distributors, despite severe pressure from many customers, including the U.S. government, who wanted to

do business directly. Dell Computer, having experimented with selling through office product retailers, has now gone back to its originally strategy of selling only directly.

However, the exemplar of a firm, which has stayed with one mode of distribution, is Caterpillar, Inc. (CAT). CAT dominates the construction industry market, worldwide. According to a recent report, its distribution system, consisting of over 65 dealers in the United States and 122 foreign dealers, is its most important asset.[18] In fact, CAT frequently makes the point that the net worth of its dealers exceeds its own, $4.57 billion to $2.9 billion in 1994. With the exception of Russia and certain other countries where dealers simply do not exist, CAT has fostered, developed, and protected its dealers when necessary; making them a primary vehicle for their success. In sharp contrast to many firms who seem to begrudge a distributor's financial success, CAT has reportedly said its objective is to make the owners of CAT dealerships rich individuals.

The CAT example, and others, suggests that the degree of success that can be achieved going to market through intermediaries. For most firms, however, except for those that elect to serve only a very homogeneous market, or produce a limited product line, both forms of distribution will be used; in many cases with multiple forms of intermediaries. For example, Eastman Kodak Co.'s Business Imaging Systems Division has established multiple channels for microfilm, supplies, and imaging systems and software.[19] These channels include an organization with direct sales representatives, a set of independent brokers and distributors, and a components marketing organization that markets system components to systems integrators and value-added resellers (VARs). These VARs are responsible for more complex systems, such as Kodak Mainframe Software and optical disk records management systems; products involving long sales cycles, and requiring extensive product knowledge and after sales service.

The extent to which a mixed pattern of distribution is used will be influenced by the degree to which competition between the direct and indirect channels can be avoided. Agreements with agents can clearly stipulate the customers or territories to be served, avoiding any conflict with the manufacturers' own sales force. Agreements with distributors are another matter. Although a distributor may be selected on the basis of the industry or territory served, U.S. anti-trust laws provide that once a distributor buys a product from a manufacturer the distributor is free to sell the product to any customer, regardless of size, industry, or location, thus raising the possibility of competing with either the manufacturer or some other distributor.

Competition between channel members cannot be totally avoided. Firms can, however, take steps to reduce the potential for conflict. Distributor agreements can indicate what markets the distributor is expected to serve. Distributors can be limited as to the product line to be handled. Ingersoll-Rand, for instance, sells its large compressors direct but sells smaller compressors through distributors. Prices can be established on the basis of volume rather than function, such that large customers can buy at the same price as a distributor, a typical practice in the steel industry.

An interesting variation on a mixed pattern of distribution is the *virtual distribution* channel. In this approach, various distribution-operating activities are unbundled to independent organizations that are highly efficient in one specialized area of distribution. For example, one company may be responsible for selling and taking orders. Another company takes care of the physical movement products, which may include packaging as well as transportation. A third may handle after-sales service.

The foregoing discussion suggests that decisions with respect to distribution are complex, and are likely to become increasingly so. They must take into account the processes by which firm finds, selects, and manages intermediaries.

Finding and Selecting Agents and Distributors

Finding and selecting the right channel intermediaries is crucial to the success of the marketing strategy. Unfortunately, there are all too many stories of problems, indicating the lack of sufficient attention to this issue. For example, a senior executive of an international mining equipment supply company told one of the authors that out of 100 distributors world-wide, his company replaced approximately 30 distributors annually, raising questions not only about the selection process but also about the firm's relationships with its distributors and the impact of this turnover on prospective distributors.

With over 400,000 merchant wholesales and many thousands of manufacturers' agents in the United States alone, the magnitude of the search and selection process may appear to be overwhelming. An organized approach, however, can materially assist the process. We like to think of this as involving five steps:

1. First, establish a profile of what the intermediary is expected to do. We previously listed some of the activities necessary to move good from producer to customer. Table 13.3 provides a more comprehensive list of dimensions on which to establish such a profile.

• Accounting systems	• Marketing capabilities
• After-sales service	• Market research
• Bank relations	• Organization
• Collections	• Packaging
• Commitment	• Physical facilities
• Cooperativeness	• Pricing strategy
• Credit	• Product handled
• Customer complaints	• Promotions
• Customers	• Reputation
• Customer relations	• Risk carrying
• Exclusivity	• Sales force
• Experience	• Size
• Geographical coverage	• Specialization and focus
• Government relations	• Storage requirements
• Inventory control procedures	• Technical services
• Language abilities	• Track record
• Legal actions	• Transportation

Table 13.3: Characteristics of Business Distributors

2. Locate distribution prospects. Potential domestic and international agents and distributors can be identified from many sources. Current or potential customers can identify intermediaries they respect. Trade associations and organizations such as the Manufacturer's Agents National Association, can provide lists of members and can also provide advice on how to ensure a good match. Trade shows are excellent venues in which to meet and evaluate prospective intermediaries. Internationally, export and trade organizations are often helpful in identifying potential candidates. In the United States, the Department of Commerce sponsors several activities specifically designed to link U.S. firms with international distributors.[20] We have previously referred to JETRO, which can be a valuable source of assistance for locating representatives in Japan. The Compass series of directories, published by-country, is available for most industrialized countries, and provides substantial details about potential agents and distributors. As in the United States, international trade shows are excellent sources for identifying potential distributors, particularly in Germany and Japan. Additional sources for locating international business marketing channels are listed in Table 13.4.

3. Screen and evaluate prospective agents or distributors against the established profile and reduce the list to three or four prospects for personal interviews.

4. Conduct personal interviews. The personal interview should be used both to ensure that a certain level of personal comfort can be established between the parties and to identify the principal dimensions on which the agreement is to be based.

5. Select the preferred candidate and negotiate an appropriate agreement. It is important that this agreement be as clear and as comprehensive as possible. Potential elements of such an agreement are shown in Table 13.5.

- Ask potential customers who is the best representative.
- Examine trade publications.
- Talk to trade show attendees.
- Enlist the help of international freight forwarders.
- Contact trade associations in the targeted market of membership lists.
- Consult the World Trade Index
- Place ads in local papers or trade journals.
- Contact foreign embassies, consulates, and trade offices.
- Use the Department of Commerce's Trade Opportunity Program.
- Use the Department of Commerce's Agent-Distributor Service.
- Contact overseas chambers of commerce.

Source: Richard A. Powell, "64 Ways to Find An Overseas Trading Partner," *Agency Sales Magazine*, March 1994, pp. 28-32. Reprinted with permission from Agency Sales Magazine © 2005 Manufacturer's Agents National Association, One Spectrum Pointe #150, Lake Forest, CA 92630, phone (949) 859-4040, e-mail: MANA@manaonline.org, www.MANAonline.org.

Table 13.4: Ways to Find Overseas Trading Partners

I. General	• Inspection of distributor's books
• Identification of the contracting parties	• Trademarks and patents
• Duration of the agreement	• Information to be provided to the distributor
• Conditions for cancellation	• Advertising and promotion
• Definition of covered products	• Responsibility for claims and warranties
• Definitions of territory	• Inventory requirements
• Sole or exclusive rights	**III. Rights and Obligations of the Distributor**
• Arbitration or resolution of disputes	
II. Rights and Obligations of the Seller	• Safeguarding the supplier's interests
	• Payment arrangements
• Conditions of termination	• Contract assignment
• Protection of sole and exclusive rights	• Consignment arrangements
• Sales and technical support	• Competitive lines
• Tax liability	• Customs clearance
• Conditions of sale	• Observance of conditions of sale
• Delivery of goods	• Inventory requirements
• Prices	• After-sales service
• Order refusal	• Information to be provided to the supplier

Table 13.5: Elements of a Distributor Agreement

Managing Relationships with Intermediaries

Finding and selecting intermediaries and negotiating agreements with them are the starting points of a successful distribution strategy. Channels of distribution, however, involve dynamic relationships among many independent organizations with diverse objectives, conflicting motivations, various operating characteristics and form, managed by human beings with a variety of personalities and cultural backgrounds. How, then, should firms work together in this dynamic relationship to best achieve the collective objectives of all the members of the channel? We consider this from two aspects.

In broad terms, relationships within a channel of distribution can be considered in terms of four concepts; channel leadership, channel control, channel conflict resolution and channel cooperation. In most channels, members look to some entity, to provide leadership. The leader, often called the channel captain, is expected to influence other members of the channel to act in ways that are advantageous to all members of the channel. The leader may be a manufacturer, as in the case of Caterpillar, or large wholesaler, as in the case of Graybar Electric. In either case, the leader is expected to determine the basic nature of relations between members of the channel and to generally ensure that there are clear-cut rules of the game, adhered to by all participants. Large manufacturers, for instance, are expected to minimize competition between intermediaries by careful selection of intermediaries or through policies with respect to pricing, service requirements, and so forth. Leadership suggests the ability to influence, or control, the behavior of channel members. Sources of ability to control can be economic or non-economic. Economic control comes principally from provision of financial incentives to other channel members.[21] Non-economic control is more related to the general reputation of the leader on such factors as past leadership, superior products, and technical competence. No matter how well a channel leader manages, there is likely to be channel conflict. Major reasons for channel conflict include competition, as we previously discussed, variation in objectives and approach, differing perceptions, and unclear roles between the channel leader and other channel members. In order to prevent channel conflict channel members establish formal channel cooperation. Channel cooperation may be formalized through industry associations and implemented through mutually beneficial programs. Channel members have the option of exercising, or following, leadership, depending on their situations, or of electing to operate independently, on the assumption that untrammeled pursuit of self-interest will serve their interests better than some form of cooperation.

Regardless of the leadership situation, individual manufacturers are faced with the challenge of effectively managing relationships with each member of the channel. Their ability to effectively do so will depend to a large extent on the attitude of individual intermediaries, some of whom expect to have close relationships with suppliers, and feel their interests are best served by actively representing the supplier, while others operate on an arms length basis, feeling their best interests are served by acting more as a purchasing agent for their customers. The majority of intermediaries fall in the first category. In addition, their relationships with suppliers, and the effectiveness with which they represent them, can be materially enhanced by an active program of support. In Table 13.6 are listed some of the activities suppliers can engage in to create an effective support program. By virtue of such activities, Parker-Hannifin, a major producer of fluid power systems, electro-mechanical controls, and related components, in the United States has been hailed as a firm which has been able to establish an unusual level of rapport with its distributors. One indication of the trust which has been built up in the relationships is that PH distributors share complete information with PH on their monthly sales of the firms products; information which PH then uses to assist distributors in development of more effective selling strategies.

- Frequent personal contact by salespersons or management.
- Frequent follow-up contacts by phone or mail.
- Requests for monthly or quarterly reports on sales, service, and competitive activity.
- Visits by distributor personnel to headquarters or production facilities.
- Incentive programs with monetary rewards and prizes.
- Recognition programs.
- Regional or international distributor conferences.
- Training programs, technical and business assistance.
- Joint customer visits.
- Joint development of objectives.
- Distributor involvement in strategy development.
- Distributor participation in advisory boards.

Table 13.6: Factors that Tend to Improve Distributor Performance

Issues Related to Physical Distribution
We conclude this chapter with a brief discussion of physical distribution. Once viewed simply as a matter of shipping goods direct from factory to customer, or from factory to warehouses for reshipment to customers, physical distribution has come to be recognized as a major element of marketing strategy, with significant potential for creating

competitive advantage, and as a major element of controllable cost, with significant potential for improving the firm's profitability.

It is beyond the scope of this text to extensively address the many aspects of physical distribution. There are a number of key considerations that business marketers should take into account in designing distributions strategies.[22]

The starting point is to recognize the need to balance logistics costs against the competitive advantage to be obtained by virtue of high levels of delivery performance. Rail freight, for instance, or low levels of inventory, may be less expensive than some forms of motor freight and higher inventory levels but may not provide the desired level of customer service. On the other hand, shipment by air, backed up by extensive stocks, may provide outstanding levels of customer service but not provide enough competitive advantage to permit the firm to price at a level that will recover its costs. Conceptually these tradeoffs are shown in Figure 13.2. In the example shown, sales gained by improving the service level from 74% to 85% justified an additional expenditure of some $500,000. This approach suggests an optimum service level with benefits in terms of increased sales estimated by marketing and costs controlled by those responsible for warehousing and transportation.[23]

How Much Should you Spend to Improve Service?

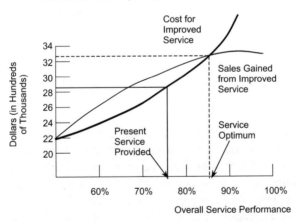

Source: "Does Your Customer Service Program Stack Up?" Traffic Management (September 1982), 55.

Figure 13.2: Cost/Service Relationship

While conceptually attractive, the notion of an optimum service level, easily calculated, is not without problems. Competitive pressures and the moves by many firms to just-in-time manufacturing are forcing firms to continually raise the level of customer service, as a matter of competitive survival. In many instances improvements in transportation methods such as container vessels, logistics systems provided by specialists such as Federal Express, improved information systems, closer working relations with distributors, and value added logistics are enabling firms to improve levels of customer service, with modest or no increase in cost. In these situations, service levels tend to be *moving targets*, requiring constant attention.

For business marketers, a key question concerns the extent of their involvement in physical distributions activities and the determination of customer service levels. Responsibility for physical distributions activities, and indeed the definition of what is a physical distribution activity, varies among firms. In Table 13.7 are listed some of the more common physical distribution activities. As indicated, many of these are outside the scope of marketing. Nevertheless, those in marketing need to be involved in the determination of customer service levels and to work closely with channel intermediaries to ensure their appropriate involvement in physical distribution.

• Production planning	• Field warehousing
• Material procurement	• Inventory management
• Inbound transportation	• Order processing
• Receiving	• Shipping
• In-plant warehousing	• Insurance
• Sales forecasting	• Documentation
• Distribution planning	• Customs clearance
• Packaging	• Customer service
• Outbound transportation	

Table 13.7: Key Physical Distribution Activities

Summary

The design and management of channels of distribution is one of the most important activities of the business marketer. During the last decade, channels of distribution have become increasingly important as increasing numbers of firms go to market through distribution and are likely to be crucial for the rest of the decade. Decisions with respect to the design of a channel make the fundamental choice between direct and indirect distribution and need to take into account the functions required, the types of intermediaries, the markets they serve, and the availability of intermediaries to the firm. Decisions with respect to management of intermediaries need to take into account the relations of channel members, their aspirations, and their attitudes toward their suppliers. International distribution involves the same basic considerations, with the added complexity of different distribution structures, different cultural, and different legal systems. A business channel relationship requires significant management resources to motivate independent intermediaries to behave in ways consistent with the business marketer's strategy. Finding and selecting intermediaries is a key management activity that can materially contribute to successful channel strategies. Business marketers must be involved in physical distribution, even where they do not have direct responsibility for physical distribution activities. Perhaps most critical to overall success of distribution strategies is to recognize the incredible changes taking place in distribution channels, to understand the forces driving these changes, and to modify distribution strategy to respond to them.

Further Reading

Daniel C. Bello and Ritu Lohtia, "Export Channel Design: The Use of Foreign Distributors and Agents," *Journal of the Academy of Marketing Science* 23, no. 2 (spring 1995): 83–93.

James R. Brown, Chekitan S. Dev and Ng-Jin Lee, "Managing Marketing Channel Opportunism: The efficiency of Alternative Governance Mechanisms," *Journal of Marketing* 64 (April 2001): 51–65.

Anne Coughlan, Erin Anderson, Louis W. Stern and Adel El-Ansary, "Marketing Channels," 6th ed., (Upper Saddle River, NJ: Prentice Hall, 2001).

John Fahey and Fuyuki Taguchi, "Reassessing the Japanese Distribution System," *Sloan Management Review* 36, no. 2 (winter 1995): 49–61.

Gary L. Frazier, "The Severity of Contract Enforcement in Interfirm Channel Relationships," *Journal of Marketing* 65 (October 2001): 67–81.

Jonathan D. Hibbard, Nirmalya Kumar and Louis W. Stern, "Examining the Impact of Destructive Acts in Marketing Channel Relationships," *Journal of Marketing* 38 (February 2001): 45–61.

James E. Johnson and Donald F. Wood, Contemporary Physical Distribution and Logistics 4th ed. (New York: Macmillan Publishing Company, 1990).

W. Benoy Joseph, John T. Gardner, Sharon Thach and Frances Vernon, "How Industrial Distributors View Distributor-Supplier Partnership Arrangements," *Industrial Marketing Management* 24, (1995): 27–36.

Leonard J. Kistner, C. Anthony di Benedetto, and Sriraman Bhoova-raghavan, "An Integrated Approach to the Development of Channel Strategy," *Industrial Marketing Management* 23, no. 4 (October 1994): 315–322

Fred Langerak, "Effect of Customers and Suppliers' Perceptions of the Market Orientation of Manufacturing Firms on Channel Relationships and Financial Performance," *Journal of Business-to-Business Marketing* 8, no. 2 (2001).

N. Mohan Reddy and Michael P. Marvin, "Developing a Manufac-turer-Distributor Information Partnership," *Industrial Marketing Management* 15 (1986): 157–163.

---

[1] E. Raymond Corey, Industrial Marketing: Cases and Concepts (Englewood Cliffs, NJ: Pren-tice-Hall, Inc., 4th ed. 1991), 1.

[2] Laurie Sullivan, "Outsourcing Trend Test Survival Skills of Manufacturers' Reps," *Electronic Buyer's News* 29 (July 2002): 1.

[3] The Directory of Manufacturers' Sales Agencies is published by the Manufacturers' Agents National Association, headquartered in California. It lists some 6,3000 agents in the United States and Canada.

[4] Svend Hollesen, Global Marketing: A Decision Oriented Approach 3rd ed. (Essex, England: Pearson Education Limited, 2004), 295.

[5] Jim Carbone, "Distributors See Slow Growth Ahead; Expect Electronics Distributors to Offer More Supply Chain and Inventory Services, But Be prepared to Pay for them," *Purchasing* 130 (May 16, 2002): 27.

[6] Svend Hollesen, *Global Marketing: A Decision-oriented Approach*, 297.

[7] *Rocky Mountain News* (July 9, 1995), 114A.

[8] John F. Monoky, "New Realities of Distribution," *Journal of Industrial Distribution* 82, no. 6 (1993): 93.

[9] Tim Clark, "Marketing Alliances Starting to Pay Off," *Journal of Business Marketing* 78, no. 5 (1993): 46.

[10] Lee Levitt, "Why Software Companies Should Direct Market too," *Brandweek* 34, no. 39 (1993): 93.

[11] Steven Wheeler and Evan Hirsh, Channel Champions: How Leading Companies Build New Strategies to Serve Customers (San Francisco: Jossey-Bass Publishers, 1999), 192–195.

[12] Mitch Wagner, "IT Vendors Embrace Channel Partners," *B to B* 87 (September 2002): 1.

[13] Chad Kaydo, "Web Masters: You've Got Sales," *Sales & Marketing Management* 151 (Octo-ber 1999): 36–37.

[14] Lawrence G. Friedman, *Go-to-Market Strategy: Advanced Techniques and Tools for Selling More Products, to More Customers, More Profitably*, (Boston: Butterworth-Heinemann 2002), 155–58.

[15] Louis P. Bucklin, Venkatram Ramaswamy, and Sumit K. Majumdar, "Analyzing Channel Structures of Business Markets via the Structure-Output Paradigm," *International Journal of Research in Marketing* 13, no. 1 (1996): 84.

[16] Friedman, *Go to Market Strategy*, 159.

Further Reading

[17]E. Raymond Corey, Frank V. Cespedes, and V. Kasturi Izangan, *Going to Market Distribution Systems for Industrial Products,* (Boston: Harvard University Press, 1989), 26.

[18]Caterpillar, Inc., A CS First Boston report by John E. McGinty, June 21, 1995.

[19]Thomas E. Furguson, "Customers' Diverse Needs Require Diverse Channels," *Journal of Business Marketing* 77, no. 3 (1992), 64–66.

[20]Richard A. Powell, "64 Ways to Find an Overseas Trading Partner", *Agency Sales Magazine,* (March 1994): 28–32.

[21]M.L. Emiliami, "The Inevitability of Conflict Between Buyers and Sellers," *Supply Chain Management* 8 (February 2003): 107–15.

[22]For a comprehensive discussion of physical distribution and logistics, see James E. Johnson, and Donald F. Wood, Contemporary Physical Distribution and Logistics 6th ed. (Upper Saddle River: Prentice-Hall Inc., 1996).

[23]"Does Your Customer Service Program Stack Up?" *Traffic Management* (September 1982), 55.